The Life Project

The Life Project

The extraordinary story of
our ordinary lives

HELEN PEARSON

ALLEN LANE
an imprint of
PENGUIN BOOKS

ALLEN LANE

UK | USA | Canada | Ireland | Australia
India | New Zealand | South Africa

Allen Lane is part of the Penguin Random House group of companies
whose addresses can be found at global.penguinrandomhouse.com.

Penguin
Random House
UK

First published 2016

004

Copyright © Helen Pearson, 2016

The moral right of the author has been asserted

Typeset in Bembo Book MT Std by Palimpsest Book Production Ltd, Falkirk, Stirlingshire
Printed in Great Britain by Clays Ltd, St Ives plc

A CIP catalogue record for this book is available from the British Library

ISBN: 978-1-846-14826-2

www.greenpenguin.co.uk

To Ashby, Lynton and Edwin, my life project

Contents

Author's note ix

Introduction 1

PART ONE: Coming into the World

1. The Douglas Babies 13
2. Born to Fail? 57
3. In Sickness and in Health 88

PART TWO: Coming of Age

4. Staying Alive 125
5. Older and Wiser 156
6. Opening Up 205

PART THREE: Coming Full Circle

7. The Millennium Children 253
8. Bridging the Divides 308

Epilogue: Where are They Now? 343

Bibliographical Notes and Sources 357
Acknowledgements 383
Index 387

Author's note

This book is about the British birth cohort studies, a remarkable series of longitudinal studies that track generations of babies from birth to death. The cohorts span over seventy years of British and scientific history, have generated a vast range of books and academic articles across many disciplines, and have involved hundreds of scientists. This book gives just a flavour of that work. Much of it is based on over 150 interviews that I conducted over the course of five years with scientists, science administrators, cohort members and others connected with the studies. I have also drawn extensively on academic publications, as well as press clippings, historical archives and other research.

The identity of people in the cohort studies is confidential and fiercely guarded by scientists. I was able to talk to just a few people who had previously revealed that they were cohort members or were willing to do so for this book, and who allowed me to write about them. In some cases, their names and other details have been changed at their request. All the data on the cohort members is meticulously and securely stored, as are the biological samples they have donated, some of which are discussed in this book. The samples are kept in facilities that meet the approval of the Human Tissue Authority, a government regulatory body.

For simplicity, I have often mentioned only a cohort director or project leader in connection with a project or piece of research, even though science is almost always a group endeavour and others may have played vital roles in the work. And regarding the number of people in each study, I have stated the number of children at its outset, but the figures used vary in the scientific literature and change over time as people die, drop out or join up.

The birth cohort studies in Britain and around the world comprise a huge scientific enterprise – and this is just one book. Please forgive its many omissions. I urge anyone wanting to know more to explore the rich academic literature, or to talk to the scientists – the real experts – themselves.

Introduction

In 1985 a young woman set out on a road trip around Britain to answer a burning question: why is it that some people succeed in life and others struggle or fail? The idea was not a new one: scientists and academics have been trying to understand all the factors that shape our lives and place us on particular paths for centuries. But this young woman, Doria Pilling, had an extraordinarily powerful way to answer this obvious yet seemingly unresolvable question: a remarkable study that was following thousands of people and charting the multitudinous details of their lives from the moment they were born.

The study had started in 1958, when scientists had carefully recorded the birth of nearly every baby born in Britain in one March week: 17,415 babies in all. They had been carefully tracking the lives of those children ever since, recording their height, health, intelligence, school performance, social class, and later their jobs, marriages and almost everything else. And, by doing this, the scientists had already discovered something profound: the children born into the most disadvantaged circumstances – the ones with poor parents and cramped homes – tended to have difficult lives from that point on, gradually racking up behavioural problems, illness and poor results at school. So troubled were these children that scientists had given them a label of unmitigated despondency: *born to fail*.

But luckily, life is never quite that simple, and no generalized label will cover every eventuality. The scientists knew that not all the children who were 'born to fail' would, in fact, do so. It was very likely that some would beat the odds, and the scientists were eager to discover who they were and how they had managed to avoid the outcomes that had been predicted for them. What is the combination of events, decisions and circumstances that can help turn things around? By the 1980s the researchers were in a good position to find out. At that stage the children had reached their twenties, and had progressed far enough in their adult lives for a judgement to be made about their success or failure, based on their educational qualifications, income and jobs. This was the project handed to Pilling, who, at this time, was still learning the ropes of her scientific profession. It became her job to find members of the study who had grown up in the most difficult of circumstances but who were now doing well in life nevertheless.

Pilling decided on the exact criteria that identified children who were 'born to fail'. She decided that a child would qualify only if he or she had grown up in a household that had one parent or five or more children, *and* whose income was low enough for the child to receive free school meals or welfare benefits, *and* lived in a home that did not have its own supply of hot water or that housed more than one and a half people per room. To put that final category into real terms, it meant that a family with just a kitchen, living room, two parents in one bedroom and four children sleeping in the other would *not* qualify as being overcrowded; a family with five children crammed in the second bedroom, however, would. Pilling found 386 such severely disadvantaged children in the study.

The majority of these children did indeed go on to struggle in some way – they achieved no educational qualifications, or they had a low income or no job. Pilling put these together into one group, the non-achievers.* But she was also able to identify 'achievers' – those who had escaped from this difficult start and had attained some measure of success. Either they had earned qualifications, such as a string of O-levels, that put them well above the average for the entire group, or they had secured a particularly high income, a skilful job, or done well enough to buy their own home. Out of her pool of 386, Pilling found 83 who made it into the achiever group. Her next task was to talk to both the achievers and the non-achievers, in order to find out what their lives were really like. So she began her journey around Britain – by train, bus and taxi – to meet these people whose lives had taken a dramatically different course and to discover what exactly had brought this about.

It took Pilling about a year to carry out all the interviews and, since this was the 1980s, she recorded them all on cassette tapes. When she was finished, she had not only to analyse her many hours of recordings, but also to look back through all the data collected up to that point – the stacks of questionnaires, interviews and other records relating to these young people that had been carefully squirrelled away throughout their lives. She wanted to find whatever it was that the achievers commonly did – and that the others did not.

A few key characteristics floated to the top. First, typical achievers had parents who were interested in their child's education and who had aspirations for their child's future. Pilling found, for example, that 56% of those who had achieved good educational qualifications had parents who had wanted them

---

* This group was considered non-achievers based on the specific criteria in the study, but that doesn't mean they were unqualified failures. Many had achieved a lot in terms of creating a stable life for themselves – in spite of difficult circumstances – and many went on to achieve more in later life.

to stay on at school, whereas only 11% of the non-achievers had parents who had stated these ambitions.

But her analysis showed that there was more to success than that. As well as ambitious parents, the achievers were likely to have had an ambitious school behind them – the combination of interested, aspirational parents and schools appeared to be a powerful cocktail when it came to children getting ahead. A typical achiever was also less likely to have difficulties at home, such as a sick parent, an unemployed father or separated parents. Another important factor was location. The achievers tended to live in areas with opportunities to find employment, and the non-achievers in areas where industry had been closed down, so the parents, and later the child, often struggled to find a job. (Pilling was travelling the country during the Thatcher years, at a time when manufacturing was on the wane and the unemployment rate was soaring; it reached a peak at nearly 12% in 1984.)

Children can do nothing about these things: they can't choose their parents, schools or circumstances at home. There was, however, one other important way in which the achievers differed from the rest – something over which they did have control – and that was motivation. A typical achiever was more likely to *want* to complete their schoolwork and continue in education – and they were often determined to escape into better circumstances than they had experienced as a child. One achiever was so set on finding an apprenticeship that he had worked his way through the *Yellow Pages*, trying every company until he found one willing to take him on. But motivation on its own was not enough. Many people in the non-achievers group were equally determined to escape, but without the combination of the other factors – the encouragement of parents and school, stability at home and the availability of jobs – they just couldn't break away from the adverse conditions of their upbringing.

Pilling summed up her findings in a book called *Escape from Disadvantage*, which was published in 1990 – 'a sort of neglected book', she calls it now. That's because at the time it came out, the book barely ruffled a feather. It joined the thousands of academic volumes that are published each year and then quickly go out of print. But today scientists view her study as one of the most powerful and positive findings that this remarkable study of 17,415 people has ever produced. It did nothing to negate the idea that disadvantage at birth does, on average, have a profound effect on the way that the rest of life plays out. But it did clearly show that those born into disadvantage were not *necessarily* destined to fail – and it identified concrete ways a child who had endured a tough childhood – or, indeed, any child at all – might prosper and thrive as an adult.

Most importantly, Pilling's book showed that fascinating discoveries emerge when scientists do something as simple as follow people carefully through their lives. This method – called a *birth cohort study* – has real power to reveal truths about the world and to bring about change.

Britain has an amazing collection of birth cohort studies: scientists here are carefully following the lives of five generations of children. These studies are unique in science and unparalleled elsewhere in the world; no other country has anything like it on the same scale. Their findings fill over 6,000 published papers and forty academic books – of which Pilling's is just one slim volume – and the results have rippled out to touch almost everyone in Britain today. They are also one of Britain's best-kept secrets: they have woven themselves quietly into the fabric of our lives, yet hardly anyone appears to know about them beyond the scientists working desperately to keep them alive.

The first cohort study was started just a few months after the end of the Second World War, when scientists recorded the births of almost every child born in one cold week in March 1946. They have been following 5,362 of them ever since, in an extraordinary feat that has now become the longest-running study of its type in the world. These people – who turn seventy in 2016 – are some of the best-studied people on the planet. The story of this birth cohort could easily fill a book on its own. Yet this was just the start. Buoyed by their success, researchers started to follow another 17,415 children, born in one week of March 1958, exactly twelve years after the start of the first study. Then, twelve years later, they started a third, which tracked 17,415 children, born in a week of April 1970. Scientists established a fourth study in 1991, and then a fifth as the millennium turned. This means that over 70,000 people, spread across successive generations and throughout the British Isles, have been the subject of intense scientific scrutiny.

These studies have amassed mountains of information – including rooms choked with paper questionnaires, terabytes of computer data, freezers full of DNA, and cardboard boxes stuffed with fingernails, baby teeth and slices of umbilical cords all carefully preserved. There is even a storage shed containing 9,000 placentas, pickled in plastic buckets. Together, these records chart the lives of ordinary British people in painstaking detail as they lived through the tumultuous decades after the Second World War.

The findings from these studies have been both prolific and far-reaching. In the 1940s they helped to shape the fledgling National Health Service, resulting in better care for pregnant women and helping to improve outcomes in all future births.

Through the 1950s, 60s and 70s, they showed that bright children from working-class backgrounds were unnecessarily falling behind at school, and they exposed the lasting impact of divorce on children. They showed that our growth and development in the womb can affect our risks of disease decades down the line – and even how long we are likely to survive.

More than anything else, however, the birth cohorts have shown that the first few years of life deeply influence all the years that follow. Children who were born into wealthier or higher-class families have been more likely to do well in school and higher education, land good jobs, stay slim, healthy and mentally sharp. Those born into disadvantage, on the other hand, have been more likely to struggle on every score. In short, our parents' circumstances have a lasting impact on ours, and this seems to be as true for the children born in 2000 as it was for those born in 1946. At the same time, the cohort studies have revealed that some routes to escaping disadvantage do exist – as Doria Pilling's study demonstrated. Things as simple as talking to children, reading to them and having ambitions for their future may help to ameliorate some – though not all – of the difficulties that come with a disadvantaged start. These discoveries are as relevant now as they have ever been, because disadvantage shows no signs of going away.

The foresight of scientists in starting these studies, and the results that pour out of them, have made the British birth cohort studies the envy of scientists round the world. 'Nothing comes close in value to the mighty British longitudinal surveys that track cohorts of babies, observing everything that happens from cradle to grave,' wrote journalist and social commentator Polly Toynbee in a 2008 report.

*

I first learnt about the birth cohorts in 2010, sixty-four years after the first study baby had been born. I was working as a science journalist and editor in New York, interested in human stories – and I came across the 1946 birth cohort, the first in the series, as I was googling around for ideas. I called Diana Kuh, the current leader of the study, and spoke to her for an hour on the phone. In that time, she talked me from the study's origins as a ground-breaking survey of births just months after the end of the war right up to its present investigations, as the thousands of people in the study approached retirement age. 'It's the best study in the world in my view,' she told me. I immediately saw that this was an amazing story that should be told.

But I also knew that I didn't have time in which to write it, because I was dealing with the challenges of my own life – and my own generation. I was born in Colchester in 1973, and had followed a love of science and of writing into a career in journalism – but now I was exhausted with a more-than-full-time job on a science magazine and two young children at home. What's more, the week after that phone call, I was due to pack up my life in New York and move back to the UK. I had to find a new house, new nursery, new school and become reacquainted with Britain, which felt very different to the country I had left eight years before. A new government had just been elected, a major austerity programme was biting, and university students were protesting about the introduction of tuition fees. I had neither the time nor the energy to research a big story about a British cohort study; taking on another commitment would be insane.

But, as I was to learn, birth cohorts cast a potent spell. So, in the end, I did decide to tell their story. I worked late nights and early mornings writing a long feature about the 1946 cohort, which came out in the first week of March 2011. I attended the sixty-fifth birthday party for that cohort, which Kuh held the same week. It was the first time most people there had met another member of the study; everyone was tipsy on wine and thrilled that the study had survived that far. These were all ordinary people leading ordinary lives, but together they added up to an extraordinary piece of science that had produced an incredible legacy, one that, I realized, deserved to be more widely known. And, with that thought, the idea for this book was conceived.

That birthday party marked the start of a five-year journey that has taken me through libraries, laboratories and living rooms. As I researched the history of the cohorts, I talked with geneticists, economists, epidemiologists and statisticians. I peered into boxes of human teeth and freezers full of urine; I thumbed through stacks of punch cards just like those on which the cohort data was once laboriously stored.

I also found myself an unwitting beneficiary of the studies. Just as I was learning about how the cohort studies had helped to usher in better maternity rights and medical care, I became pregnant and gave birth to my third son – thus experiencing some of the care and maternity leave that the scientists' work had been instrumental in creating. When I avoided alcohol and ate fish during pregnancy, it was partly because results from the cohort studies had contributed to this essential prenatal advice. When I read to my children every day, I knew, because of the cohort studies, that this was generally an excellent thing to do; and when I worried about my precarious balance between work and children, and about never being able to afford to buy a house, I knew, because of the cohort studies, that all these concerns were typical of people born in 1970, around the same time as me. My work on the cohort studies had become an illuminating frame of reference in which to view my life.

At the same time, I discovered that, ever since their inception, these valuable studies have always teetered on the brink of extinction – either through lack of money, or through the shifting winds of scientific fashion and political support. The story of the British birth cohorts is therefore one of a struggle for survival, and the heroes of that story are the remarkable scientists who have fought for them, many of whom I have been fortunate enough to meet in the last few years. It is only because of their belief, commitment, stubbornness, charm and eccentricities that the cohorts have been able to bring their benefits to the world, though the world at large has remained unaware of the extent of their achievement – until now.

The birth cohorts are one of Britain's greatest national treasures – even though they are quirky, at times farcical, run on the cheap and eternally fraying at the seams – in other words, quintessentially British endeavours. And the credit that they deserve is long overdue.

Helen Pearson
October 2015

PART ONE
Coming into the World

Paisley Central Library

68 High Street, Paisley PA1 2BB
Renfrewshire Libraries Tel: 0300 300 1188

Borrowed Items 13/07/2019 15:11
XXXXX7903

Item Title	Due Date
* The life project	10/08/2019

* Indicates items borrowed today

Thankyou for using this unit

The library is always open at
www.renfrewshirelibraries.co.uk

1.

The Douglas Babies
The Birth of a Methodology

On 5 March 1946, at a time of day that no one can recall, a baby girl forced her way out of the body and on to the bed of Gertrude Mary Palmer. The baby, to be called Patricia, was a sturdy 9 lbs 2 oz, and that Palmer had borne four children before this one didn't lessen the pain of the birth. It hurt that bad, I nearly died, Palmer would tell her daughter years later.

She told this to the health visitor too, the woman who arrived at her door a few weeks later to talk to her about Patricia's birth. The health visitor might have made the mistake of going to the grand front door of 3 Wolseley Terrace, in Cheltenham, before realizing that there was no bell for the basement flat where Gertrude Palmer lived, and that she had to walk around the house to a low, heavy door that opened off a scrappy lane at the back. Once she was inside and sitting at the large kitchen table, the health visitor opened her bag and pulled out a soft pencil and several sheets of foolscap paper, filled with typewritten questions and marked STRICTLY CONFIDENTIAL. She told Palmer that thousands of mothers all over the country were being asked these questions, and that by answering as accurately as she could, her experience would greatly help the authorities to plan better maternity services for future mothers. Then she checked her watch and started to read out the questions. Palmer dutifully answered them all.

Yes, Palmer said, the baby was legitimate. No, she wasn't

working when she started this baby. She just looked after the children and the house, and helped her husband to stoke the boilers that warmed the telephone-exchange offices above the flat, which they did in return for subsidized rent. The baby was born at home, she said, and a midwife had come to help with the confinement. About two days after the baby arrived, Palmer explained in answer to the next query, she was fit enough to do a full day's work again around the house. She knew that women who gave birth in hospital were expected to stay in bed for two weeks, but she saw no point at all in that. No, she certainly didn't have any domestics helping her: she could do the work much better herself. Palmer had grown up in service, and although the deliveries of coal and wood for the boilers meant that dirt bled into the flat, she insisted that she kept everything just so. Who looked after your husband while you were in bed, the health visitor asked her. He jolly well had to look after himself, Palmer replied.

Next, the health visitor wanted to know about any other children, and Palmer told her that she had two alive and two dead. There was Ken, who was already sixteen, and Derek, who had been robbed of his twelve-year-old life by rheumatic fever at Easter time and whose memory still made her teary at that time of year. The third child was seven-year-old Edith, the fourth child had been stillborn, and then baby Patricia made it five. She hoped there would be no more after that. How many rooms were there in the flat, excluding the kitchen and scullery, the health visitor wanted to know. Three – two bedrooms and a large living room. The bath was in the kitchen and the lavatory was outside. And had she received her full extra ration of a pint of milk during pregnancy? Yes, she had, and she'd made very sure to get her allocation of orange juice and cod liver oil too.

Now nearing the end of the form, the health visitor asked about how much the pregnancy and birth had actually cost. How many vests, napkins, petticoats, bootees, bonnets, shawls, knickers and rubber sheets had she bought for the baby, and how much had she spent on each? Palmer had spent very little, she replied; the baby was perfectly clean and comfortable in her sister's layette. And she had spent next to nothing on smocks, corsets, nightdresses, knickers and brassieres for herself, she said, as the health visitor carefully noted it all down. As she came to the end of the list of questions, the health visitor asked what her husband did in the way of work. Patricia told her that he was a labourer for a building company. What she didn't say was that sometimes she had no money, because he would spend his wages at the pub and the betting office before he came home.

By this time, the two women had been talking for around half an hour. The health visitor closed the questionnaire, tucked the papers into her bag, and they exchanged a few more niceties. Then Palmer showed her to the door. Once the health visitor was gone, Palmer got back to her routine. She needed to offer the waking baby her breast, settle her, check the boiler, scrub the floors and make supper for her husband, as she always did – perhaps cold meat, chipped potatoes and, because puddings were her speciality, a lovely spotted dick.

Gertrude Palmer was not the only new mother being interviewed by a health visitor as spring breezed into Great Britain in 1946. Just a few months earlier, a group of scientists in London had decided to try to interview the mother of *every* baby born in England, Scotland and Wales in the same week. The scientists wanted to understand what it was like for British women to go through pregnancy and bring a child into the world at that time, ten months after the end of the Second World War.

The scientists knew that surveying a week's worth of births would involve quite a lot of babies – around 17,000, in fact. No one, in the history of science, had ever attempted to collect such detailed information on such a large group of mothers and babies; indeed, few scientists had attempted to interview such a large group of people at all. The study would be completely unprecedented in its scale and ambition – if, that is, they could get if off the ground. That job had fallen to a man called James Douglas, a 31-year-old doctor who was working out of a small office at the London School of Economics. Douglas didn't have much in the way of staff, apart from his loyal assistant, Griselda Rowntree. He didn't have much money for the study either, and the cash he did have would run out in two years. He also didn't have anything so luxurious as electronic calculators, computers or e-mails to help him out, because none of those had yet been invented. But he had plenty of energy and a firm belief that he could succeed in pulling off a colossal survey of births.

Before doing anything, there were some practical decisions to be made. Most pressingly, Douglas needed a group of people the size of a small army to go out to interview the mothers. Ideally, they would have good access to the women and their health records, and have an intimate knowledge of the 'mothers' problems', as he put it, which was a euphemism for the uncomfortable and gory business that accompanies a pregnancy and birth, most of which was considered a private, vulgar topic at the time. Luckily, health visitors perfectly met all the requirements. These women, who were generally trained nurses or midwives, were already sent out to check on the health of all mothers in Britain shortly after a child was born. This meant that, conveniently for Douglas, they could do the work in the course of their duties.

Next, Douglas needed to set the date of the survey. He and his colleagues had decided to survey all the births in a single week because it would be a quick way to obtain a random sample of all births across the country. But which week of the year should he choose? He wanted to employ students to help analyse the completed questionnaires on the cheap, so he realized that it had to be early in the year, before the students left on their summer holidays. He chose the week of 3–9 March 1946. He also decided that the health visitors should wait about eight weeks after the births of the babies before they interviewed the mothers. This interval, Douglas wrote later, 'was considered to be long enough for the mother to have returned home, purchased layette, pram, &c., received bills for the confinement, and made arrangements to take her baby to the infant welfare centre.* On the other hand, details of her expenditure and experiences during pregnancy and the lying-in period would still be fresh in her mind.' Douglas put together a trial version of his questionnaire, and asked health visitors in Bristol, in Kensington and in rural Inverness to test them out on mothers, who seemed delighted that anyone was taking an interest in their 'problems'. Now if he could just scale everything up, it looked like the survey might very well work.

By this point, it was February 1946 and the birth week was dangerously close, but Douglas didn't let the pressure show. He sent out typed letters to 458 local authorities across Great Britain, addressed to the medical officers of health, who kept a

---

* These were generally cold, dusty halls where women took their babies to be checked by health visitors and where they could collect rations of milk, orange juice and cod liver oil.

register of new births and oversaw the health visitors. 'I should be most grateful if you would inform me at your earliest convenience whether you will be able to cooperate in this study,' he wrote in the clipped tone of his time, enclosing a stamped-addressed postcard to ensure a speedy reply. Almost all of the officers sent them back saying that they were happy to help. Douglas then dispatched packets of questionnaires and a detailed 'Memorandum on the Procedure', which explained exactly how health visitors should complete the survey and told them to take particular care to reach *all* mothers, including those who would not normally see a health visitor for the simple, terrible reason that their baby had died.

With everything now in place, all Douglas needed were a few thousand babies to turn up, and they did. When the designated week arrived, bitter winds were bearing down on the country, and the south of England was blanketed with snow. But the babies, of course, didn't care about the state of the world on their birth days. Nor did they care that everything about their births was about to be recorded on one of Douglas's forms, or that the form would mark the start of a life that would be more scrutinized by scientists than almost any that had gone before. And so, eight weeks later, a throng of health visitors started to fan out across Britain, knocking on the doors of the mothers – of whom Gertrude Palmer was one.

Some mothers slipped through the net. There were quite a few war brides who emigrated to America with their soldier husbands before the health visitors showed up. In some other cases, the health visitors were turned away, particularly by unmarried mothers whose babies had been adopted or who were anxious to conceal the birth. One woman said she had no time to spare because of the bomb damage to her house and the seven other children under her feet. But most of the mothers didn't dream of saying no. They were all used to doing what they were told during the war, and they felt it was their duty to carry on doing their bit.

In the end, the health visitors interviewed a remarkable 13,687 mothers – wrapping in 91% of the babies born that week. The completed forms were handed back to the medical officers of health, who posted them back to Douglas. By the end of June, the accumulating questionnaires were starting to form papery towers on his desk and floor. 'We have found the completion of these records most interesting,' read a letter from the health officer in Hull that accompanied the forms. 'The health visitors have undertaken the work most willingly, feeling that they are making a contribution to a piece of work that can be of great value.'

He had no idea how right he was. This colossal, overambitious maternity survey initiated a train of events that would touch the lives of everyone in Britain, and that would be venerated by scientists internationally over the course of time.

Douglas's maternity survey did not emerge from a vacuum. Its origins can be traced back to a group of thinkers who met for the first time in London on 15 June 1936. It was called the Population Investigation Committee, and it had come together to discuss one of the most hotly debated scientific and political issues of the day: the lack of British babies.

Up to the mid 1800s, the average woman in Britain had some four or five children, but then the birth rate had started to fall, to the point that by the 1930s she would bear just two or three. If you plotted this on a graph, the problem became obvious when you extrapolated out the line. If the trend continued, Britain wouldn't have enough people to sustain and rule the

British Empire, which at that time encompassed about a quarter of the world's population. This anxiety was a big topic of discussion by demographers of the 1930s, who studied human populations, and was captured in publications such as *The Twilight of Parenthood* (1934) and *The Struggle for Population* (1936). 'Unless people decide to have larger families,' warned one particularly hysterical commentary, 'it will go on diminishing until there is no one left.'

While extinction of the British was one possible and rather unlikely outcome of falling fertility, another was that it would drive the country into intellectual decline. That's because those having the most children tended to be working-class people who, according to one idea, tended to be less intelligent. The fear was that the clever middle and upper classes would gradually dwindle away, swamped by a rampant proliferation of working-class fools. This was a major concern of the eugenics movement, whose aim was to discourage those considered to be physically or mentally undesirable from having children. (These were not extreme views for the time: the British Eugenics Society was a thriving group in the 1930s, and it included many politicians and academic heavyweights.) The lack of babies had also become of interest to doctors and medical researchers, although for different reasons. Compounding the fertility problem was the alarmingly high death rate for babies born in Britain. This was heart-rending for families who lost a child, and a national embarrassment for the obstetricians and gynaecologists, whose job it was to deliver them safely.

It was as a result of these fears that the Population Investigation Committee came into being. It aimed to 'examine the trends of population in Great Britain and the Colonies and to investigate the causes of these trends, with special reference to the fall of the birth rate'. Thanks to its close links to eugenics, the group met regularly in the genteel white-stuccoed premises of the Eugenics Society, at 69 Eccleston Square. That this committee included demographers and sociologists on one side and doctors and medical scientists on the other made it all the more interesting, because it bridged two broad categories of academic research: the social sciences (the study of human behaviour and society) and the life sciences (the study of living organisms, including us). Today, scientists would say that the Committee was interdisciplinary.

At the Committee, social and medical scientists found common ground in their concern about births. But, for all their broad expertise, it must have been tricky for this gathering to talk about fertility at a time when any discussion of sex, contraception and abortion was desperately awkward. (Nothing on these matters was included in the final maternity survey – which today seems an almost absurd omission from a survey about reproduction.) So the Committee talked about other options instead. Were women put off by 'the unsatisfactory conditions of confinement', they mused, such as a lack of hospital beds or the pain of labour? Or was it that the expense of having children had spiralled out of reach? 'There are reasons for thinking that the medical and other costs associated with the birth of a baby may today be a serious deterrent to parenthood,' the Committee wrote.

But how much of a deterrent was it? Hardly any studies had tried to add up the total cost of having a child. Before and during the war, the costs of medical care were covered through a patchwork of private, public and charity funds – which meant that, basically, people got whatever medical care they could afford, and if they couldn't afford it they often went without. Although many pregnant women were entitled to government maternity grants of approximately £2 and a few other financial hand-outs, these were thought to be pretty paltry sums. The Committee continued to debate the fertility issue all through the war years, until, at some point, its members reached something of an epiphany. They realized that they just didn't have the information to know what was putting parents off. They needed to go out and actually talk to mothers, both poor and rich, from across the country. They needed a national maternity survey – a major investigation of British births.

By the end of the war, the idea of such a survey had gained traction, and the Committee members had drummed up a few thousand pounds to get the study off the ground. The group had already employed a young demographer called David Glass to coordinate research for the Committee, and he soon became a major champion for the study on the social sciences side. But they still needed a good hands-on man to run the survey. A medical man would be good, because he would understand all the issues around pregnancy and birth. Ideally, he would also have experience of conducting massive scientific surveys of people. Glass knew someone – a promising doctor he had met in Oxford through mutual friends. Douglas – doctor, scientist, charmer and idealist – fit the bill perfectly.

As the son of a clergyman, Douglas had grown up attending several church services a day, and the expectation was that he would be a priest or a missionary. But he didn't want to be either. Douglas was attracted far more by the cool, hard facts offered by science and medicine than by the untestable ideas of religion. In 1932 he joined Magdalen College in Oxford to study physiology and medicine – and there he was drawn into the invigorating company that cemented his faith in science and nurtured his social ideals. He was taught by J. Z. Young, just as the young biologist was starting his work investigating the electrical pulses on the spaghetti-thick neurons of the giant squid; he was friends with Peter Medawar, who went on to win a Nobel Prize for his studies of immunity. He mingled with left-wing thinkers; he played viola and he all too frequently broke hearts. There was something about Douglas's rangy body, prematurely receding hairline, brains and infectious charisma that would make women fall for him at the drop of a hat. He was, in the words of one of his many female friends, 'quite devastatingly beautiful'.

By the time Douglas had finished his medical training, however, he found that a seemingly intractable problem was attached to his chosen profession: he found some sick people to be terrible, self-obsessed bores and medical practice to be hierarchical and depressing. After qualifying, he spent a few months delivering babies in London's East End, which was so squalid that it was once described as 'the hell of poverty'; yet it opened his eyes to the miserable conditions into which so many babies were born and which quickly caused their deaths. He became convinced that he didn't want to spend his life clearing up nasty messes like these. Instead, he wanted to find out what made people ill and then prevent them from ever becoming so in the first place. In practical terms, this meant moving away from applied medicine and into the world of medical research.

At Oxford, Douglas had fallen in with Solly Zuckerman, a dynamic South African zoologist who hosted dinner parties packed with intellectuals. Zuckerman carried out animal experiments to try to understand the reproductive system in mammals, and for a while Douglas joined him in his cramped laboratory, where they studied such things as the menstrual cycle of monkeys and intersex conditions in pigs. When the war broke out, Zuckerman and other prominent scientists became concerned that the military effort was not being properly guided by scientific research, which, they argued, could help build better tanks, heal wounds, improve agriculture and a host of other things. Zuckerman was given permission by the Ministry of Home Security to start a Research and Experiments Branch (later Department) in 1939 – a crack team of scientists based in Oxford and assembled to inject some scientific analysis into the issues of war. Douglas was a pacifist. He had stated his conscientious objections at a tribunal, and as a doctor he didn't have to fight. Instead, he signed up with Zuckerman.

It was here that Douglas gained his experience of surveys, but these were of deaths rather than births. The unit undertook a vast Field Survey of Air-Raid Casualties, a truly extraordinary scientific enterprise that was designed to work out how, exactly, bombs do harm. The morning after an air-raid, the unit would dispatch teams of men to selected bomb sites across London, Birmingham and Hull, where they would tour the first-aid posts, hospitals and mortuaries, classifying and counting the deaths and injuries, and detailing their causes. It must have been awful, of course. Ghoulish humour was one way to cope: a skull might have been separated from a man's body, but look, the men would say, Brylcreem kept his hair perfectly in place.

Douglas was mostly on the numbers side of things, collating and analysing all the data as it came in. By converting all the air-raid reports into 'standardized killed rates' and 'standardized casualty rates', the Unit shattered a commonly held myth that bombs killed people by blast waves, concluding instead that a victim was far more likely to die by being 'violently displaced' by collapsing roofs and walls, or by a host of other tragic means. (This accorded well with the researchers' own experiments using explosives, rabbits and goats.) Douglas wrote all this into extensive, classified reports that he dispatched to the War Office, marked TO BE KEPT UNDER LOCK AND KEY. He hoped that the reports would help politicians to work out ways to save lives during air-raids. So he was horrified when he discovered that they were also being used to devise more devastating bomb attacks abroad. Douglas learnt that scientific data can be powerful, but that once scientists let it go, they have no control over how it is used by politicians – an observation that he would make again when he was doing surveys of a different kind. He didn't appear to let his disillusionment show. Douglas 'rendered brilliant service', Zuckerman wrote of him, making it 'certain that he will prove a success in almost any venture to which he turns his attention'.

That venture, as it turned out, was the 1946 maternity survey. With his experience, Douglas was almost uniquely qualified to lead it, and he landed the job. The survey fitted with his ideals: by helping to reduce infant mortality, he hoped to prevent the ill-health and tragedy he had seen in London's East End and perhaps to smooth out some of the gaps between rich and poor. Douglas, the medic, worked very closely with Glass, the demographer, to devise the survey. In the end, each loved the survey in his own way. Douglas set about organizing the birth survey with all the ambition, speed and can-do attitude that he had used to survey bomb sites during the war. And a few months later, the completed maternity questionnaires started to flood in.

For Douglas, collecting the 13,687 questionnaires was just the starting point – he still had to extract the information from them and work out what it all meant. This was laborious, to say the least. First, his cheap students worked through each form by hand and converted every answer into a pre-assigned number, which they wrote on the form. Next, Douglas passed the forms to a team of women whose job was to transfer the information to punched cards: small, cardboard rectangles the size of a dollar bill in which a piece of information is represented by punching out a hole at a certain spot.* One questionnaire might fill six or more cards, and with 13,687 babies you can see that all this added up to a lot of cards. Douglas stacked them up in rows of wooden filing cabinets and then fed them into a tabulating machine, a thumping device about the size of a piano that used the holes to sort the cards into piles and then count them up.

Take social class, for example, which would turn out to be one of the most important pieces of information on those cards. Douglas worked this out based on the occupation of each mother's husband, which was the standard way it was done.** The wives of professional and salaried men – the doctors, lawyers, businessmen and managers – were at the top end of the scale, followed by black-coated wage-earners – those who brought home a weekly salary doing clerical work, for example. Manual workers and agricultural workers occupied the bottom rungs of the ladder. (The few unmarried mothers, who could not be assigned a social class because they had no husbands, were simply hived off and later studied as a separate phenomenon.)

Douglas worked incredibly hard, and within two years of the

---

* According to computing legend, the very first punch cards were made for the US Treasury and were dollar-sized so that they would fit in discarded boxes that had once been used to store newly minted paper notes. The cards look like large beige baggage labels with the numbers 1–80 printed along the long edge and the numbers 0–9 printed in columns below each one.

** Douglas used the same social class classification as the country's Royal Commission on Population. Today, scientists classify people's socioeconomic status using an updated list of occupations, as well as measures of education and income.

survey he had written a remarkable red book called *Maternity in Great Britain*, explaining what all the holes in the thousands of punched cards amounted to in real terms. The data he had collected allowed him to address the question that had originally brought the survey into existence: why national fertility was in decline. Except that, by 1948 – as many of you will probably have realized by now – fertility wasn't in decline at all. It was going through the roof.

In 1945, when millions of men returned from the war to their wives and girlfriends, they instigated a surge in births now famously known as the baby boom. This surge was most dramatic in the United States, but the UK also saw a sharp increase in the birth rate – and the 1946 survey had unknowingly captured the very first members of the boom. By the time that Douglas was writing up his results, babies were spilling out so quickly that any concerns about the country's fertility had been laid to rest. But that didn't stop Douglas's book from shocking the nation when it was published in November 1948. That's because his data showed, in simple numbers, what it was really like to be born in Britain – and the picture that emerged put the nation in a far from flattering light.

Almost every result that tumbled out of Douglas's tabulating machine showed a country divided by class. The babies in the lowest class were 70% more likely to be born dead than those in the most prosperous, and they were also far more likely to be born prematurely.* Part of the problem appeared to stem

---

* Douglas defined premature babies as those who were born weighing 5.5 lbs or less. This is different from the terminology in use today: a preterm birth is one that occurs before 37 out of the usual 40 weeks of gestation; and a low-birth-weight baby is one that weighs less than 5.5 lbs, or 2.5 kg.

from the dismal antenatal care that the working classes received. The working-class mothers accessed medical care later in their pregnancy, were less likely to see a doctor for the birth and less likely to deliver their baby in a hospital or nursing home — for the obvious reason that they couldn't afford it. 'In all aspects of maternity care well-to-do mothers get better attention than those who are poor,' Douglas wrote. (Upper- and middle-class families were also, in general, the richer ones, so when Douglas was writing up his results, he generally considered money and social class to go hand in hand.)

The contrasts between those at the top and those at the bottom were stark. A well-off woman would typically spend two weeks in hospital for the birth. This wasn't exactly fun: the matrons in charge were so strict that they sometimes allowed a father in to see his baby only once a week, and they were known to check a woman's feet for dirt to make sure she hadn't got out of bed. But it was a different world from that of a poor woman giving birth at home. One woman in the survey delivered her baby in the family bed, while her husband and three other children waited in the room next door. With only two rooms for the five of them, there was nowhere else to go.

When Douglas totted up the costs of pregnancy and childbirth, he was in for a shock: having a baby turned out to be eye-wateringly expensive. That might not be news to parents today, who spend an arm and a leg on the latest items for dressing, washing and transporting their babies, but Douglas was adding it up for the very first time, and he revealed that there was plenty of pricey paraphernalia to be bought seventy years ago too. The wives of professional and salaried workers, the highest social class, commonly spent some £47 for all medical fees, chemist's bills, layette, cots and prams for their first child; whereas the wives of agricultural workers, in the lowest class, spent less than half that. For both rich and poor, the total cost of childbirth consumed about six weeks of the family income – a massive bite and far more than most poor families could afford. It was blatantly clear that those £2 national maternity grants fell hopelessly short of covering even the most basic expenses. At the start of the survey, the scientists had set out to ask if the costs of childbearing deterred parents from having children. Now they had their answer, and it had come with a twist: yes, the costs were punishingly high, but the baby boom made it obvious that this hadn't stopped parents from having children. The costs just made people poorer with every child that they had.

All this made poverty seem like an inescapable trap, but perhaps the most remarkable thing about the results is that they didn't cause widespread concern. It's not because no one cared, or no one noticed – for a few months, policy-makers and politicians were brandishing copies of Douglas's book. It was because the country already had the means to put things right. Britain was about to be transformed – by the welfare state.

A few years earlier, in November 1942, the economist William Beveridge had published a radical report on the way that Britain should be rebuilt after the war. It attacked the evils of what he called 'Want, Disease, Ignorance, Squalor and Idleness' and urged politicians to abolish them by introducing a major system of national insurance that would cover all citizens and help them through difficult times. His ideas were wildly popular, because they seemed to encapsulate what everyone was fighting for – ending the pre-war world in which poverty and class were deeply entrenched and putting a better, fairer world in its place. Douglas whole-heartedly agreed.

The reforms inspired by this now-iconic report built the

welfare state that still supports Britain today. Shortly after it was published, Winston Churchill's government tackled 'ignorance' with the 1944 Education Act, which was intended to even out inequality in the education system. The following year, when Labour Prime Minister Clement Attlee came to power, his government took on 'disease' with plans for a National Health Service that would provide free healthcare for everyone. The NHS was designed and brought into existence in 1946, and launched in practical terms in 1948. The results of the maternity survey showed how much needed to be spent on better provision for pregnancy and birth – and they appeared just in time to be integrated into the plans for the NHS. The survey may have exposed deep inequalities in maternity care, but the hope was that they could be eradicated by the NHS and other aspects of the welfare state. Douglas's report 'was a blueprint for the maternity service we've had ever since', one obstetrician later said.

When the NHS launched in late 1948, the medical care associated with pregnancy and birth became free; around the same time, more generous maternity allowances were introduced that stretched for up to thirteen weeks after the birth and were later extended. Douglas still didn't think this would be enough, and wanted to see costs cut even further, either by more generous grants or by retailers slashing the cost of baby clothing, cots and prams. The latter never happened, but the former did. By putting maternity care in the spotlight, Douglas helped to create the lasting belief that pregnant women deserved support by the state, which over time grew into the maternity leave and benefits that families receive today.

Douglas's work revealed many divisions between the well-off and the poor, but amongst his most important findings were those that related to pain relief in childbirth. Much to his surprise, he found that a huge number of women received no pain relief – during home births, only 20% did – and that it was the lower classes who suffered the most. Women had been fighting a long battle for respite from labour pains, and the survey made it plain that the battle was yet to be won. For decades, there had been widespread opposition to pain relief in labour, because it was deemed to go against the word of God. ('In sorrow thou shalt bring forth children,' the sinful Eve was told – Genesis 3:16.) But two events started to turn things around. One was the discovery that chloroform had anaesthetic properties. The other was that Queen Victoria secretly called a doctor to the birth of her eighth child, Prince Leopold, in 1853 and demanded that he give her some of this new-fangled chloroform to get her through.* The palace denied the event for several years, but it nevertheless helped to disseminate the idea that taking pain relief in labour was an acceptable thing to do. By the time of Douglas's survey, there was an array of means available for dulling labour pains, including chloroform, a potent drug called 'twilight sleep', and gas and air (also known as 'laughing gas'), which is a mixture of oxygen and nitrous oxide that sets the head spinning. So it was a shock to find that most women weren't getting anything at all.

One reason for this was that doctors and midwives were discriminating against the lower classes and dismissing their pain out of hand. Another, more practical one was that midwives had great difficulty in administering gas and air. Many weren't qualified to do it, or could do it only if a doctor was present, and those

---

* That doctor was John Snow, who is better known for being a father of epidemiology for his work in tracing a cholera outbreak to a London water pump in 1854.

that could often found the apparatus too heavy to carry to the birth. (It was impossible to transport on a midwife's bicycle and sometimes an ambulance would be called in to deliver it to a home birth.) When all this came to light in Douglas's book, women's groups and newspapers got worked up. It prompted newspaper headlines such as 'Needless Pain', and a few years later it spurred the introduction of a Private Member's Bill in the House of Commons that would give every woman the legal right to pain relief in childbirth. The bill was eventually defeated, because of arguments that the NHS would already be providing women with better care. But the whole episode did, over the next few years, bring about changes in the rules, with the result that midwives could administer gas and air more easily and the right of women to receive pain relief during birth was established.

One week before Douglas's book was published, on the evening of 14 November 1948, a boy was born at Buckingham Palace to Crown Princess Elizabeth. The story goes that Prince Philip played squash while his wife was in labour, but then brought her carnations and champagne once the baby – who was Prince Charles – had safely arrived. There could hardly be more contrast between the birth of a future king and some of the impoverished births captured in the maternity survey of 1946. But the arrival of a celebrity baby on the heels of Douglas's book certainly thrust the subject of maternity into the public mind and may well have helped to increase the impact of his findings. Douglas had done all the hard work on this ambitious maternity survey, but in the end it was the royal family who inadvertently helped to get it the attention that it deserved.

As Douglas and Glass were writing up the results of the maternity survey, they had an idea. It's unlikely that this idea emerged from nowhere; although science stories like to portray bright ideas as light bulbs, lightning bolts or inspirational moments experienced in the bath, the truth is that most ideas are more organic in their genesis, sprouting like a seedling from a soil of pre-existing knowledge and fertilized by the interests of the time. So it was with this particular idea, one that was so important that, years later, they diplomatically liked to say that it had occurred to each of them independently at the same time. And the idea was this: wouldn't it be wonderful to keep following these thousands of children all through the course of their lives? In other words, would it be possible to turn their maternity survey into a cohort study?

A 'cohort' is a group of people with something in common. The word originates from the Latin *cohors*, and was used in Roman times to refer to a military unit of several hundred soldiers.* When Douglas carried out the 1946 survey, he was, in effect, identifying a birth cohort: a group born at the same time. But the original aim had been to collect information on them only once. Scientists call this type of study a 'survey', or a cross-sectional study, because it captures information on a slice of the population at one moment in time. We might call it a snapshot – the data gives a picture of a crowd as if it were frozen at that instant in time.

Britain has a long, rich history of surveying its people in this way. The Domesday Book, completed in 1086, is a colossal, detailed survey of much of England and Wales conducted on the orders of King William I and unprecedented for its time. William wanted to find out how much land and resources everyone owned, so that he could work out how much tax and

---

* Ten cohorts made up a legion, and together the legions commanded by Julius Caesar crushed the local tribes of Gaul – modern-day France and Belgium – and expanded the Roman Empire across Europe.

military service he was owed; the survey was so detailed that it sometimes recorded each donkey and goat. The name 'Domesday' is thought to refer to God's final Day of Judgement – doomsday – when every soul would be judged and against which there would be no appeal. The idea was that the Domesday Book would have the last word on who owned the land.

Although William's survey is often called the first national census, it was several centuries before the first modern census was carried out in Britain. In 1801 a simple headcount was conducted, largely because of fears that the country would be unable to support its growing population. A census has been conducted almost every ten years since. It was part of an explosion of interest during the 1800s in collecting data about populations, ranging from their total numbers, ages and sex to how many were arriving and leaving through birth and death.

But all these were forms of surveys. A cohort study differs from a survey in that scientists follow the group they have identified over time in order to work out the incidence of a disease, death or some other outcome. In a birth cohort study – which is what the 1946 survey was about to become – the group are all born around the same time; but scientists can also define a cohort that they wish to track by using other characteristics. Everyone in the group may live in a particular region, or hold the same type of job, or behave in a certain way. A cohort that is studied over time also becomes known as a 'longitudinal study'.

Adding the dimension of time to a human study is powerful, because it allows scientists to address questions that are tough to tackle in other ways. Let's say that we went out tomorrow and carried out separate snapshot surveys of all the newborn babies and all the five-year-olds in one town and then worked out which were poor or sick. This would tell us a lot about how many children of each age fall into these groups – but it would tell us nothing about whether the poor babies were the ones who grew up into sick children. The only way to do that is to track the newborn babies over time. Cohort studies allow scientists to make connections between events and characteristics that happen at one point in time and events and characteristics that arise later on.

The truth is that everyone on this planet is already engaged in a type of cohort study. We watch our children take shape alongside their cohort of siblings, cousins and friends, and we diligently document the process through diaries, height charts, photos and school reports. A generation before that, we started to participate in our own cohort study as we grew up surrounded by our peers; we are watching them still, and wondering quite how their lives diverged from ours. There is a deep and endless fascination with watching human life unfold.

Cohort studies have become a particularly powerful tool in epidemiology, the branch of medical research that studies the patterns of health and disease in populations in order to understand their causes. Here, cohort studies are used to follow people over time and to investigate who falls sick, and why; thus, the history of this methodology is entwined with that of epidemiology. Epidemiologists need to calculate the rates of disease or death in different groups of the population – poor and rich, for example – and show that any difference between the two groups is meaningful. (Let's say, for example, that our study has shown that more poor children die in infancy than rich ones, as Douglas found. Chance alone could have meant that there was an unusually high number of deaths amongst poor babies in our particular town or in the week that we carried out our survey – much like tossing a coin several times can, on occasion, produce an unusually high run of heads by chance. We need to use mathematics to prove that this association between poverty and infant mortality is unlikely to be explained by chance.)

The idea of comparing death and disease rates in different groups can be traced to a self-taught statistician of the 1830s named William Farr. He worked at the Office of the Registrar General, as the first 'Compiler of Abstracts'. There, he did something for which epidemiologists will be forever grateful: he established a careful system for recording vital statistics – births and deaths – as well as a disease classification system, the descendant of which is still used by all doctors today.* Such systems are critical to epidemiologists, because the data allows them to tease out patterns about who is dying, when, where and why. The motivation for the 1946 birth cohort emerged from Farr's legacy; ultimately, it answered questions about fertility and infant mortality, and allowed Britain to see that, while the former was declining, the latter was not.

Farr dived deep into the data and began to calculate the mortality rates – number of deaths over time – for people in particular social classes, regions or occupations, or with particular diseases. He built one of the first 'life tables': it showed the risk of someone of a particular age dying that year (and a shocking 14% of babies died in their first year in 1841). But Farr can also lay claim to one of the earliest cohort studies in epidemiology, which tracked a group of people through time. (There is no true 'first': ask twenty cohort scientists to direct you to the first cohort study, and they will give you twenty

---

* The International Classification of Diseases (ICD) is a standard tool used around the world to categorize diseases. It ensures that all doctors mean the same thing when they refer to a myocardial infarction (a heart attack), for example, which is given the code I21 in the latest iteration of the ICD.

different answers, but Farr's has a pretty good shot at the title.)
He presented his study, called 'Report upon the Mortality of
Lunatics', at the Statistical Society of London on 15 March 1841.

Farr's report was commissioned after Parliament became
interested in the conditions of hospitals that housed London's
lunatics – the term used then for those with severe mental
retardation or mental illness – who were often committed to
an asylum for life. Farr counted the lunatics being admitted
into a series of asylums in London over nearly a decade, and
then followed them up to work out which ones recovered
and which worsened and died. Farr was shocked to find that as
many as 27% of paupers died in some asylums – a mortality
rate as high as that experienced 'by the population of London
when the plague rendered its habitations desolate!' he wrote.
His pioneering analysis used advanced statistical methods to
compare the mortality of different population groups and
to trace those groups over time.

Scientists have toyed with cohort studies ever since. As the
nineteenth century neared its end, some became interested
in measuring not just numbers of people but also more
detailed aspects of their bodies and minds, such as height,
weight, growth and intelligence. In the United States, in the
1920s and 1930s, scientists set up a handful of small studies to
trace cohorts of young children so that they could understand trajectories of growth and development. Perhaps the
most famous of these today is one that was started in 1921
by Lewis Terman, a psychologist at Stanford University who
was involved in developing intelligence tests. Terman was a
eugenicist interested in nurturing the most intelligent children, and his study was designed to show that portrayals of
these super-bright children as wan, freakish, social outcasts
were wrong. He scoured schools for some 1,500 exceptionally

bright children and then traced their mental and physical development in a study called Genetic Studies of Genius, which continues to this day (although only a handful of the 'Termites', as they are known, are still alive). Terman showed that the children were mostly healthy and well adjusted, and that they matured into successful adults. However, the problem with this study was that the children didn't mirror the world at large: the vast majority were white and from affluent families (Terman even enrolled his own children in the study). Many of the other cohort studies that were started at this time were also relatively small, with a few hundred children or so in each, or they used fairly ad hoc methods to recruit children. And, unlike the Terman study, many of the US child cohorts were put on ice once the children reached a few years of age. (Some years later, a new member of staff asked Douglas if it was worth flying over to the US to learn about the studies there. Douglas had replied that there was nothing to be learnt.)

It is little wonder, however, that there were no larger cohort studies at this time: they were expensive, time-consuming and *hard*. Handling data was an almighty chore when it involved punching thousands of cards, sorting them on a deafening tabulating machine and then calculating statistics with paper and pencil. The idea of following a generation of children was a wonderful notion, but until that point scientists had been too daunted by the task.

Nonetheless, when Douglas and Glass conceived the idea of following their 1946-born children, cohort studies were very much in the air. Yet there was nothing out there that quite paralleled what they were planning to do. Their study would have a larger cohort than almost any other; it would span an entire country; and it would capture an entire generation from the moment that it arrived in the world. The cohort members would also be starting from dramatically different positions in life, ranging from the very poor to the very rich. Douglas and Glass wanted to know if these inequalities persisted as the children grew up, like permanent scars left by birth, or if class inflicted only shallow wounds that healed up and faded away. Before them lay a unique, tantalizing scientific opportunity that would ultimately prove to be impossible to resist.

When Douglas and Glass had launched the maternity survey, they expected to wave the babies on their way into life; after all, they had learnt what they wanted to know about childbirth and they had no money at that time to follow them further. But now they could envisage a different future. For one thing, they had proved that it was possible to pull off a national survey of this type, so there seemed to be no reason why they couldn't do it again.

There was also, the two men realized, something unique about these children. Because of the moment in time in which they had been born, they would be the first to pass through a country that had been radically reshaped both by war and by Beveridge's report. The children may have been growing up on rationed food, but they were also amongst the first to benefit from free school meals and milk as part of the expanding welfare state. They would be the first to be treated for free by NHS doctors and at hospitals, and the first to pass through a remodelled school system. 'It was clear from the start,' Douglas wrote of the group, 'that its experiences would be very different from its predecessors and successors and in recording them we intended to provide benchmarks for comparison with future generations.' Douglas and Glass's timing had been serendipitously impeccable. They would be able to document the lives of these children much as if they were the guinea pigs of the welfare state and work out whether political reforms evened out the dramatic inequalities that had been observed at their births.

When Douglas first decided to follow the children, he realized that he needed to tweak the study design. Most importantly, he felt that he couldn't keep tracking all 13,687 children because the calculations would be too cumbersome, and he had neither the money nor the staff. So Douglas selected a more manageable sample of the children. To do this, he threw out the illegitimate children, because many of them had been adopted and would have been difficult to trace. He also jettisoned the twins, because he felt that they would have to be analysed in a separate group and there weren't enough to make it worthwhile. And then, because nearly three quarters of the sample were from the lowest social classes, he whittled down the group by choosing, at random, just one in four of these children. This left him with a total of 5,362 children: there would be roughly equivalent numbers in each social class, but still distributed across the entire country.

The whole process of crafting the questions, recruiting the health visitors and tabulating the results had to be started all over again. Douglas worked like a machine, and sent health visitors back to the mothers when the children were two; again when they were four and a half; and when they were six. The children themselves became known as the Douglas Babies and Douglas, in turn, came to view this vast family very much as his own.

The questions that the mothers answered were eclectic, to say the least. Has the child ever had an accident in which he was burnt or scalded, broken a bone, or been badly cut or bruised? Has the child any habits such as thumb-sucking, nail-biting, nose-picking, tics or general fidgetiness? In 1950, when the children were four, the mothers were asked to list everything their children had eaten the previous day. (One typical child had breakfasted on bread and dripping; lunched on meat, peas, potatoes and blancmange; and eaten bread and butter for supper.) Douglas also asked the health visitors to make some notes on what they saw at the home. Was the child's clothing in a satisfactory or unsatisfactory state of repair? Was the home amongst the most clean/average/the least clean? And Douglas took a detailed interest in the children's toilet habits, in order to test a hypothesis of Freud's that forcing children to toilet train very early in life could backfire and lead to mental health problems in adults. How old was the child when you left his napkins off at night? How frequent were the child's motions? How often did the child receive a laxative purge? (Although Douglas never did tackle Freud's idea explicitly, some thirty years later other scientists did show that bedwetting as a child was associated with depression and other psychiatric disorders in adults.) The reason for all these questions was that Douglas wanted to keep the study as broad as possible. He was determined to keep his hypotheses wide, so that the cohort wouldn't run out of steam when, after a few years, more narrowly focused hypotheses would have been fully tested. The study had arisen from both social science and medical science, and Douglas wanted it to keep spanning the fields. It helped that Glass, the social scientist, was still taking a very active role behind the scenes. Douglas wanted to understand the health and development of the children, but he was also keen to shed light on some of the urgent social issues of the day, such as the impact of social class.

Unfortunately, the narrative that emerged from all this was

on the continuing and profoundly negative impacts of being born at the bottom end of society. The children in lower-class families were the most likely to fall ill or die in the first few years of life, perhaps, said Douglas, because they were more likely to 'meet infection than . . . the more cloistered child of the well-to-do'. The lower-class children also grew more slowly and ended up shorter on average than those in the higher classes, even when Douglas took account of the parents' heights. Douglas attributed this to their poorer diets: even with rationed food, free milk and other welfare benefits, a poor family still couldn't afford enough to eat. He estimated that about a quarter of all families in Great Britain with children under five were suffering in this way. None of this reflected particularly well on the brand-new welfare state, which, in spite of the ideals and good intentions of its creators, appeared to be doing little to even out differences in class.

It seems obvious today that social conditions such as poverty or poor housing should affect people's health, but this wasn't always the case. Although social scientists had been documenting these problems for many decades,* some people in medicine were painfully slow to catch on. In Britain, before the war, many doctors didn't give their patients' social background much thought. That was largely because hospital consultants, the most senior people in medicine, secured their income from private practice and therefore saw well-off patients who could afford to pay – and these tended to be the ones suffering from

---

* For example, in 1901 Seebohm Rowntree published *Poverty: A Study of Town Life*, which contained the results of his investigations into the population of York. Of the 46,000 people surveyed, the study revealed that a shocking 20,000 were in poverty and that many of these were so poor they could not afford the food, fuel and other necessities important to sustain their health.

heart and lung problems or cancer, or who needed surgery. The patients with infectious disease, mental illness, poor growth and all the other conditions in which poverty played a huge part were not admitted to the hospitals where they worked. In an era in which huge swathes of the population were struggling to get enough to eat, the sorry truth is that many doctors just weren't that concerned about the effects of poverty on health.

But at the point Douglas was getting his maternity survey together, things were beginning to change, in part because of the burgeoning interest in social equality that blew in after the war. Universities started to establish departments in this new field of social medicine, which explored the relationship between health and social factors such as poverty, poor living conditions and poor nutrition. Douglas's studies, then, added fuel to the fire; and the idea that social and economic factors have a powerful influence on health and disease has grown stronger ever since.

Douglas tackled many other urgent health and social issues of his day – and of ours. One topic of great debate in the early 1950s was working mothers, or, as Douglas charmingly phrased it in one of his early book chapters, 'Expectant Mothers in Gainful Occupation'. During the war, many women had taken up work for the first time to fill positions that had been vacated by men. By the time of the 1946 maternity survey, 28% of pregnant married women worked full time and, while many quit during the pregnancy, Douglas found that just over 15% of women were in full- or part-time work by the time their children were four years old.

This raised a conflict in many people's minds. They could see that women should have the right to work, and that these women helped to relieve shortages in the workforce and brought in money to needy families. On the other hand, there was a general feeling that the children of these women were paying a terrible price, and that this new era of working women could spawn a future generation permanently damaged by their mother's absence. So who was right? Douglas had the data to find out.

The answer, as so often in science, was hardly black and white. When Douglas crunched the numbers on stillbirth and prematurity, for example, he found that there was no increased risk associated with working early during pregnancy, but that there was an increased risk of prematurity for working late.* But he defined 'working late' as working in the last five months of pregnancy, which seems outdated today, when many women work so late in pregnancy that they sometimes take a taxi from the office to the hospital for the birth. And the calculation was scuttled by class, as Douglas freely admitted. The association between working late and prematurity could have been explained by the fact that those working late were also much more likely to be the poorest mothers who needed the income, making it impossible for him to properly separate the effects of work from those of class. Douglas did go on to find a more reassuring answer when he looked at older children, in which there was little evidence that children whose mothers had worked were suffering physically or emotionally. They were about the same height as the children of stay-at-home mothers, had the same number of accidents, and no greater frequency of nightmares or 'bad habits' such as bedwetting.

Even as all these results were emerging in the 1950s, they already seemed out of date. Rationing had ended, the welfare

---

* As explained earlier in this chapter, Douglas was using his definition of prematurity — babies born weighing 5.5 lbs or less — rather than the modern one.

state was maturing, living standards were improving, and Britain was leaving behind the shadow of war. It was altogether a different world, and Douglas and Glass wondered whether the next generation would grow up in the same way as the last. They started to think how wonderful it would be to have a second cohort study and perhaps, in future, a third, so they could compare the experiences of different generations as they grew up. Fortunately, they weren't the only ones to be thinking this way.

In late 1954 Douglas received a note: would he kindly attend a meeting to discuss the idea of a second, nationwide survey of British births? On 16 November he met with a small group of doctors and scientists at London's Ministry of Health on Savile Row. This time, there were no eugenicists and demographers present, because the questions to be addressed by the study all related to medical research. There were two major reasons to launch a second survey of births. The first was the alarming rate at which babies were dying, a concern that had fed into the founding of Douglas's 1946 maternity survey too, but that time was doing little to assuage. Doctors talked then in terms of the perinatal mortality rate, which is the number of stillbirths combined with the number of children who die in the first weeks of life. In 1948 there were still 38.5 perinatal deaths per 1,000 live births. The number was high compared with the rate in many other countries – in Norway, for example, it was closer to 26 – and in the years that followed this figure had been stubbornly refusing to go down.

The second reason for launching a new survey was that it could serve as an appraisal of maternity services under the NHS, which by then had been running for six years. By that point, the spiralling costs of the NHS had become a major political and medical embarrassment. When the health service had been launched, the hope was that its costs would quickly fall as doctors dealt with a backlog of illness and the population's health improved. But what actually happened was that the costs rocketed because people started seeking treatment for conditions that they had weathered stoically before. Doctors were now under pressure to show that they were offering an efficient standard of care. The thought was that a new maternity survey, which could be compared with Douglas's benchmark survey of 1946, would show whether the introduction of the NHS had improved care for women and their babies, and that information could be fed to the Ministry of Health and streamline the way that things were run.

Douglas was hugely enthusiastic. If they had pulled it off once, surely they could do it again. Everyone else at the meeting was too, and the study, called the Perinatal Mortality Survey, started to take shape, modelled on Douglas's method of collecting all the births in one week. The study landed in the first week of March 1958 – exactly twelve years after its predecessor. But, because the focus of this survey was on understanding why babies had died, the Committee wanted information on more deaths than would occur in a single week, so that they would have sufficient numbers to carry out statistical tests. They therefore did something that turned a copy-cat survey into a ground-breaking one: in addition to collecting information on a week's worth of births, they also decided to take in all the newborn babies that perished throughout March, April and May, and to carry out post-mortems on as many of them as they could. No one in the world had attempted to do such a detailed investigation of perinatal mortality before; very few have done so since; and the decision to study dead babies has subsequently proved to be so important that it is still helping to save babies' lives today.

Running such a survey sounded like an appallingly grisly job, and it wasn't one that Douglas wanted to do. He had recently relocated to Edinburgh, and he had his hands full with his own 5,362 children. Luckily, there was another doctor present at the meeting who was delighted to take on the task: an astute paediatrician called Neville Butler.

Butler knew all about births and was known to describe his own, in 1920. He 'was born at an early age, domiciliary delivery', and his 'head was the wrong way round', he joked. His grandfather and father were doctors, and Butler, who was something of a prodigy, was running two medical practices by the age of twenty-one. After the war, Butler moved into paediatrics, the branch of medicine that deals with the growth, development and disease of babies and children. He established his credentials at the famous Hospital for Sick Children, Great Ormond Street, in London.

Unlike Douglas, Butler loved helping those who were ill. He was a superb and instinctive paediatrician, able to identify a child's problem as quickly as a hawk could spot its prey. But Butler was also intellectually curious, and wanted to know what made children ill in the first place – he was something of an epidemiologist, because he was interested in the origins of disease, unlike many doctors of the time. He was therefore captivated by the idea of a massive maternity survey that would be able to discover what it was about some children's backgrounds that put them at particular risk. Butler was known to showcase an almost permanent, amiable grin, and he wafted his enthusiasm like perfume. Whoever he talked to would be swept up by his energy, imagination and vision, and quickly come to believe that collecting reams of information on colossal numbers of children was the most worthwhile undertaking in the world, even if no one had yet invented the computers necessary to easily analyse the data. 'I would do anything for this study,' he would say years later.

When Butler took the reins of the Perinatal Mortality Survey, he launched himself into it like a rocket, blasting around the country to find money and help. And working alongside him was an extraordinary organization called the National Birthday Trust Fund, a charity started in 1928 by a group of well-to-do women who campaigned for better maternity services, and without whom the survey would never have got off the ground. Together, Butler and the Trust wrung money from the Joseph Rowntree Village Trust – the same Rowntree who established one of Britain's chocolate empires – the Tobacco Research Council and the Variety Club of Great Britain, thus helping to pay for the survey with profits from chocolate, cigarettes and show business, amongst other sources. They cajoled doctors, pathologists, midwives and medical officers into performing the grunt work for free, and lined up pathology centres around the country for the autopsies. They even borrowed time on the tabulating machine at the National Coal Board, which was around the corner from the survey headquarters. There was little choice: at the outset, the survey had a budget of less than 10 shillings per child.

This time, midwives were to fill in the forms within twenty-four hours of each birth and to include many more earthy details than Douglas had collected. What was the expected date of delivery? Where had mothers booked, or planned, to have their babies, and where had they actually delivered? How long before delivery did the membranes rupture? Did the baby's crown, feet, shoulder or face emerge first? Just after the survey questions had been signed off, Butler – who was becoming known for his extravagant disregard for deadlines –

raced in and told the team to recall the survey from the printers. He had heard of an odd American study suggesting a link between smoking and birth weight, and he absolutely had to add a question about whether pregnant women had smoked. The survey was dutifully retrieved from the printers, Butler inserted Question 23 and renumbered the rest. This would, one day, prove to have been an invaluable delay.

When the clock ticked past midnight on 3 March, they were off. However laborious it was to fill in the questionnaires, there is no doubt that dealing with the deaths was infinitely worse. As winter gave way to spring 1958, the dead babies started to stack up at the pathology centres in cardboard boxes, infant coffins and wooden crates. The pathologists had the miserable task of unpacking each tragic bundle and then completing a detailed questionnaire. It started by asking whether the body was macerated – softened by soaking – which showed whether the child had perished while still in uterine fluid or after the birth. It closed, eleven pages later, with a diagnosis for the baby's death. It was a terrible task, and some pathologists autopsied an average of fifty children each. 'My lab looks a bit like a battlefield,' wrote one in dismay.

When the window of data collection finally closed, at the end of May, it was clear that the amount of information collected in this survey far outstripped what Douglas had gathered twelve years before. A remarkable 98% of mothers – amounting to 17,205 women – in England, Scotland and Wales completed the survey during the March week, who together bore 17,415* babies in all; and the team had managed

---

* Many of the subsequent data analyses focused on the 16,994 mothers of singleton babies, including babies who did not survive beyond a week but excluding multiple births. A lot of literature today says that the study includes around 17,000 children.

to gather additional records on 7,618 mothers whose babies had died and 5,000 or so meticulous autopsy reports. But, while Douglas had processed his data within a few months, Butler's analysis was hit by delay after delay.

Some of it was unavoidable: every questionnaire had to be scrutinized personally to ensure it was accurate; every tissue slice taken from the lungs of the dead babies was reviewed; and when the 184,000 punch cards were found to be inaccurate, they had to go back and check 20,000 original questionnaires. Butler was so determined that the work be accurate that he was running his clinic during the day and working unpaid to write up the survey through the night. 'Please do try and get more sleep,' a colleague wrote to him in May 1960. 'If you continue to work at such a pace without more sleep and proper food, you will end by killing yourself – on the roads if not by illness.' As the analysis stretched on, doctors, midwives and funders were all growing increasingly impatient to know what had been found.

Eventually, Butler and his team threw a press conference in a private room of the House of Commons to announce the results. It was scheduled for lunchtime on 25 October 1962, four and a half years after the survey had taken place. All the major British newspapers were invited, as well as representatives from the BBC. Butler knew that the data could cause a stir, because nothing is more exquisitely sensitive than the subject of babies who have died, particularly if some of those deaths could have been prevented. To make sure that he got the right message across, he worked from a script that was carefully dictated, typed, retyped and re-retyped by his hard-working secretaries. Butler and a roster of eminent, male obstetricians were on stage. Douglas was in the audience.

Butler stood up to disclose what this vast birth investigation had revealed. To start with, he now knew where every woman in the country went for her pregnancy care and where she eventually gave birth. The survey had shown that 49% of births took place in hospital units staffed by consultants, and most of the rest happened at home or in a medical unit led by GPs. (The 'elsewhere' category on the forms, Butler said, had shown that a few babies had been born in lay-bys, taxis or Turkish baths.) The survey had confirmed that the perinatal mortality rate had fallen somewhat since Douglas's survey in 1946, but that it was still unacceptably high. There were more perinatal deaths than there were deaths in the rest of the first thirty-five years of life put together. This raised the obvious question: why?

One glaring answer had emerged when Butler divided the data by class: he found that babies of unskilled labourers died at a far higher rate than those of the professional classes – which was exactly the same class pattern that Douglas had found in 1946. Poor babies were still far more likely to die than rich ones – providing a terrible condemnation of the NHS, which had been introduced to iron out inequalities in health, but hadn't managed to come close to overcoming the class divide. The length of a pregnancy was also of immense importance, the numbers showed. Babies that were delivered prematurely, before 38 weeks out of the usual 40 weeks of gestation, were at much higher risk of death, but so too were those born late, at 42 weeks or more. Women attempting their first birth through the 'untried pelvis' were also at high risk, as were those having their fourth or fifth child. The data did show that the results from Douglas's earlier survey had helped to make birth a marginally more comfortable experience: 56% of women received the painkilling drug pethidine and over 54% took gas and air.

At the press conference, however, all this sailed smoothly under the bridge. Instead, the focus of attention moved quickly to where women gave birth, a topic that was already causing major ructions in the obstetrics field. Many medical consultants – who are the most senior doctors – were pushing to get more births into hospitals, where they would be in charge and where women had access to the latest equipment and expert care. They thought that too many babies were born at home or in medical units under the direction of GPs and midwives, and that this put them at greater risk. (Needless to say, many GPs disagreed.) The consultants assumed that data from the new maternity survey would help make their case, because it would confirm that hospital was the safest place to give birth. But science is rarely so generous as to provide simple answers, and that is not what the survey actually showed.

Butler and his colleagues had divided up the women according to where they had 'booked' (meaning where they planned to deliver) and where they actually gave birth, and then calculated the perinatal mortality rate for each. They found that mothers who booked and then delivered their baby at home, as well as women who booked and delivered in a GP unit, had mortality rates that were about half those of women who had booked and delivered in hospital. Women who had booked to deliver at home or in a GP unit, but who had ended up giving birth in hospital, had some of the highest mortality rates of all. On the face of it, this suggested that hospital was the *worst* place to give birth – but Butler and the obstetricians interpreted it in a different way. They argued that the higher death rate at hospital was due to their being relegated the higher-risk pregnancies: women who were known to be at risk of complications were more likely to book for a hospital delivery, and others were rushed there in labour when something started to go wrong. Some of the figures did support this assertion. One in three of all deaths occurred because babies lacked oxygen at birth, for example, and facilities available only at hospitals might have been able to help.

In fact, it was impossible to say, based on their simple analysis, whether home or hospital was safer precisely because they had not taken account of the different types of women who ended up in each – their age, class, how many children they had previously had, and so on. Often, the best way to test a hypothesis in science is to carry out an experiment. The ideal experiment for comparing home and hospital births would be to randomly assign pregnant women to give birth in hospital or at home and then compare the outcomes. Then, as now, this is almost impossible to do, because it's unethical to tell high-risk women to give birth at home if they need medicines or equipment available only at hospital; and even if researchers include only very low-risk women in such a trial, these women are understandably reluctant to be told where they have to give birth. That's why, as of writing this over fifty years after the 1958 survey, there have been no major clinical trials of this type.

At the press conference, the consultants were starting to get worked up. They were of the firm opinion that hospital births were best, and they wanted more obstetric consultants, more money and better conditions for midwives. ('Let them get married and have their own children,' said one; 'they are far better midwives if they have had children.') Then a member of the press cut to the chase: So should all women have their babies in hospital? he asked. 'That is my opinion,' one eminent obstetrician replied. 'Surely the days of taking out an appendix on the kitchen table have gone,' cried another, 'and yet delivery under similar conditions is perpetrated!'

Butler, looking on, was appalled. The data suggested that low-risk women were safe giving birth at home or with their GPs. He thought that doctors should do a better job of identifying women who were most at risk – like the lower-class mothers and those who were overdue – and getting them into hospital. The press should *not* conclude that the survey showed that all women should have their babies in hospital, he said, urging the journalists to get the facts right. Those attached to the survey 'would be drummed out of the Brownies if they made ex cathedra statements like that', he warned.

The next day, the kitchen-table story went big. It headlined on the BBC and Independent Television news, and Butler was interviewed on *Woman's Hour*. Newspapers had a field day, portraying babies perishing during filthy home deliveries. 'Lack of care kills 50 babies a week. Survey shows home is not best,' wrote the *Guardian*.

Just as Butler had feared, GPs were absolutely outraged at the assertion that they provided second-rate care; they were now being maligned by a study to which they had contributed much of the work. It is 'unjustifiable and irresponsible to state categorically that more babies will be saved by delivery in hospital', fumed one doctor in the pages of the prestigious *British Medical Journal*. Butler blamed the misinterpretation of the facts on the media. 'If all the contributions had been entirely scientific and the reporting entirely scientific everything would have been all right,' he said. The whole episode was a fine lesson in the difficulty of trying to convey complicated information and a nuanced message – *some* women would be better off giving birth in hospital – through a press conference and a media that errs towards simplistic messages – *all* women should have hospital births.

And before too long the misconstrued results of the 1958 Perinatal Mortality Survey were having a momentous effect: they helped drive a rapid decline in home births. By 1968 the number of births taking place in hospital had risen from 49% to over 80%. This happened in large part because hospitals shortened the time that women stayed after the birth, so that more women could pass through the same number of beds. The change can't be pinned solely on the 1958 survey – medical practice was moving that way anyway – but it almost certainly contributed. The debate about the safest place to give birth rages to this day, and the answer is, still, a nuanced one: hospitals are considered very safe indeed but the recommendation depends on the health of the mother and how many babies she has had, amongst other things.

The survey and the move towards more hospital births did help to drive down the rate of perinatal mortality, which has steadily fallen in Britain ever since. And the survey had another unexpected impact on the practice of childbirth. The finding that overdue babies were at high risk of death meant that obstetricians began to induce labour as a matter of course before women reached 42 weeks of pregnancy. By the 1970s this had become so common that an 'epidemic of induction' was said to be under way – a change that some doctors later came to question.

In 1962, however, these after-effects had yet to be felt. And as Butler and Douglas walked away from the press conference, they already had other things on their minds. Butler desperately wanted to revisit his 17,415 children and turn the 1958 survey into an ongoing cohort study like its predecessor. But he didn't have the support or the funds.

For Douglas and the 1946 cohort, meanwhile, memories of birth were fading away. The children were already facing the next biggest challenge that life throws at us: school.

2

Born to Fail?

Cohorts Go to School

For Patricia Palmer, 5 March 1957 was a special day. It was her eleventh birthday and, although she was still hardly aware of it, the eleventh anniversary of her entry into Douglas's cohort study. It was also, however, a school day, and that was not something to celebrate. It was her final year at primary school, and her teacher appeared to enjoy smacking children around. Once, he had punched Palmer so hard in the chest that he knocked her to the ground. Palmer was terrified, and she would lie on her bed at night without any covers, hoping that she might catch a cold and be able to stay at home. But that day in March she had to go in, because Palmer, along with all the other children in her school year, was going to sit the 11-plus exam.

This exam was another manifestation of Beveridge's re-forms, and had been introduced to give everyone a more equal chance at school. In the years before the war, the country had a bewildering array of schools: public, grammar, endowed, proprietary, elementary, first, primary, secondary, preparatory and more. Some were free and some charged fees – but the upshot was that the type and quality of schooling, much like healthcare, depended on what your parents could afford. This meant that only a small percentage of children passed from primary to secondary school in Britain, compared with other countries in Europe, and the secondary schools were dominated by children of the middle and upper classes. Then had come the 1944 Education Act, which had been designed to level the playing field. The Act made full-time education compulsory and free for all children aged between five and fifteen, and initiated a tripartite system of secondary schools: grammar for the brightest, followed by secondary modern and technical schools, which were supposed to teach hands-on mechanical and engineering skills to those with less of an academic bent. Students would be streamed into the grammar school based on their performance on the 11-plus – named for the age that children would be when they entered the school. The exam was an intelligence test, with all kinds of words and number problems, and the idea was that the cleverest children would pass the exam and win places in the academically rigorous grammar schools, regardless of their social class or disadvantages at home.

Palmer had plenty of disadvantages. Her father had left home when she was five, and had died shortly afterwards. Whether it was the drink or the violence that eventually made her mother force him out, Palmer didn't know and no one ever said, but her mother was now holding down housekeeping jobs to keep the family afloat. Palmer didn't like wearing third-hand clothes and hated that she was the only one in her class who received free school meals. But she had cruised through primary school, and her mother told her that she had always done very well on any tests sent out by that study she was part of in London. 'They've always said you've above-average intelligence.'

On the day of the exam, however, none of that mattered, because her teacher appeared to have written her off. On the front of the 11-plus exam paper, Palmer had to fill in her name, birth date and that day's date. Because it was her birthday, she wrote down the same date twice, apart from the year. But when the teacher saw what she'd written, he assumed she'd made a mistake and couldn't even get her own birthday right. He grabbed her from the seat and walloped her across the head. 'I don't know why you're sitting this,' he spat at her. Palmer was shaking as she filled in the exam – so when the results came through, she was unsurprised to find that she'd failed. Perhaps it didn't matter anyway. When her brother Ken had passed the 11-plus, he hadn't been able to go to the grammar school, because her mother couldn't afford to buy the blazer, cap and tie.

In 1957 Douglas also found out that Palmer had failed her 11-plus, just as he found out the results of every member of his cohort who had sat the exam. By this stage, he had stored away nine detailed questionnaires on the children, and it was hard to think of much he hadn't asked. But at that time Douglas was absorbed by the performance of his cohort children at school.

To some extent, time had dictated this change. It's just like any parent observing their own children: their anxieties tend to focus on whatever the children are doing at the time, meaning that parents obsess about their birth, then their growth (and bowel habits), and then, from about the age of four or five, about how they are doing at school. So it is with birth cohorts. Time and age frame the questions that are asked. Douglas had already observed his cohort through birth and early development, and it now made sense to trace their educational progress too.

At the same time, there were growing concerns about the education system that the cohort could help to address. From a distance, the 1944 Education Act appeared to have been a roaring success, by helping all bright children get ahead. But things were a lot more messy on the ground, where each local education authority was left with the job of imposing the new tripartite system on the patchwork of schools that it already had and without enough money to build a roster of new ones.* The number of grammar school places available differed dramatically from one region to another, and various cut-off lines were being used to decide who was clever enough to attend. What's more, each area used its own 11-plus exam as well as more subjective measures, such as teachers' reports, to decide which children were grammar school material and which were not. Douglas and many others strongly suspected that the system was unfair and that poor children were not getting in.

Meanwhile, children were coming under increasing pressure to pass the test, because parents saw it as the way for their offspring to get ahead. Those who passed won praise and sometimes more. (When John Lennon passed the 11-plus in 1952, his family gave him a new green Raleigh bicycle – although he eventually failed all his O-level exams and went on to other things.) Those who didn't pass, on the other hand, were often left with a lifetime sense of failure and thoughts about what might have been.** It didn't help that some of the schools that they did end up in did little to soothe the pain. 'Some [secondary] modern schools gained a well-justified reputation as dumping grounds for the rejected with little hope for their futures,' read one educational policy review.

With so much riding on the 11-plus, then, it was imperative that the system actually worked. But did it? Had class ceased to matter; were brains all it took to get ahead? With

* One consequence of this was that hardly any secondary technical schools, which were the third prong of the tripartite system, were ever built.
** For the sake of transparency, I should state that in 1984 I failed my 11-plus.

the cohort, Douglas had the perfect tool with which to find out, because he could trace children of different social classes and see how many secured a spot. He set about it with his usual brisk pace. Douglas returned to the children again and again during the school years, and this time he recruited teachers and school doctors to send him updates on the children's progress. At the ages of 8, 11 and 15, Douglas asked the children to sit mental-ability tests too.* This was vital, because in order to know whether all the bright children got places in grammar school, he needed to have an assessment of their intelligence that was completely independent of the 11-plus.

Douglas published what he found in 1964, in a book called *The Home and the School*. Its cheery, lemon-yellow dust jacket belied a sobering body of work. Bright children from the middle classes were far more likely to do well at school and pass the 11-plus than working-class children. When he compared children who were equally bright, based on his tests, it could be seen that just over half of children from the upper middle classes secured grammar school places, while only 22% of those from the lower manual working class managed to do so.** 'This is a distribution of selective secondary school places that can hardly be justified in terms of social equity or, for that

---

* 'The political dangers of monopoly seem to have been much exasperated/excised/exaggerated/expropriated/expostulated', read one question for the eight-year-olds. This was, admittedly, one of the hardest questions. The first on the list, and the easiest, read: 'Come with me to the shops to buy some fire/water/stone/sweets/motors.'

** Douglas assigned children into four social class groups: upper and lower middle class; upper and lower manual working class. (Those at the top of the class ladder – what we might today call 'upper class' – were included in his 'upper middle class' category.)

matter, of national interest,' Douglas wrote. Not only that, but the performance gaps between the middle and working classes appeared to widen as the children passed through school. In short, the educational system was anything but fair, and class mattered as much as it ever had.

The attrition of smart but poor children became known as the 'waste of talent'. Douglas's results paint 'a picture of a nation, educationally, slopping about the house in broken down bedroom slippers. It is a story of wastage,' lamented the *Observer* when his book was published. The outcry quickly turned Douglas's book into a must-read educational reference for student teachers, and many of those teachers remember it still. 'It is hard to imagine a rival in fascination and importance,' read one review in the *Guardian*.

The results were fascinating – but they also made waves because they arrived at just the right time. On the national and international stage, Britain was under more pressure than ever to improve its educational act. There was growing recognition that if the country was to compete in a modern, industrialized world, it needed an educated workforce – brains were the foundation for economic success. This was famously articulated in a political speech by Labour Party leader Harold Wilson in 1963, when he pointed to the scientific and technological revolution that was storming the world. The new Britain was 'to be forged in the white heat of this revolution', he said. Except that it wasn't if, as Douglas's results suggested, the education system was haemorrhaging so many of its bright young things just because they were working class.

In 1965, the year after *The Home and the School* was published, the new Labour government drove through a massive expansion of comprehensive schools, designed to replace the selective school system with a one-size-fits-all approach.* Douglas and his data were in the thick of it; he gave evidence to politicians and interviews to the media; and there was talk of his moving into educational policy. He was 'the custodian of a vast reservoir of information', read a profile in the *Guardian*: 'a man powerful to influence welfare and educational policy'. But Douglas stuck firmly with the cohort. He felt that the science was too complex to say definitively whether grammar schools or comprehensives were the best system. Perhaps he remembered the fate of those wartime air-raid reports, and that politicians could twist information in ways that the scientists who produced it had never intended. 'I think we've given people a lot of ammunition,' Douglas said simply. He handed it to the politicians and left them to get on with the fight.

In 1963, just before Douglas published his book, the education system was coming under scrutiny in another way. The 1944 Education Act had established a Central Advisory Council for Education to advise the government about matters related to education. Nearly twenty years later, Sir Edward Boyle, the Minister for Education, asked the council 'to consider primary education in all its aspects, and the transition to secondary education'. Lady Bridget Plowden chaired the council – and the Plowden Committee, as it became known, was interested in commissioning some research. One idea was to conduct a big survey of primary-school-age children across the country, in order to explore how all kinds of educational measures – ranging from reading ability to behaviour – were influenced by all kinds of other things, from class size to social background and

---

* Local education authorities were asked, rather than required, to make the change, which is why some still have grammar schools and the 11-plus.

child health. The 1944 Education Act had focused attention on all aspects of the education system, from its tips to its roots, and the roots – the primary schools – turned out to be especially in need of reform. Primary schools of the 1950s were pretty wretched places: children were often being taught in classes of forty or more, and many schools were Victorian-era buildings that lacked basic amenities such as electric light, hot water, a playground or proper plumbing. Corporal punishment such as caning was standard, and it was thought that children needed to be disciplined as much as taught. Furthermore, the number of children attending school rose on the back of the baby boom – from 4.5 million in 1944 to nearly 7 million in 1955 – and the schools were struggling to cope.

As researchers cast around for a group of children to study, they realized that they already had one. It wasn't the 1946 cohort – they were already leaving secondary school by then. It was the 17,415 babies whose births and backgrounds had been carefully registered in the second survey, in March 1958, and who were now in their first years of school.

After the press-conference fiasco of 1962, Butler had put his 1958 survey on the shelf. He yearned to turn it into an ongoing study like Douglas's, but he couldn't drum up the money or the support, and no one had even kept track of where the children lived. Now, with interest and money from the Plowden Committee, there was an opportunity to restore it to life. But, while Butler had the passion to do this, he lacked the necessary expertise in education. The study was in need of a new driving force, and it acquired it in the form of Mia Kellmer Pringle.

Kellmer Pringle once told a colleague that she'd had three hurdles to overcome in Britain: she was a foreigner, she was a woman and she was clever. She had grown up in a Jewish family in Vienna, but fled the country as the war approached, and arrived in London with her mother and little else. But Kellmer Pringle possessed a phenomenal intellect, and had the drive and ideas of a woman decades ahead of her time. She kept up a gruelling schedule of part-time jobs while winning a first in psychology, a PhD and then a position as an educational psychologist at the University of Birmingham. 'If there is one person who laid the foundations for the current focus on . . . the importance of the first five years of life and the role of parents, it is Mia Kellmer Pringle,' a colleague wrote. Internationally, she was building a reputation for her work on childcare and development; at home, she was also gaining one for her glamorous Continental accent and for flinging her mink coat over her car engine to keep it warm. Kellmer Pringle was always on time, and she always knew where she was going. Because of her poor childhood she had had to walk everywhere in London, because she couldn't afford the bus. So in later life she had a shortcut to every destination at her fingertips, and she would walk – fast – to get there.

Tragedy threw Kellmer Pringle in the path of the 1958-born children. Her husband had died suddenly, and colleagues in the education world thought that a new challenge might help her to make a fresh start. She was invited to move from Birmingham to London, to head up the National Bureau for Co-operation in Childcare (later, the National Children's Bureau), an energetic new organization in Fitzroy Square designed to improve best practice in childcare. Kellmer Pringle wasn't sure – 'I shake a little in my shoes,' she admitted – but accepted nevertheless. 'Anything anybody can do to make it easier to help children is what matters.' She had been in the job only a few months when she met Butler, and heard about the idea of following up the children from the 1958 survey. Kellmer

Pringle found Butler a little peculiar – and Butler found her difficult too – but she could see that if she adopted a huge national study of British children, the results could put the Bureau and herself on the map. It was agreed that Butler and Kellmer Pringle would co-direct the follow-up study, and together they devised a plan to trace the children and find out as much as they could about their education, social circumstances and health at the age of seven. Because the follow-up study meant that the children were now being monitored through time, the 1958 survey transmuted into a birth cohort study, just like its predecessor.

Scientists call the follow-up studies of a cohort 'sweeps', because they have to gather up all the children in a single stroke. This first sweep turned out to be a rush job, because the deadline imposed by the Plowden Committee meant the children had to be found, the survey completed and the results written up in the space of eighteen months. Butler and Kellmer Pringle didn't pare down the numbers in the study, as Douglas had, so they had some 17,000 seven-year-old children to reach; and, because no one had kept in touch with them, their whereabouts had to be traced from scratch. This was an almost comically laborious task that involved writing to every school in the country to ask if they had children whose birthdays fell in the 1958 birth week and then trying to match them up with the birth records by hand.

An educational psychologist called Ron Davie was appointed to do the sweeping; at times, Davie slept on a fold-up bed at the office so he could put in the extra hours. The record-matching took so long that the scientists eventually gave up any hope of completing it in time for the Plowden Report – an omission that they later put right. And yet, despite all this, huge numbers of the questionnaires were collected and analysed, with answers provided for questions relating to 'Backwardness', 'Creativity',

'Handedness', 'Happiness' and 'Dental Decay'; and thousands of children completed a test called simply 'Drawing a Man'.

Getting the results written up and submitted to the Plowden Committee went down to the wire. On the morning in March 1966 that the final report was due to be completed, the entire staff of the National Children's Bureau were still working flat out, frantically printing sixty copies of the report on squealing Banda copying machines. One person would quickly proof-read a waxed, typed stencil of each page. Then others would attach the stencil to the machine and start cranking the handle, sending damp, sweet-smelling copies flying out the other side. They knew that the reports had to be finished by 3 o'clock, when a van was arriving to pick them up. So you can imagine their horror when the van arrived several hours early – the reports simply weren't done.

The van driver explained that he couldn't wait: it was his wife's birthday, and he had to be home on time or his life wasn't worth living. The study's secretary explained that he had to wait: a nationally important survey of British schoolchildren would all be for nothing if the finished reports weren't dispatched that day. The van driver relented and headed off to make another delivery first, and the entire Bureau went back to reading and cranking, with just a pause for sandwiches eaten with ink-stained fingers. Later that afternoon, when the van returned, the reports were finished – a little smudgy, but finished all the same – and the van driver loaded them up and drove off. Whether or not he was late for his wife's birthday, we don't know. But we do know that the report reached the Plowden Committee in time to be read.

The results from the 1958 cohort study came out in the Plowden Report, *Children and Their Primary Schools*, in 1967. There was no evidence that this next generation was doing any better at breaching the barriers of class than had Douglas's Babies. Children born into lower-class families were still struggling to keep up with their upper-class counterparts. And the study also went further, by showing just how wide the gaps had grown when children were still at a young age: 56% of children in the top social class were judged to be 'good' readers, compared with 23% in the lowest class. As one newspaper crudely put it, 'Slow reader may lack an indoor loo.'

The cohort informed some of the Plowden Report's sharp criticisms of Britain's schooling. 'The more dismal corners of primary education produce plenty of evidence of parochialism, lack of understanding of the needs of children and of the differing homes from which they come.' The Committee's recommendations centred on the idea that teachers would provide the best education if they considered what was best for the child, something that sounds obvious but wasn't necessarily so at the time. It suggested various ways to iron out some of the class divides by offering nursery education to all children after the age of three and providing extra support to schools in deprived neighbourhoods. It also said that corporal punishment should be banned.

In the short term, however, the Plowden Report didn't produce any dramatic changes in schools. The Conservative government that commissioned it had been replaced by a Labour one by the time it came out, and policy changes were already moving schools in roughly the direction that Plowden recommended. But in the long term its suggestions were adopted: free nursery provision was introduced for all three-to-four-year-olds in 1998. And corporal punishment was banned from state schools in 1987 (though private schools were, remarkably, free to use the cane until 1999).

★

From a distance, the two cohorts were swimming smoothly along, producing important results; but beneath the surface scientists's legs were frantically kicking to keep them afloat. Every time Douglas wanted to collect a new round of information on the first cohort, he had to beg for money from various charitable sources. He had won funding from the Nuffield Foundation, Great Ormond Street, the Ford Foundation, the Eugenics Society and fourteen regional hospital boards, but that was before the children had entered school. The entire operation was hand-to-mouth, and Douglas wanted to get the cohort on to firmer financial ground. Cast out any stereotype you may entertain of academics having deep thoughts in their ivory tower; the truth is, someone has to pay for the tower.

Things turned around for Douglas when he ran into Harold Himsworth, who was head of the Medical Research Council, the organization that held the government's research budget in its hands. Douglas knew that the MRC was about his only option if he wanted government funding, which at that time was still a little ad hoc. Today the UK government has seven research councils that fund all aspects of academia in the arts, sciences and engineering; then it had just the Medical Research Council and the Agricultural Research Council. So Douglas could turn to only one place. Fortunately, Himsworth was intrigued by the cohort, and invited Douglas to his office to chat some more. 'We'd better have an MRC unit, old boy,' Himsworth told him.

The casualness of that remark belied its significance for the study: financial salvation was now assured. A research project earning the status of an MRC 'unit' is comparable to a shaky start-up company being bought out by a corporate giant. It meant that the government agreed to fund Douglas and his team, subject to five-yearly reviews, until Douglas retired. 'From then on our problems, our financial problems, vanished,'

Douglas later said. The unit, which got going in 1962, occupied poky corridors at the London School of Economics. The funding also meant that Douglas's research operation could be scaled up – it need no longer be one man and his study, but could encompass an entire team. They were even able to start spin-off studies in other groups of children to explore some of the questions raised by the cohort, such as why impoverished children struggle on so many scores. (In one such study, scientists explored how a group of mothers spent every ten-minute slot within a 24-hour period with regard to consequences for the children's IQ and development, discovering that warmth and absence of hostility correlated with better outcomes more than 'any other damn thing', as one researcher put it.)

Technology was changing too. When Douglas first started the unit, the racket of the tabulating machine and the clattering of the mechanical calculator meant that researchers kept paracetamol in their drawers for the headaches this cacophony sparked. By 1968 things had started to quieten down. That year, the University of London opened a vanguard computer centre in Guildford Street for the use of scientific research, with a top-of-the-line supercomputer. Douglas purchased a high-speed data link – otherwise known as the Research Unit Bicycle – and from then on researchers would pedal through the city carrying the latest pack of punch cards held together with elastic bands. (By this time, punch cards weren't used for the tabulating machine; they had found a second use, telling the computer in machine language what calculations to do.) Some years later, the bike was left in the hall. The 3 million punch cards that the study had accrued were all transferred to computer-readable magnetic tape, 'a most painful change', Douglas said, to ensure they were a faithful replica of the original. The study had collected more than twenty years of irreplaceable data about

Britain and its children on those cards, but this was the first time it had been backed-up.

While Douglas was getting to grips with new technology, Mia Kellmer Pringle was pulling every string she could to keep the 1958 cohort on the road. The money from the Plowden Committee had covered only one visit to the children, when they were seven, and she needed to find more money if she was ever going to see them again. Kellmer Pringle set about getting it with all the determination of Douglas but launched a somewhat different campaign.

Kellmer Pringle couldn't turn to the MRC for funding; it was already paying for Douglas's cohort and besides, her interests and background were in education and social science. Ever since the war, social science researchers in the UK had been engaged in a battle for academic recognition and funding, without much success. In the 1950s the Conservative Party politician who was responsible for research felt that public money should go to the natural sciences instead; social science was a 'happy hunting ground for the bogus and the meretricious', he said, reflecting the view that the field was not rigorous and revealed things that everyone already knew. But, with time, more and more scientists and politicians argued in favour of the field, and in 1965 the government established the Social Sciences Research Council, which would distribute funds to the discipline – a major mark of recognition for the field.

For Kellmer Pringle, the SSRC was the obvious place to turn for funds to do another sweep – but she was asking for a lot of money, and it looked as if the Council would turn her application down. This wouldn't do. To counteract this, Kellmer Pringle organized a relentless letter-writing campaign to the director of the Council, until he thought he was under siege. She also made sure that she had the appropriate support behind the scenes. If officials said no, she went straight to the politicians, whom she'd already secured as friends with a heady cocktail of intellect and charm. 'The civil servants had worked out they couldn't afford to do whatever it was Mia wanted – but the next thing they knew the minister was saying yes to it,' one colleague of Kellmer Pringle's recalls. Before too long the SSRC came up with the funds.

This was a triumph for Kellmer Pringle, but it was also a significant moment in the life of the young cohort, because it meant that it was moving down a slightly different path from its predecessor. Kellmer Pringle was manoeuvring her cohort into the social sciences, whereas Douglas had positioned his in medical research, something that would shape the trajectories of the two cohorts from that point on. (Butler, the doctor who had started the 1958 cohort, was still a major presence in the study, but when the first book on the seven-year-old children came out, Kellmer Pringle had made sure her name came first on the spine.)

With the money in hand, the scientists sent out the survey of eleven-year-olds in 1969. It's painful to admit, but the children had to be traced from scratch all over again.

Twelve years after Patricia Palmer failed her 11-plus exam, Steve Christmas failed his. Christmas was one of the 1958 cohort – he was born in a hospital near Clacton-on-Sea in Essex, and his life had followed a pretty glum route ever since. His parents were busy running a café and had little interest in school; neither did Christmas, who was permanently tired. His dad frittered away most of what the family earned on a bottle of whisky a day and then he kept his children up until the small hours with his drunken ramblings. When Christmas got to the 11-plus exam, he didn't really know why he was taking the test. He opened the paper, wondered what the hell to do, and left it blank.

The scientists' 1969 questionnaires asked all the usual things about health, school, social circumstances and intelligence, but they threw in a little twist. Every child was asked to spend thirty minutes writing about what their lives would be like at the age of twenty-five – something that would arrive in the almost inconceivably distant future of 1983. The scientists received 13,000 essays back. Eleven-year-old Christmas drew a picture of himself with one eye, stubby arms and a long but-toned-up coat. Some people have interpreted this as his being trapped and helpless in a terrible home; Christmas says he just couldn't draw. But he also dutifully penned an essay about his future life – and this is what he wrote:

> *In my 25 years of 25 years old I go gardening and some times Do sports. My real Job is a sargant in the police. in the police it is a hard Job some times you get hurt very cireas and some times you die of your shot womns To Join the police you have to be nearly 6 foot I am marid with 4 children thear ages are 1 4, 7 11 thear names are Jhon aged 1 robin aged 4 and bob aged 7 and last of all Charles aged 11. My wife is the same age as me and her name is Jane. and I have changed my name to mark Stephensons and Jane Stephensons. I live at 61 payvew cresent wayels. our house has 6 bedrooms and a kichen and a toilet in the bath room. when my children grow up I want them to be a police man and drive a police car and do well and then be a police constbele and be married like me and have some little boys and girls and be happy. 2 of my children go to school thay are bob and charls.*

Along with the other most deprived 1958 cohort children, Christmas would come to feature in the ground-breaking studies about inequality that emerged some years down the line.

*

Kellmer Pringle had been disappointed that the Plowden Report failed to call much attention to the National Children's Bureau, and now she was determined that the cohort would make a splash. In 1972 the cohort scientists were about to publish their latest results in a book called *From Birth to Seven*. Somebody at the Bureau knew someone high up at the *Sunday Times*, with the result that the Bureau and the *Sunday Times* struck an agreement: the paper would get an exclusive on the book and run a major article in its colour supplement; in exchange, the paper agreed to mail a copy of the article to every cohort family as a thank you for having taken part. The story was titled 'The Unequal Start' and showed that lower-class children were not just falling behind at school: they were an average of 1.3 inches shorter than their rich counterparts; they had six times as many speech difficulties; and nearly a third had never visited a dentist, in comparison with 1% of the highest class.*

The article was due to be published on Sunday, 4 June 1972, and all other reporters were told that the book was embargoed until Monday, 5 June. But every national newspaper broke the embargo by two days. 'Must these children be lost?' asked the *Daily Mirror*. 'Education Minister Margaret Thatcher should be alarmed by a report [showing that] the youngsters of manual workers lag far behind their middle-class schoolmates.' The papers were shocked by the enormous social, health and educational gaps that separated children at such a young age.

From Douglas's perspective, none of this was a shock at all: he'd already documented all kinds of setbacks suffered by

---

* In this analysis, the researchers divided the group into five social class groups based on the occupation of a child's father. Broadly speaking, occupations in social class I required higher professional qualifications such as medicine or law; social class V was made up of unskilled manual workers.

children born into the lower classes as they grew up. Scientists before him had seen it too. But memories are short, and the fact that something has been discovered before never seems to stop scientists from discovering it again. On top of this, its timing was right. In the early 1970s, when the cohort results came out, the class conversation was getting louder once again. The British economy was in decline, and industrial disputes had soared; a vicious dispute over the pay for coal miners was causing nationwide power cuts to conserve fuel. Many people in working-class jobs felt that they were suffering, and the cohort results served to reinforce the view that life for some was incredibly unfair from the start.

In 1973 a slim paperback digest of the cohort results, called simply *Born to Fail?*, went on sale in station bookstores for 30p. It went on to sell 80,000 copies. It focused on the most deprived children in the cohort, the one in sixteen who lived in families with one parent or with five or more children, *and* inhabited cramped houses or ones without bathrooms and hot water, *and* had a low income of some £15 or less after rent and bills. Then it sketched out how these children tended to struggle from the moment they were born. They were more likely to have been born prematurely, more likely to have been in care, more likely to have skipped school because of illness and were less likely to have been vaccinated. More than half of them had to share a bed and many of them, at the age of eleven, still wet it. 'The disadvantaged group suffered adversity after adversity, heaped upon them from before birth.' The book spelt everything out in simple language and added some black-and-white photos of glum children from a forlorn 1970s housing estate. This way, anyone could pick up a copy, race through it and get completely depressed on the train.

Born to Fail? – and the scientists behind it – argued that reducing inequalities that cripple the life chances of disadvantaged children should be an urgent priority – and that this could be done by a redistribution of income and major improvements in housing. But it held out no hope that this would be done. Peter Wedge, one of the authors of the book, quoted the English historian and socialist R. H. Tawney, who, in a 1913 lecture, said that 'The continuance of social evils is not due to the fact that we do not know what is right, but that we prefer to continue doing what is wrong. Those who have the power to remove them do not have the will, and those who have the will have not, as yet, the power.'

Many people did have the will and the power, of course, and there were signs that all this focus on disadvantaged children was starting to hit home. In Britain, politicians on both sides in the early 1970s were talking about the expansion of nursery education – the idea being that universal nursery provision would create a more equal start for all children. The United States was already ahead of the game in this regard: in the 1960s President Lyndon B. Johnson introduced the Head Start Program, which was designed to boost the development of disadvantaged children through early education and family support; the programme still runs today. The birth cohorts were helping to drive this type of thinking and action.

In 1972 Conservative politician Sir Keith Joseph, who was then Secretary of State for Social Services, made a ringing speech about cycles of deprivation – the idea that parents who had been deprived became parents of another generation who were also deprived, and so on and so on, with little chance of escape. Kellmer Pringle already counted Joseph as a close friend – she 'charmed him no end', one Bureau member recalls – and now Joseph referred to the cohort findings, which supported his ideas. The speech itself generated an uproar, because Joseph suggested that unintelligent or inadequate parents were having too many problem children, and that they should stop – ideas that smacked of eugenics. But the speech spawned a research programme to discover whether cycles of deprivation really did exist. Seven years later, this concluded that they did but that it was complicated – because everything depends on how you define and measure 'deprivation'. There was evidence that educational attainment, occupational status, crime, psychiatric disorder and family difficulties did continue over generations, but there was also ample evidence that many individuals could break out of the cycle and escape a disadvantaged background; equally, there was evidence that people could sink into disadvantage, even though they hadn't started out that way.

The cohort scientists were running up against exactly this idea. Whenever Wedge presented his *Born to Fail?* results at meetings, he was always met with the same retort. Someone would stand up and say, but how can this be true? I grew up with all those terrible things and I did just fine. Wedge would try to explain the seeming contradiction. 'We've looked at thousands of children and this is, on balance, what happens,' he would say. But just because *many* people born into disadvantage go on to struggle doesn't mean that *everyone* will follow that path. As we saw in the introduction, some people do beat the odds – and the scientists were at this point starting to give serious thought to the fascinating question of why this was so. Who does fail, and who succeeds?

The cohort gave them a chance to find out, because they could follow the disadvantaged children on into their lives and see who beat the odds. Take Steve Christmas – what would happen to him? By this point, Christmas had gone to the local secondary modern, where he was put in the remedial class. He would emerge five years later unable to address an envelope.

Sometime afterwards, the bailiffs turned up at his house to take away the family possessions, because his father couldn't pay the tax bill. It was certainly looking like Christmas was born to fail, and with time he – and the scientists watching him – would find out if this was true.

All this angst about class did have one positive effect, as far as Kellmer Pringle was concerned: it convinced politicians that the 1958 cohort was worthwhile and that they should pay scientists to carry out another sweep when the children were sixteen, in 1974. There is no doubt that they made the right decision: the 1958 cohort would contribute evidence to every major inquiry on child health or welfare in Britain that took place during the first two decades of its life. And in the field of education, almost every issue that is currently debated about schools today was presciently raised by them some forty or fifty years ago. For example, the 1958 cohort ended up testing policy changes that its predecessor had helped to create, when Douglas discovered that grammar-school places were more likely to go to those who had had every advantage from the start, and helped bring about a change to secondary education.

The members of the second cohort were entering secondary school during the period when many education authorities were switching from the grammar school system to comprehensives. With children passing through both the old system and the new, the opportunity arose for a never-to-be repeated natural experiment that could be used to test which system better served them. It was a particularly good experiment, because the type of school that each child attended was simply a reflection of the policy in the area in which they lived, so, to a large extent, the children were randomly assigned either to a selective school system (grammars and secondary moderns) or to a comprehensive one. The cohort scientists saw this, linked up the children's school type with their performance on standard reading and maths tests, and then tried to rule out social class and other confounding factors – i.e., any factor that gets in the way of accurate results by producing a spurious or misleading link.

However the cohort scientists looked at it, they couldn't find much difference between the grammars and the comprehensives – certainly the brightest children appeared to do equally well in each. The Bureau wrote up the results in a special issue of its journal, *Concern*, and circulated several thousand copies to local education authorities around the country. The results landed smack in the middle of a renewed debate about which was better: selective or comprehensive education.

This argument had never really disappeared entirely, but it surfaced afresh in 1979, when Margaret Thatcher was elected prime minister. Thatcher, whose father ran a grocery shop, had attended the local grammar school and went from there to Oxford. The very first Act she passed as prime minister was designed to expand selective education through the 11-plus. But some local authorities were deeply opposed to going back to the selective education system, and the whole issue had become polarized along party lines. When the cohort paper suggested that there wasn't much evidence to support one system over the other, the Bureau found itself under attack – accused of political bias and fiddling the data. On a radio show to discuss the results, one cohort scientist found himself introduced as the man in the red corner – the left-leaning, comprehensive school supporter – facing off against his opponent, the grammar school advocate, over there in the blue. But the scientists had confidence in the data. 'We had the entire statistics profession on our side,' recalls one.

The grammar school question didn't go away – and cohort researchers have been tackling it again and again, with increasingly sophisticated methods, ever since. Many scientists think that any differences between the school types are small at best and that the answer to which offers a better education depends on the ability of the child, their social background and the quality of the various schools on offer where they are.

The 1958 cohort took on a multitude of other questions about schooling. Worried about the effect of big class sizes in school? The cohort scientists examined this in the 1970s and found that seven-year-old children in small classes did no better than those in large ones. (In those days, 'small' classes were those with 30 children or fewer in them, and 'large' classes were those with 40 or more, whereas classes today rarely exceed 30.) The finding incensed teachers, who at that time were pushing strongly to reduce class size, and the relationship between class size and student performance remains contentious today.

What was the best way to teach children how to read? Seven-year-old children who learnt reading by phonics – building up words from their component sounds – tended to progress more quickly in reading than those who did not, the cohort showed, but in the end the scientists concluded that what mattered most was the confidence of the teacher in the technique and his or her relationship with the children.

Were independent schools better than state schools? Here, it was particularly difficult to separate out the influence of social class, but it looked like the benefits of independent schools were marginal at best. 'It is doubtful whether any advantage in measured attainment could justify the additional costs involved for parents,' the team wrote.

Sometimes it seems like the same old questions go round and round like clothes in a washing machine. Each generation confronts these important and complex problems for itself, only to find there are no simple answers; but cohort studies have nevertheless come to be an essential tool in cutting through the complexity. Sometimes, a cohort study that started decades earlier still offers some of the best evidence for policy-makers trying to arrive at informed choices in their own place and in their own time.

Children's life chances are of course determined by many factors in addition to the type of school on offer. In the 1960s, for instance, Douglas had found that good parenting appeared to be hugely important for children's educational progress; one of his findings was that interested parents could partly compensate for some of the disadvantages brought about by poverty or social class – in other words, home was just as important as school. So it is unsurprising that, with the advent of a rising divorce rate, the 1958 cohort scientists came to consider the consequences of family break-ups upon their subjects.

Just 3% of children born in the 1946 cohort had seen their parents separate or divorce by the time they were six; whereas 8% of the children in the 1958 cohort had parents who had split by a similar age. The black-and-white TV ads of the sixties portrayed the breadwinner husband with a contented stay-at-home wife and her rosy-cheeked children. But things weren't looking so rosy in real life: in 1969 an Act of Parliament made it much easier to file for divorce in Britain, and the rate of break-ups went through the roof. The rising rate of divorce quickly became a political hot topic. The traditional family model was shattered, and the fear was that single parents were being left destitute and children were being harmed.

As a consequence, the government convened a group called the Finer Committee on One Parent Families, which examined the impact of this major demographic shift. As the Committee was starting to collect evidence in 1969, a young woman at the National Children's Bureau called Elsa Ferri pitched in. The children in the second cohort were amongst the first to experience divorce in significant numbers, and the study offered an opportunity to find out what repercussions this would have. Ferri scoured data from the cohort on one-parent families* and then went out to interview some of them to find out what their lives were really like.

It pretty soon became clear that there were lasting effects from not having two parents around. These children were more likely to do poorly at school and suffer behavioural problems than those who had two parents at home. (Much later, studies showed just how enduring these repercussions were: the children of divorced parents grew into adults who were more likely to be unemployed, earn less, suffer mental health problems, fall sick, drink too much and see their own relationships crumble. In fact, by some measures, divorce seemed to have more of a negative impact than a parent's death.) But, as usual, the picture was complicated, because children of single parents also tended to be of a lower social class, have less money, live in smaller, grottier homes and suffer other disadvantages – there were, in other words, plenty of confounding factors getting in the way. The researchers wanted to filter these out and to pinpoint whether having one parent per se was associated with children's problems, or whether it was these other factors that really mattered. And when Ferri did this, a more nuanced picture emerged. Yes, having one parent

---

* Of the families she studied, Ferri found that 54% were considered to be one-parent due to separation or divorce, well over a third because a parent had died; and the rest fell into the category because the children had been born to unmarried mothers.

was associated with difficulties for children – but much of that association could be explained by the poverty and disadvantage that went with it. Ferri was excited by the finding: it meant that the key to helping children lay in lifting them out of poverty, not necessarily in stemming the tide of divorce. She was called in to the Department of Health and Social Security to talk about her results. It was a high-level meeting with a senior civil servant who was one down from the permanent secretary. 'OK, so we've read your findings,' he said. 'Now what do you think is the most important policy message?'

'Well, quite clearly,' Ferri replied, 'the main area for policy reform is poverty.'

One-down-from-the-permanent-secretary's eyes glazed over. 'Oh, well, yes of course we know all that,' he said. 'But, given that's not going to happen, what would you recommend?'

Ferri was crestfallen – like Douglas before her, she realized that policy-makers can use research however they choose. However, when the Committee on One Parent Families did finally issue its report, in 1974, it acknowledged that single parents often struggled for money and recommended that they receive extra financial support from the government. Its recommendations were not taken up.

The 1958 cohort continued to attack the issue, with one study in particular revealing the value of studying children throughout their lives. For years it was assumed that children of divorced parents suffered setbacks because of the divorce itself and what happened afterwards. But the scientists were able to use the cohort data to look at the children *before* the divorce had even happened – and they showed that whatever was going on at home was affecting children's educational performance and behaviour long before their parents eventually separated. Even further down the line, researchers were able to compare cohorts born at different times to examine whether the increasing frequency of divorce was lessening its effects on children's life chances, as measured by their performance at school. It wasn't.

With two successful birth cohort studies on the go, scientists and doctors met in February 1966 to discuss the possibility of a third. The idea did not have universal support – if we had two already, did we really need three? Some obstetricians, for example, wondered what more could possibly be learnt about the routine process of birth. 'Few countries can equal the self-critical analysis to which obstetricians in Britain regularly submit themselves,' wrote one jaded member of the profession. And GPs were still upset about the fallout from the 1958 survey, which had been interpreted by some as suggesting that births were unsafe in their hands.

But there were champions for the idea, and Butler was, tirelessly, one of them. Before the first meeting, he had prepared a whole list of reasons to carry out a third birth survey, the main one being that perinatal mortality was still a big concern. Although the 1958 survey had helped to drive down the rate, it wasn't falling as steeply as everyone would have liked, and another survey might reveal why. Butler wanted to know whether high-risk mothers – such as those from the lower classes – who had not been getting to hospital in the previous survey were now getting better care. Computers promised to make the analysis much easier too. Butler was also determined that this study, unlike the last one, would be planned as a cohort study from the start, rather than having to resurrect it after a few years. His reasoning was that if you already had two birth cohorts, why *not* make it three?

At the meeting, Butler's arguments appeared to convince everyone. 'Is there anybody who thinks it is not worthwhile?' the chairman asked the group. No one spoke up, and preparations for the third cohort soon got under way. The survey would take place in the week of 5–11 April 1970, twelve years after the 1958 survey, just as there had been twelve years between the first and the second. A scientist called Roma Chamberlain was hired to lead it, along with an obstetrician, Geoffrey Chamberlain (who was widely assumed to be married to Roma but was not).

It would be hard to argue that this survey was easier; the passage of time and changing face of science had made sure of that. The 1946 survey had answered almost solely to one organization, the Population Investigation Committee; the 1970 survey involved twenty-three charitable bodies, government departments and professional bodies, and they all wanted a seat at the table. In fact, one table was nowhere near big enough. Four separate working parties were established to figure out what questions to ask in the survey (What brand of the Pill was used? Which of sixteen types of pain relief were administered?), and another to grapple with how to administer it.

The biggest problem for this third survey, however, was the price tag. All the additional people, bureaucratic procedures and sophisticated computers caused the costs to spiral out of control.* As the week of the survey approached, the organizers still didn't have the money in the bank, and luck wasn't doing much to help. The day the forms left the printers, a violent

---

* The National Birthday Trust at this time employed a young man named Jeffrey Archer as its director-general, with the aim of raising enough to fund the survey. Archer had big plans, including one to launch a campaign called Britain's Million Mothers, in which every new mother would receive a card shortly after the birth of her child suggesting that she make a 'thank offering' to the Trust of £1. He confided to the steering committee that it would be a 'nice blackmail' and that, in a decade, money would be a dirty word in these discussions because they would not have to worry about it. Shortly afterwards, with the birth survey still desperately short of funds, Archer left to pursue greater things.

snowstorm paralysed the country. The first batch of forms to be sent to Northern Ireland, which was included for the first time, was lost at the docks, so a second had to be dispatched by plane.* The post office went on strike during the survey, and it took two weeks for any completed forms to reach London.

Yet, for all these setbacks, the scientists pulled it off again. The survey reached 17,196 babies – including, in a wonderful reproductive loop, one born to a 24-year-old mother who was a member of the 1946 cohort. The newspapers were happy to publicize the survey – everyone loved a baby story in 1970 as much as they did in 1946 – and pictures of newborns were everywhere in that April week. 'Computer probes 15,000 births,' marvelled the *Sun*.

Two years later, when the computer had finished its job, the Chamberlains revealed the results – although, having learnt a lesson from the kitchen-table incident, they released them in the medical literature rather than at a press conference, in a book called *British Births 1970*. The after-effects of the previous two surveys were evident in the figures: 66% of women gave birth in hospitals; 26% of women had their labour induced; the majority of women received some form of pain relief; and the perinatal mortality rate was falling. Other things hadn't changed so much. The survey showed that there was a higher perinatal mortality rate attached to hospital births than to home ones, which some doctors again explained away by saying that high-risk births were directed to hospital.

And when it came to class, nothing had changed at all. Babies born into the lower classes were still much more likely to die than those born into the more privileged ones. It was a bleak

* Although the births in Northern Ireland were included in the survey, they were not followed up after this.

discovery, as the scientists wrote in their book. 'There is nothing to contradict and everything to support the theory that social class differences are widening rather than diminishing.'

3

In Sickness and in Health

Cohorts and Epidemiology

There was an unusual bustle in Philip Cheetham's house on a Saturday morning in 1959. His mother had asked him to stay in bed, and he could hear people coming and going downstairs, their voices full of concern. But he couldn't hear his father's voice and, with the intuitive sense that children possess, he soon worked out why. His father had died, and the commotion was because his mother and her neighbours were laying out the body, making it presentable for when the undertakers arrived.

Cheetham's life was already taking up a thick file in James Douglas's records of children born in 1946. Actually, it was something of a surprise that he even had a life at all, given that his mother's first two children had been stillborn and she had suffered a terrible pregnancy with him. When baby Philip had arrived – on 6 March and at a surprisingly robust 9 lbs 4 oz – it was at home, and his mother haemorrhaged and nearly lost her life.

There were three bedrooms in the terraced house in Croston, Lancashire. His grandparents took one bedroom, his parents the second, and he had the third. The toilet was a wooden plank with a hole in, covered by a shack and situated 200 feet down the garden – or at least it was until his grandparents died, at which point Cheetham's bedroom was converted into an indoor toilet and he moved into their room. Cheetham doesn't remember wanting for anything when he was a child, but he was firmly in the working classes, according to the cohort files. His mother worked as a weaver in the local cotton mill and his father looked after the railway tracks. The heart attack that had killed his dad, however, came without warning.

Cheetham was clever, but that wasn't enough to propel him through the 11-plus. Besides all the problems at home, the local school was in such a state that six teachers arrived and left during the year of the exam. (Some years later, Cheetham read about the 'waste of talent' that James Douglas and the cohort study had revealed – the bright, working-class children who failed to secure a grammar school spot – and realized that this described him perfectly.) But Cheetham's story perhaps shows how a streak of ambition and parents who take an interest can beat the odds. His mother switched him into a good secondary modern school, where he shone at metalwork and technical drawing. He found a local apprenticeship at the age of sixteen and was promoted by his supervisors; he later went on to win a scholarship to study for further exams. He forged a career in aircraft design, computing and specialist software for engineers. It certainly looked as if Cheetham had overcome the inherent disadvantages of his working-class upbringing.

But there was one aspect of his history from which he could not break free, and that related to his health; he may have inherited a susceptibility to cardiovascular disease. And it was the cohort study that alerted him to this fact. Cheetham had generally cruised through the medical tests that the cohort scientists subjected him to, except for a red flag that popped up in 2010, at the age of sixty-four, which showed that his cholesterol level was worryingly high. He started to take statins to bring it down.

Too late. One night in 2011, he woke up in the small hours

and didn't feel quite right. The left side of his face was aching, and when he reached for his water, he couldn't swallow it. Within an hour, an ambulance had taken him to the local hospital, where doctors pushed an endoscope down his nose and throat. 'I have good news for you,' the doctor told him. 'You don't have cancer.' But Cheetham was quickly losing the ability to speak – and when he tried to write down what he wanted to say, his scrawl wandered off the lines. He was soon diagnosed as having had a stroke.

Cheetham didn't believe that a poor diet or an unhealthy lifestyle caused his illness: the doctor had told him that even if he were to subsist on a diet of lettuce leaves, his cholesterol wouldn't drop. So it was most likely a genetic problem, aggravated by the socioeconomic assaults to which he had been subjected cumulatively throughout his life – all of which would have been carefully noted by the scientists conducting the cohort study. Because, as it turns out, medical records on 5,362 people are a very valuable commodity indeed.

All the while the scientists had been tracing the first two British birth cohorts through school, they had never lost sight of their health. Douglas had been diligently asking school doctors and nurses to regularly examine the children, as well as asking mothers about their children's health. (Has this child ever had bronchitis, broncho-pneumonia, or pneumonia? Has this child ever had discharge of pus from his ears? How often has he had a snuffly or running nose during the last year? Is this child sick when travelling / sick when excited / sick when he over-eats / sick on other occasions / not frequently sick?) And soon enough, all this information found a practical use.

It was an otherwise normal Friday in December 1952, when the Douglas Babies were six and a half, that London nearly choked to death on its own toxic fog. The city was no stranger to pollution, which was belched unreservedly from factories and regularly pooled into filthy smogs. But that day was different. It was bitterly cold, and everyone stoked up their coal fires, sending smoke pouring out of the chimneys. At the same time, a weather system conspired to trap the smoke and mix it up with all the noxious factory effluent, as well as a cloud of pollution that happened to be blowing over from the Continent. A fog began to form, then it thickened and congealed. Soon pedestrians couldn't see their feet.

The fog worked its sour taste into people's mouths and left their noses coated with black grit. From there, it worked its way deep into everyone's lungs. For four days over that weekend, the city was forced to inhale an airborne stew that couldn't have been more poisonous if witches had brewed it up themselves. Scientists later worked out that each day of smog contained about 800 tonnes of sulphuric acid and 1,000 tonnes of smoke particles. A tonne is roughly comparable to the weight of a VW Beetle, a fashionable vehicle in 1952. So, to put it in perspective, that's about 800 Beetles' worth of sulphuric acid wafting around and being inhaled.

By the time the London fog cleared four days later, it had taken an astonishing toll. Several prize cows at the Smithfield agricultural show suffocated. More to the point, some 12,000 people are thought to have died from the fog and many more struggled to breathe. The 'London fog' – now considered one of the most dramatic episodes of air pollution in history – woke everyone up to the country's massive pollution problem, which had been growing unabated in tandem with industry. This had to stop. Four years later, partly in response to the fog, politicians passed the 1956 Clean Air Act, which forced the use of smokeless fuels in some towns and cities. The Act was so effective that smoke emissions plummeted, and London – believe it or not – actually became a sunnier place. The number of hours of winter sunshine shot up after the Act by more than 50%.

The London fog also left its mark on scientists, because it fuelled a wave of medical research into the effects of air pollution. One of the questions was over its long-term effects. The London fog had shown that a sharp increase in air pollution could kill – but what happened if you breathed a lower level of pollution, in and out, every day, year upon year, as many people living in towns and cities did? Did that cause health problems too – and, if it did, did they clear up if you escaped into cleaner air? This was important to know, because respiratory diseases, including tuberculosis, bronchitis, emphysema and asthma, were rife.

Douglas had a unique way to explore the problem. The thousands of children in the 1946 cohort had spent the first ten years of their lives breathing polluted air before the Clean Air Act kicked in, and he already had careful records of their respiratory health – how many coughs, colds, runny noses, cases of tonsillitis, bronchitis and pneumonia they'd had as they grew up. All he needed now was a measure of how much pollution each child had been exposed to.

Douglas found this in a rather ingenious way: by collecting old records from Local Fuel Overseers, the people who kept a note of how much coal was distributed when fuel was still being rationed. He used the records to classify every region of the country into four categories, ranging from very low pollution (typically the rural areas) to high (the densely populated parts of towns and cities). Then he matched up the addresses of the cohort children with the level of pollution in their home region and with their health records up to the age of fifteen.

When you think that he had 2,689 different regions, thousands of cohort children and fifteen years' worth of health data, you can see that the study was pretty complex – although not as complex as Douglas might have liked. He knew that he had no way of taking into account the effects of a child's journey from a high pollution area to a school in a less polluted one. And, to make the analysis manageable, he ignored children who had moved house during the study from one pollution level into another. Still, it was the best he could do, and the pattern that emerged, when he published the results in 1966, was as clear as London's newly cleaned skies.

Douglas found that children growing up in the most heavily polluted areas were significantly more likely to suffer from coughs and infections of the lower respiratory tract, such as bronchitis and pneumonia. They were also more likely to be absent from school with illness – and were a touch more likely to have 'discharging ears', which are a sign of ear infections. For once, social class was irrelevant. Working-class and middle-class children were equally affected if they lived in polluted regions – even the affluent have no way to scrub the air clean. The results also followed a gradient: the more pollution children were exposed to, the more health problems they suffered – and, most surprising of all, the lung problems lasted until at least the age of fifteen, even though the new legislation had drastically cut pollution levels from the time that the children were ten. This suggested that exposure to pollution as a child interferes with the lung in a way that causes lasting damage – a finding that sounds obvious after the fact, but wasn't before the research was conducted. We now know that children are born with very immature lungs, and that these undergo incredible growth and reorganization in the first few years of life, making them acutely vulnerable to pollutants. If that growth is interrupted, they may never fully recover – one reason why exposure to air pollution is now considered one of the biggest public health threats in the world.

The pollution study demonstrated, yet again, the value of tracing children over many years – not only to reveal their educational paths but also to observe their changing health. And, by this point, scientists didn't need convincing that massive child cohort studies were useful for understanding infant and child health. The British birth cohorts were not growing up alone: a whole spate of them had been started up around the world. In 1959 US scientists started the biggest of these when they collected information on some 55,000 pregnant women and started to follow their children in an effort called the Collaborative Perinatal Project, designed to explore how factors during pregnancy and early life contribute to disorders of the brain and nervous system such as cerebral palsy. That same year, a related effort called the Child Health and Development Study began to recruit what would eventually be over 20,000 pregnant women in California in a broad study of the influences on prenatal and child health. There were perinatal projects examining thousands of births in Denmark and Finland, and smaller ones had emerged in Newcastle, Aberdeen and other places besides. There was, in fact, quite a cohort of cohorts – although some of them did not survive, as we'll see. Like Douglas and Butler, scientists and doctors had come to recognize that cohort studies provide a fascinating window on human health. Their place in the field of epidemiology had become unshakable.

During the birth and childhood of Douglas's cohort, epidemiology had been undergoing a transformation. Through the late 1800s and early 1900s the discipline had been concerned almost entirely with infectious disease, because that was what

was killing us. Cholera, tuberculosis, measles, typhoid, diph-
theria – the list of infections went on and on. Epidemics of
these killers gave the discipline its name, which stems from the
Greek words *epi* ('upon' or 'among') and *demos* ('the people').

But, with time, epidemiologists started to conquer these
conditions with scrupulously planned scientific investigations.
In 1854 a doctor called John Snow – the same one, curiously
enough, who relieved Queen Victoria of her labour pains earlier in this book – carried out a study that became seminal in
the history of epidemiology, when he investigated the reason
why people were succumbing to an outbreak of cholera that
was rampaging through the Soho area of London. Snow went
out and interviewed households that had been affected,
mapped their locations and eventually traced the outbreak to a
water pump on Broad Street, where the victims had drawn
drinking water that appeared to be contaminated with sewage.
Snow is considered a founding figure in epidemiology for
showing that carefully analysing the patterns of a disease could
point to its cause – even though it took another twenty years or
so to find that cause, a bacterium called *Vibrio cholerae*, which is
expelled in the faeces of people with the disease and passed on
to new victims when they drink water contaminated with the
bacteria. Over the next few decades, scientists identified the
microscopic bacteria and viruses responsible for other infectious diseases and were soon beating those bugs into retreat.
Improvements in sewers and the supply of clean water helped
to stop their spread; vaccines arrived for tuberculosis, polio and
whooping cough; and in the 1940s penicillin became the first of
several antibiotics available to treat infections. So successful
were these campaigns that by the Second World War epidemiology had lost its interest for many doctors in Britain.

Sometimes in medicine, however, patching up one problem

just exposes another. The enormously influential medical statistician William Farr had systemized the classification of deaths
in the mid-nineteenth century, and, a few decades later, those
death counts were generating some particularly scary-looking
graphs. From the 1920s onwards, doctors in industrialized
countries noticed that the number of people dying from heart
disease and cancer was climbing fast, along with those dying
from stroke, diabetes and chronic lung disease. By the time the
Second World War had come and gone, some were saying that
such chronic diseases had replaced infectious diseases as the
modern epidemic. Suddenly epidemiology had an enormous
new problem on its hands. This drove it into a new era of
research in which cohort studies were thrust into the spotlight.

The most famous example of this lies in the story of lung
cancer, which, seventy years ago, was on a particularly sharp
upwards curve. In 1920, 1.5% of cancer deaths in British men
were caused by lung cancer; by 1947 this had rocketed to nearly
20% and was showing no sign of slowing down. It's easy to see
now that this rise was happening hand in hand with a growing
appetite for cigarettes. In 1900 every adult in the United States
smoked an average of around 50 cigarettes each year; by 1965
this had risen to more than 4,200 – and around a half of men
and a third of women smoked. In the UK, some 80% of
men smoked by 1948. But the very fact that smoking was so
incredibly widespread made it hard to see that smoking could
be a cause of lung cancer – because lots of people smoked but
only a small fraction of them got the disease. There were
reports from the 1920s onwards suggesting that smoking was
the root of the problem, but they did not get the international
attention that they deserved. Many of them came from Germany – before and during the Nazi period – and they were
written in German and overlooked elsewhere in the world.

In Britain the Medical Research Council decided to launch its own investigation of the cause of lung cancer, and it turned for help to a leading statistician called Austin Bradford Hill,* who in turn recruited a medical researcher called Richard Doll to help. The work that these scientists went on to do became a landmark in epidemiology. Doll and Hill first launched a type of epidemiological investigation called a case-control study. They scoured London hospitals for people who had lung cancer – the cases – and compared them with a 'control' – a group of people who were in hospital for different illnesses. Then they asked the participants about their smoking habits in the past and tried to eliminate confounding factors, such as age, class and exposure to other pollutants. By the time they had tabulated their results, in 1950, it was clear that the ones who had lung cancer were much more likely to be smokers than the ones who had escaped the disease.

At the time, study after study was finding the same link between lung cancer and smoking. But other scientists had huge incentives to rip the work apart. Few people liked the idea that the highly popular and enjoyable habit of smoking was potentially lethal – particularly the tobacco industry, which was putting up a robust defence. That aside, there were some good scientific reasons to question the link between smoking and lung cancer too.

The first of these touches on one of the thorniest issues in epidemiological studies: distinguishing a correlation from a cause. Just because there was an association between smoking and lung cancer didn't mean that smoking *caused* lung cancer. One way to explain the problem is by imagining a room containing a light switch and a bulb. If you flick the switch and the

---

* Everyone knew everyone in those days: James Douglas had worked with Bradford Hill in Solly Zuckerman's scientific research unit during the war.

light bulb comes on, you might safely assume that the switch was the cause. But what if flicking the switch only turns on the light bulb some of the time; and what if the bulb comes on a few years or decades after you flicked on the switch? That's the case with smoking and cancer. Huge numbers of people smoked – they flicked a switch – but only some of them developed lung cancer, often years after they had started to smoke. To make matters more complicated, some people got lung cancer even though they had never smoked: the light bulb went on by itself. This makes it extremely hard to work out if the switch is actually operating the bulb. Which explains why, in the 1950s, scientists were reluctant to rule out other explanations for the smoking–lung cancer link. It was possible that lung cancer somehow caused people to reach for cigarettes – or perhaps something else entirely caused people to smoke *and* increased their risk of lung cancer.

The second big objection to the smoking–lung cancer link arose from the method that Doll, Hill and many other scientists had used. Case-control studies are fraught with possible error, because the diagnosis of a disease can actually influence the way that we behave. A patient who knows they have lung cancer might be looking for something to blame and overestimate the number of cigarettes that they had been smoking. Alternatively, doctors might interrogate cancer patients about their smoking habits in a more rigorous way than those in the control group. Distortions such as these may have biased the studies, suggesting that cancer patients smoked more often than they really did.

Given the widespread scepticism, Doll and Hill knew that they needed a better approach. The most convincing way to nail the link between smoking and cancer, Hill realized, would be to identify a large group of people whose smoking habits were known and then follow them to find out whether the smokers developed cancer more often than the non-smokers, and whether the heavy smokers were struck more often than the lighter smokers. In other words, they needed to set up an adult cohort study – although they didn't call it that at the time. They called it a 'prospective' study, and the idea was so new to medicine that when Doll and Hill later published their work they printed the *Oxford English Dictionary*'s definition of the word at the base of the page. ('Characterized by looking forward into the future', it read.) The concept was simple, they admitted, but had not been put into action before because such studies are time-consuming and expensive. Now that it was clear so many lives were in jeopardy, the effort was considered to be worthwhile – and the expense was covered by the government. For the smoking prospective study, Hill suggested that doctors might make a good group. They would probably be interested in responding to a scientific study, and they would be easy to follow up because they had to keep their names listed on the Medical Register in order to practise. And, of course, they smoked just as heavily as everyone else.

On 31 October 1951 Doll and Hill launched their cohort study by posting a questionnaire to 59,600 British doctors on the register. The questions, which covered just one side of paper, asked simply if the recipients were smokers now or had been in the past, and, if they smoked, how heavily they smoked and for how long. (Hill was a stickler for short questionnaires and said that before any question is included, a scientist should stop and ask five questions about whether it was necessary to include it at all.) The strategy worked: 41,024 people replied, and it took about a year simply to open the envelopes and get the responses on to punch cards. The researchers also asked the Office of the Registrar General (the one that once employed

Farr and that keeps statistics on births and deaths) to provide them with copies of death certificates for anyone whose occupation was listed as doctor. Then they just waited for people to die.

After nearly two and a quarter years, thirty-six men had died from lung cancer.* Every one of those cancer cases occurred in doctors who had smoked. But Doll and Hill went the extra mile to make their case that smoking was not just correlated with lung cancer, but was the cause. They showed that the risk of lung cancer rose steadily with the amount of tobacco that a person smoked. The same year, 1954, the results came through for another massive cohort study, of nearly 190,000 American men. This had been launched around the same time as Doll and Hill's with the express purpose of disproving any association between smoking and lung cancer. Instead, it convincingly proved that there was a link.

After these cohort studies were published, there was still massive resistance to the smoking–cancer link, but slowly, very slowly, the dominoes began to fall. In 1957 the Medical Research Council issued a firm statement saying that tobacco was the most likely cause of lung cancer, and the United States Surgeon General openly agreed. The results of the two cohort studies are now considered seminal in the history of epidemiology for cementing the link between smoking and cancer and fuelling the process by which tobacco was thrown into the dungeons of public health. Five years after Doll and Hill started their cohort, which is now known as the British Doctors' Study, they were able to publish results showing that smoking is also associated with heart disease, chronic lung disease, peptic

---

* In their preliminary analysis, published in 1954, Doll and Hill focused only on men aged 35 or above.

ulcers and tuberculosis; forty years into the study, a link was demonstrated to thirty causes of death. Hill's work on this study led him to think more generally about the type of evidence required to prove a causal link between a specific factor (such as smoking) and a consequence (a disease such as lung cancer); his conclusions, published in 1965, came to be known as 'Bradford Hill's criteria for causation' and are still widely used in epidemiology today.

A few years earlier, another adult cohort study – which would prove to be equally iconic in the history of medicine – had started to take shape: this one was conducted in the small town of Framingham, Massachusetts. Its origins can be traced to the death of a US president. When Franklin D. Roosevelt started his term as president, in 1932, in the midst of the Great Depression, his doctors noted that his blood pressure was pretty high, at 140/100 mm Hg. In 1945, after an historic twelve years in office and most of a world war, it had risen to a stratospheric 300/190 mm Hg, and Roosevelt could barely stand. He collapsed and died of a stroke that year, bringing his presidency to a premature end. This was a tragedy, but not a surprise. By the 1940s about half of all deaths in the United States were caused by cardiovascular disease – the constellation of conditions that affect the heart and circulatory system, often resulting in heart attack or stroke. But medicine was at a loss to know what to do about it. There was so little known about the causes of heart disease that most people just accepted that this was the way they would exit the world.

Roosevelt's death spurred some action: shortly afterwards, President Truman signed the National Heart Act into law, and half a million dollars were allocated to a twenty-year study of heart disease. One proposal that swam to the top was to conduct a cohort study – one that would follow a typical population over time to work out what predisposed them to the condition. The organizers chose the mainly white, industrial community of Framingham, Massachusetts,* because its physicians were thought to be willing, it was close to cardiologists at nearby Harvard, and it had already participated in a major study of tuberculosis. On 11 October 1948 the first Framingham resident was brought in and given a thorough cardiovascular exam; notes were made of their blood pressure and heart sounds. Over the next four years, the study recruited over 5,000 adults, and then regularly examined them again and kept track of their heart health. The cohort even included its fair share of women, which was quite a novel gesture for epidemiological studies at that point.

Nearly ten years after it started, the Framingham Heart Study showed that townspeople with high blood pressure – defined as 160/95 mm Hg or above – were succumbing to heart disease at a far higher rate than those with lower levels. Over the next two decades the study went on to nail down all the major factors that put people at risk of cardiovascular disease: smoking, diabetes, high cholesterol levels, obesity and lack of exercise. The study leaders are even credited with coining the phrase 'risk factor', which is a standard part of the vernacular with which we now discuss chronic disease. This cohort study helped to change medical practice, making it routine for doctors to try to identify those at high risk and to encourage them to lessen that risk through weight loss, diet, exercise or drugs. It has been so influential that today doctors

---

* In the America of that time, little thought was given to conducting such a study in a poor and/or black community. It was only much later, in the 1970s, that most epidemiologists came to the realization that they had to consider the different risk factors in different social and ethnic groups.

evaluate a patient's chances of having a heart attack using an algorithm called the Framingham Risk Score, or related scoring systems.

The Framingham Heart Study and the British Doctors' Study were instrumental in transforming the field of epidemiology, pivoting it away from its traditional focus on infectious disease and towards the causes of chronic disease, giving it a whole new authority in the process. Suddenly students in epidemiology lectures woke up, and a wave of bright, curious young things were attracted to the field. And at the very heart of all this was the cohort study. There couldn't have been a better demonstration that the method was a sharp knife with which to dissect the causes of disease. From this point on, cohort studies became one of the most crucial elements of modern epidemiology and were launched on an ascent to scientific fame.

The British Doctors' Study and the Framingham Heart Study have also been described as two 'intellectual levers', because they swung scientists around until they were completely focused on adult lifestyle as the driver of chronic disease. This idea had an added appeal, because it offered an easy escape route. Avoiding the cigarettes or other risky behaviours could lower the chance of disease, even though we know now that changing people's behaviour is painfully hard to do.

In the 1960s, as the world was coming to terms with the idea that smoking could kill adults, the scientists working on the 1958 cohort turned their attention to a related question. Could smoking kill babies too?

Butler had been ahead of the curve when he threw his last-minute question on smoking into the perinatal mortality survey; at that time, just one study had suggested that smoking while pregnant could reduce a baby's birth weight, and no one gave the matter much thought. All the focus in the 1950s was on smoking and lung cancer, and few people were paying attention to the alarm bells starting to clang in the medical literature about smoking during pregnancy. So, after the mid-wives in the 1958 survey had faithfully recorded the smoking habits of over 17,000 mothers, Butler had done some preliminary analyses and then put the data to one side.

With time, however, the issue started to heat up. Through the 1960s and 1970s, a series of studies confirmed that smoking in pregnancy was associated with lower birth weight, but controversy swirled around the results. The first point at issue was whether smoking was really the cause of the reduced birth weight. It was another light-switch-and-bulb puzzle, just like the one over smoking and lung cancer – the infernal struggle to extract a true cause from an epidemiological association. Was smoking really the switch, or were confounding factors getting in the way? There was some evidence that the women who smoked were different: they were more likely to be in the lower social classes, or were older, or were having their third or fourth child – all factors that could have made them more likely to have small babies anyway. This explanation for the link was sometimes called the 'constitutional hypothesis', because the thought was that women with a certain 'constitution' were more likely to smoke *and* to have small babies.

The second point at issue was about whether smoking had any consequences for babies' health, even if it was responsible for lowering birth weight. The evidence here was contradictory: some studies showed that women who smoked during pregnancy had babies who died at a higher rate, but others found no such thing. A few doctors argued that there was no harm done if babies were a shade thinner, and it might even have a beneficial effect by slimming down babies that were considered to be unhealthily overweight. And then, layered on top of all this, was the paternalistic view that women – especially very emotional, pregnant ones – shouldn't be burdened with undue pressure to give up smoking, which might backfire by causing the poor things stress. In 1973 a painfully condescending editorial in the leading scientific journal *Nature* said that cigarettes had the double bonus of helping expectant mothers calm their nerves and not gain excessive weight. For this reason, any pressure to stop them smoking was misguided and could backfire by worsening their health.

Luckily, Butler and his colleagues didn't listen to that. Butler knew that the 1958 cohort contained unparalleled data to resolve the debate, and, once the Plowden Report was out of the way, he and the Bureau scientists had an opportunity to dust it off. The original mortality survey included detailed information on the women's age, social class and other potential confounders, which allowed them statistically to rule these out. It recorded how many cigarettes a woman had smoked and whether she had given up or cut down during pregnancy. But the survey's biggest advantage was its astonishing number of perinatal deaths – far more than any other study that had tried to get at the smoking problem. In the spring of 1958, the survey had recorded all the perinatal deaths over three months, over 7,000 in all. This was important because perinatal death, although a commoner event in 1958 than it is today, was still rare; and scientists needed a huge sample of deaths in order to detect a difference between the perinatal mortality rate of smoking and non-smoking mothers in a way that would be statistically significant. Now those death records would be put to excellent use, and they eventually helped to save many more lives than were lost.

The fierce debate about smoking and lung cancer had also generated an invaluable aid in getting to the truth about smoking in pregnancy: 'Bradford Hill's criteria of causation'. If an association in an epidemiological study met several of Hill's criteria, it would strengthen the case that the link was a 'causal' one – that it was as cast-iron, say, as the link between smoking and lung cancer. Hill's criteria said that the association should be strong, just as smoking dramatically increased the risk of cancer; that it should be consistently observed across studies in different places and circumstances; that it should show a biological gradient, just as Doll and Hill had found that the risk of lung cancer went up with the number of cigarettes smoked; and that it should have a plausible mechanism. It was a high bar to cross, but the cohort had an ace in its hand: a statistician called Harvey Goldstein, who had once worked with Doll and was the numerical powerhouse behind many of the cohort results. Sometimes, when the Bureau scientists gathered in the coffee bar, they would strike up a game of mental chess, trying to move through a game by holding the board in their minds; most people could hold five or six moves, but Goldstein could retain eight, nine or more.

When Goldstein, Butler and the cohort scientists had completed their analysis of smoking during pregnancy, they were able to build a case bit by bit. Certainly the association between smoking, reduced birth weight and perinatal mortality was strong. The analysis showed that cigarette smoking during pregnancy cut babies' birth weight by an average of 170 g and that heavy smoking elevated the rate of perinatal deaths by 28%. There was also a clear biological gradient. Goldstein was able to show that the perinatal death rate went up with the number of cigarettes women smoked, and that women who gave up smoking before the fourth month of pregnancy had perinatal death rates equivalent to those who had never smoked. Goldstein also eliminated confounding factors such as social class, mother's age and number of previous children. Even with all these removed, the association between smoking, reduced birth weight and perinatal mortality was rock solid.

In fact, the confounding factor of social class offered an explanation for some of the conflicting results from the past. Babies from all social classes were born lighter if their mothers smoked, but the babies of the working-class mothers already tended to be lighter than those from higher social grades. Goldstein proposed that smoking, by shaving off those extra grams, would push more of the working-class babies over the threshold from survival to death. (Death rates start to spike when birth weight drops below 2,500 g.) This was very clarifying, because it suggested that the reason some earlier studies had found no increased death rate associated with smoking was because they had focused on women who were mostly middle class and so for whom the reduced birth weight from smoking had less impact.

Taken together, Goldstein felt the evidence was strong enough for medical authorities to discourage pregnant women from smoking. There were too many lives at stake – and, to make his point, he worked out exactly how many that was. Assuming that about 30% of women smoked in pregnancy – a pretty safe bet in 1972 – Goldstein calculated that some 1,500 babies would be saved in the UK if they all gave up – a thick slice of the 18,000 who died each year. In the United States, some 4,600 babies would be saved out of a total of about 87,000 deaths a year. At some point during the analysis, by the way, Goldstein gave up smoking, as did his soon-to-be-pregnant wife.

When Butler and Goldstein's meticulously argued paper appeared in the *British Medical Journal* in April 1972, many doctors and scientists were finally convinced. The analysis satisfied many of Hill's criteria for a causal association, and although it didn't nail down the mechanism by which smoking cut birth weight, scientists already had a good sense of that: the carbon monoxide in cigarette smoke was thought to deprive the baby of the oxygen it needed to grow.* 'No reasonable doubt now remains that smoking in pregnancy has adverse effects on the developing foetus,' stated an editorial in the *BMJ*. 'It is the smoking itself rather than the type of woman who smokes that is responsible for these effects.' But the results still didn't move from the medical journals into the wider world – until, that is, the *Sun* newspaper picked up the story and splashed the 'shock report' over its front page under the headline 'Mums' cigs killed 1,500 babies'.

The tabloid story heralded a far wider acceptance of the risks of smoking during pregnancy. In 1973 hoardings sprang up across Britain featuring a poster of a naked woman with a ripe pregnant stomach and a cigarette perched casually in her hand. 'Is it fair to force your baby to smoke cigarettes?' it read, before explaining that over a thousand babies' lives could have been saved if pregnant women had chosen not to smoke. The poster campaign, which was considered very risqué at the time and was launched at great expense by the Health Education Council, did what it set out to do and turned heads; surveys commissioned by the Council before and after the campaign showed that the number of women who smoked during pregnancy dropped from 39% to 29%. Efforts to prevent women smoking during pregnancy haven't stopped since, although the posters, public health campaigns and support teams have still

---

* It is now thought that many constituents of cigarette smoke are toxic to the growing foetus.

not had sufficient impact: some 12% of women smoke during pregnancy in the UK today, and a similar figure in the US.

An avalanche of studies has since arrived to highlight the risks of smoking during pregnancy, which is now known to include a higher risk of miscarriage, birth defects and sudden infant death syndrome. And the cohort scientists, like many others, went on to explore whether smoking during pregnancy had longer-term effects on a child. It did. When the team analysed their data on seven-year-old children, they found that those whose mothers had smoked during pregnancy were shorter on average than those of non-smoking mothers and performed less well on educational tests – their reading age, for example, was about four months behind that of those whose mothers had not smoked. There was no sign that these effects vanished with time. By the time the 1958 cohort reached early adulthood, the children of mothers who smoked during pregnancy had fewer educational qualifications and were more likely to be obese, despite having started out as smaller babies. None of these differences went away when researchers took social class and other confounders into account.

While cohort studies were starting to gain widespread fame and admiration from medical researchers, the 1946 cohort was hitting a rough patch. The problem stemmed from the wide breadth of the study. It sprawled across disciplines like an overgrown bramble bush; its roots had been in demography and maternal medicine, it had branched into child health, educational policy and pollution, and sprouted into many other things besides. The famous adult cohorts, however, were planted squarely in medical research and dedicated to a single condition – cancer or heart disease. You could say in one sentence what they were about. This simplicity was their strength.

Douglas's cohort study had matured, and the questions that he had asked of it shifted to reflect both the age of the children and the scientific and political questions that arose along the way. This shouldn't have been surprising – in fact, it makes perfect sense. It's just like life itself. At the birth of a child, her parents may have some idea of how her life will pan out, but no one really knows where she will end up. Time passes, the child blooms and the world changes around her in ways that shape her path and that could never have been anticipated.

But the changes in science itself were making it harder for a sprawling cohort study to justify its existence. At the start of the study, when it was Douglas, a secretary and a few thousand pounds, he had been pretty much free to do what he wanted. Now, in the 1970s, with tens of thousands of pounds in government funding from the MRC, Douglas was held more firmly to account. The research council regularly scrutinized what he was doing and brought in other scientists to review the cohort's work. Many of these reviewers ended up scratching their heads. They could see that the cohort was producing good medical research – for example, the impact of class differences on children's health and the lasting effects of pollution. But they were a little nonplussed that this 'medical research' unit was also spending so much time publishing on grammar schools and educational inequality.

It was true that the MRC funding had been a lifeline for the cohort, but it was also forcing the study into a disciplinary box. The fact was that an interdisciplinary birth cohort just didn't *fit*. Neither did Douglas himself, who found himself an outsider in every field. His interest in educational research meant that the medical profession had cut him off – he wasn't a practising doctor any more – yet those in educational research frequently attacked him for not being one of them. 'You got a sort of sense', one colleague from the time recalls, 'that he was not quite part of the whole caboodle.'

The other inexorable problem for Douglas was that his cohort was growing up, and this meant he had to adapt the study yet again. The question now was what could be learnt from his subjects in their twenties and thirties – and, to be honest, Douglas wasn't really sure. Almost all of them had finished education, found jobs and houses, and settled down. Now they were busy raising children, taking seaside holidays and doing all the other things that filled utterly mundane British lives. At one point, Douglas toyed with the idea of wrapping the whole thing up when the cohort reached twenty-five. He couldn't do it – but his malaise showed when he sent out the next survey, which rambled through a broad landscape of questions about family, health, jobs and more. Are you now single, married, widowed, separated or divorced? Do you have an indoor lavatory? How tall are you? What machines or machine tools do you use in your work, including vehicles and typewriters? Are you a member of a social club or working men's club? How do you think you will vote in the next general election? And this sweep cost more to administer than any of the previous ones: now that the cohort had left school, he could no longer get his data for free from teachers and doctors, and he'd had to hire a team of professional fieldworkers to do the interviews, at a cost of over £36,000. After all that, some of the data languished, and was hardly used.

This wavering about the future of the cohort was fuelled by his colleagues in the epidemiological world. All the exciting results spilling out of the adult cohort studies on cancer and heart disease were focusing medical attention firmly on the health of middle-aged adults, those in their forties, fifties and beyond. That's because chronic diseases mostly strike people in middle age, and the prospective cohort studies were finding that the behaviours of these middle-aged adults – smoking, putting on weight and so on – were important in driving the onset of their ill-health.

No one at this time gave much thought to the idea that events in childhood and young adulthood could have an influence on chronic diseases. It just seemed too much of a stretch to think that what people did as children could have an impact on the lung cancers and heart attacks that struck them years down the line. And, even if childhood experience did influence adult health, most researchers thought it would be too difficult to study. An observational study would have to start following children at birth and then trace them for decades until they collapsed and died – which would probably be long after the scientists themselves had passed on. Who on earth would do a crazy study like that?

Of course, Britain already had three such studies, but they were still young in chronic-disease terms. They also hadn't achieved the fame of the British Doctors' Study or Framingham, which meant that many epidemiologists didn't pay them too much mind. By 1972 the members of the first cohort were only in their mid twenties. From many epidemiologists' points of view, nothing interesting would happen to them until they eventually started to sicken and die, which would be in a couple of decades' time. It seemed both pointless and expensive to keep following them through the prime of their lives.

This type of thinking had drastic consequences for some of the other birth cohorts in the world – particularly the Collaborative Perinatal Project and its sister cohort, the Child Health and Development Study in the United States, both of which had been started in 1959. If scientists had continued to follow these children, their results would have completely eclipsed those of the British birth cohorts and you probably wouldn't be reading this story today. But they didn't. In the 1960s, when the children in the American cohorts were seven and five respectively, the studies were stopped. The funding organisations just weren't convinced that the enormous expense and hassle of tracking thousands of children any further would be worthwhile, a decision that some scientists still regret.*

Yet, as Douglas neared the end of his career, a couple of his studies challenged this belief. He looked at the prevalence of chronic cough in his cohort members – a good proxy for bronchitis and other respiratory illness – at the ages of twenty and twenty-five. There was no surprise when he found that smoking was associated with lung problems – but there was when he pulled out associations that traced right back to the start of life. He found that children who had suffered bronchitis or pneumonia before the age of two were at higher risk of adult respiratory illness in their twenties, and so were those who had been born into the lower social classes. (Douglas also revisited his pollution data to show a weak link to childhood pollution exposure too.) This was very intriguing. It pointed to the idea that whatever experiences we have as children could shape our health all the way into young adulthood, and perhaps throughout the rest of our lives. The cohort, if it continued, would be in a unique position to find more of these links, because it had comprehensive health records going back to birth.

Douglas, however, was getting on, and the rules of the MRC stated that the study unit must come to an end when its director retired, which would be in 1979. A great debate ensued

---

* Scientists did continue to follow some small samples of the children, and decades later some of the mothers' blood serum samples were used in a study of risk factors for schizophrenia. So ultimately, a lot of good came from these studies.

about what to do with the cohort. The MRC commissioned reviews, solicited proposals – and then sat on the fence. It knew the study was special, but then again, it had cost a lot and perhaps it should just be allowed to die. It wasn't clear what the cohort was for any more, and it also wasn't clear who would lead it.

What Douglas needed was a successor – someone with a vision for the cohort's future. That man had walked in the door just a few years earlier.

Michael Wadsworth had starched his collar, cleaned his jacket and fastened his cufflinks for his job interview with the cohort in May 1968. Douglas hadn't. He sat opposite Wadsworth, in his boxy office, wearing a tweed jacket and with the door thrown open, just as it always was, so he could boom down the corridor to his staff. Douglas may have been a little unsure about Wadsworth, because he hadn't read medicine or studied at Oxford like most of the young men he knew, but, as he quickly discovered, Wadsworth knew someone who had: John Butterfield, a professor of experimental medicine at Guy's Hospital in London, whom Douglas had taught at Oxford during the war. So, in the middle of the interview, Douglas picked up the telephone and rang Butterfield, holding the receiver, as he customarily did, an inch or two from his ear.

'I've got one of your boys here,' Douglas barked.

'Yes, yes, he's a good bloke,' Butterfield bawled back.

Wadsworth was only four years older than the cohort and had the zeal for science that Douglas had lost. He had even followed a path that the cohort data could have predicted: as a bright, lower-middle-class boy, the son of a teacher and a probation officer, he had passed the 11-plus exam and made it to grammar school. He studied English and philosophy at Leeds

University, but then landed a job with Butterfield, who was studying type 2 diabetes, another chronic disease that had been mysteriously rising in incidence since the war. When Butterfield sent him out on a bicycle to talk to patients about their health, Wadsworth found himself doing a crash course in epidemiology, computing and the art of carrying out surveys. All this – and the loud endorsement he was getting from Butterfield on the phone – seemed enough to convince Douglas that the young man in front of him would be a good hire.

'Well,' said Douglas at the end of the interview, 'I'm going to give you the job – but let's go out to tea and we'll talk about it. There's a very good place at Lincoln's Inn Fields where we can have tea and watch the girls play netball.' The two men shared a drink and admired the view – and that was how Wadsworth entered the study that would dominate his life.

At first, Wadsworth leapt from branch to branch of the 1946 cohort. He carried out a study for Home Office bureaucrats, who wanted to know why the rate of delinquency wasn't going down even as the nation's incomes were rising. He found that the delinquents – whom he defined as those who had committed major offences including burglary, violent crimes or sex crimes – were much more likely to have suffered psychological upset earlier in life, through, for example, parental separation or divorce. He went on to launch the Second Generation Study, a massive effort to trace cohort members' children and to give them the same tests of reading and vocabulary that their parents had taken at the age of eight, except with the outdated words – 'muslin' and 'guinea' – scratched out. Wadsworth also shouldered a mundane but essential cohort duty. Back when the cohort members were teenagers, Douglas had started to send out birthday cards to them, so that he could keep them interested in the study and keep track of where they lived.

(Patricia Palmer was always thrilled to receive hers, which was usually the first of her birthday cards to arrive.) The task of designing and writing these thousands of birthday cards fell to Wadsworth, something that he found a terrible chore.

But while Wadsworth was agonizing over what to write in the cards, he was also starting to think about the future of the cohort itself. He knew that Douglas was losing steam, and that there were questions about what more could be learnt from these young adults. Wadsworth, however, could see an answer – and it all stemmed from Butterfield, diabetes and a town's worth of wee.

Type 2 diabetes arises when the body loses the ability to control levels of the sugar called glucose, often as a result of being overweight. If it goes untreated, it can lead to heart disease, stroke, nerve and eye damage, kidney disease and more unpleasant things besides. In the 1960s, when Butterfield became involved, most doctors diagnosed diabetes when patients showed up reporting the classic symptoms of thirst, fatigue and frequent trips to the toilet to urinate. Then the diagnosis would be confirmed by testing to see if the patient's blood glucose had climbed abnormally high. A quicker, cruder test can be done using urine, which, in the case of diabetics, contains glucose because sugar is running so high in the blood that it spills over. So that was how diabetes was detected – but what many doctors didn't do then was to give much thought to how the disease had developed over time. One day you weren't diabetic, and then one day you were, and no one knew a great deal about what had happened in between.

Butterfield decided to use the urine test as a means to examine the 'in between' bit in a staggering piece of epidemiological investigation that took place one Sunday morning in 1962. He

asked every resident on the Electoral Roll of the town of Bedford to eat their Sunday breakfast – cornflakes, eggs, porridge,
it didn't matter as long as it would give their blood sugar an
opportunity to rise. Then he asked them to urinate in a pot and
to leave the sample on their doorstep, from which a team of
volunteers gathered them up, like a throng of milkmen collecting their bottles.* Once they were in, the team lined up all
25,000 amber-filled vials, and started to test the sugar levels in
every one. Legend has it that when one man handed in a sample of sherry instead of urine, Butterfield went to his house
and said, 'You may have made medical history, my boy, but,
just to be sure, can you please do it again?'

When the testing was over, Butterfield had a surprising
result that lifted the lid on the development of chronic disease.
He found that over 1,000 Bedford residents had sugary urine,
even though they'd had no obvious symptoms and hadn't been
diagnosed as having diabetes. He confirmed that many of
them had blood sugar high enough to qualify as diabetic and
he also showed that blood sugar tended to rise slowly with age.
The experiment had quite an impact on the field, because it
showed that the disease could take five, ten or even twenty
years to develop, as a person's body slowly lost its ability to
regulate glucose and their blood turned from sweet to syrupy.
This meant that some people were suffering all the damaging
effects of unhealthily high blood sugar for years before they, or
their doctors, noticed that they had deteriorated. (It's now
thought that a staggeringly high number of adults – in the US,
more than one third – have this type of 'prediabetes', in which
blood glucose levels are higher than normal but not high

---

* To help, Butterfield recruited the local medical officer of health, as well as members of the Round Table, Boy Scouts, Women's Institute and more.

enough to be classified as diabetes itself, and guidelines for ways to delay its onset have been established.)

As Wadsworth watched all this go on in Butterfield's group, it left a major impression, because he realized that other chronic diseases also probably develop over decades, and that the disease itself – the heart attack, stroke or lung condition – was just the end of the line. If you looked for them, there were plenty of signs in the medical literature that this was true. One of the most striking examples emerged in the 1950s, when army doctors carried out autopsies of American soldiers who'd been killed in action in the Korean War and opened up their coronary arteries. It was known that these arteries become clogged with fatty plaques that block the flow of blood and can eventually cause a heart attack – but this process, called athero-sclerosis, was thought to be confined to middle age or later, when heart disease emerged. The soldiers being autopsied were fit young men, often in their twenties – but the doctors nevertheless found clear signs that their arteries were starting to fur up. It was a strong indicator that atherosclerosis devel-oped over decades, just as diabetes did. And those practising another branch of medicine – mental health – knew there were plenty of reasons to study people throughout life, because it was well established that psychiatric illnesses such as schizo-phrenia and depression reared their heads in adolescence and young adulthood.

This mattered for the future of the 1946 cohort, because it showed that the early adult years – the twenties and thirties – weren't boring or irrelevant to health. In fact, they would be exactly the time when the first signs of disease emerged. And this gave Wadsworth an idea. Butterfield had used a simple test to show that blood sugar tended to rise with age, before the diagnosis of diabetes. Wadsworth became convinced that if he carefully assessed the health and nutrition of the cohort members using other simple tests — such as those for blood pressure, lung function, weight and mental health — and charted them into the future, he would be able to glimpse the early signs of chronic disease. The first round of tests would serve as a baseline measurement, and then he would do them again and again to see how they changed.

As Douglas's retirement loomed, Wadsworth wrapped up all these ideas and wrote them into a report that he submitted to the MRC, which pleaded for a new life for the cohort. In response, he heard nothing. The MRC leadership dithered. The uncertainty over the cohort's future was excruciating and every other member of the unit left.

On a Monday in July 1979, with just two weeks left on the unit's lease in Hanway Place, the phone rang for Wadsworth. He picked up: it was a scientific secretary at the MRC calling to deliver the verdict. You're moving to Bristol with the study, the secretary told Wadsworth, and you will work from the epidemiology department there. (The MRC liked its units to be directed by a medic, so it chose a qualified doctor, John Colley, to be honorary director while Wadsworth did most of the day-to-day work.) We'll give you five years to show you can do something with the cohort — and after that, we'll review you, decide if we like the direction you're going in and whether to keep the study alive any longer. Wadsworth hardly heard the rest. All he registered was that the study was going to survive.

A few weeks later, as the movers came to clear the office, Douglas came to see him. 'Let's go and have a sandwich,' he said. The pair sat outside in Soho Square, around the corner from the unit, and quietly ate their lunch. 'I'm sure you'll do a good job,' Douglas said, but Wadsworth could see that he was upset. It wasn't that he wanted the cohort to end. Douglas had come to see the scientific value of carrying on – and he even suspected that the biggest returns on the money and work he had invested in the study were still to come. But, after having set up the study and nurtured it for thirty-three years, he was finding it difficult to accept that he would no longer be involved. It was a little like seeing a son or daughter leave home.

Wadsworth, however, was eager to pick up the reins. The following month would see him travelling down the motorway to Bristol in a convoy of three enormous Pickfords removal trucks stuffed with punched cards. He had arranged for the defunct tabulating machine to go to London's Science Museum, but he needed to keep the cards, which still served as a vital data back-up, even though much of it was now stored on computer. After loading up, the movers had told Wadsworth that the trucks would have to spend the night in the storage depot at Peckham and travel down the next day. Thirty years of irreplaceable, confidential data were to sit in a car park at a time when data security consisted of a locked van door. Wadsworth thought it was horrendous and hardly slept that night.

When he arrived at the study's new home – an old public health laboratory on the top floor of a Bristol University building – there wasn't enough room for the cards, so the removal men sweated the cases down to the disused mortuary and piled them on the floor and on the old concrete slabs. It was an appropriate resting place for bodies of data awaiting further dissection.

Wadsworth could hardly wait to begin. Working with Colley and a small team, he began to put together a survey of health and nutrition with a level of detail that had never been previously attempted. He advertised in the *Nursing Mirror* for a team of nurses to visit the thousands of participants in their homes and put them through a battery of tests. The cohort members had to fill in questionnaires about their physical health (Do you usually bring up any phlegm first thing in the morning? Have you done anything that made you perspire in the last four weeks?) and their mental health too (Has life seemed quite hopeless? Did you ever feel like ending it all?). The nurses took careful measurements of blood pressure and lung capacity, which involved blowing hard into a tubular peak flow meter. When the nurses were being trained, Wadsworth would pretend he was having a massive heart attack and crumple to the floor, in the event that the lung test triggered such an event. (It never did.) At the end of the visit, the cohort members were also asked to keep a diary of everything that they ate or drank over seven days, measured to the nearest ounce. (Mince and onion, 4 oz, read one standard 1982 supper. Sponge, fatless; Beer, bitter, ½ pint.) Even with the growing help of computers, collecting and coding all this data would keep Wadsworth and his team fully occupied for the next three years.

Douglas was gone, and the unit had folded, but the cohort study had a reprieve. Now there was Wadsworth, 5,362 cohort members and a big idea to prove.

PART TWO

Coming of Age

4.

Staying Alive

Cohorts Struggle for Survival

In the spring of 1979, as Wadsworth was pleading to keep the first British birth cohort alive, the scientists leading the second threw a tragic kind of birthday party.

The children who had been born in 1958 were now twenty-one, and Kellmer Pringle wanted to celebrate. The original idea was to hold a party somewhere like the Café Royal, the famous restaurant and bar in Piccadilly – but of course the budget didn't stretch to anything as glamorous as that. Instead, the party took place at the National Children's Bureau itself, which is located on a London block, choked by busy roads. The scientists at the Bureau invited about one hundred members of the cohort, as well as members of the press. As luck would have it, someone had a connection with a catering company, which was persuaded to supply a birthday cake – a big, fancy iced one that would be delivered by van.

Backslapping, speeches and interviews were all scheduled for the day. Everyone was excited to receive a congratulatory telegram from Andy Gibb, the younger brother of the Bee Gees and at that moment a pop idol with a string of US number-one hits. Gibb was one of several people to have been born in that 1958 week who were now rising stars. A few months earlier, in the televised finals of the Miss Great Britain beauty contest, the woman representing Hammersmith West had gone up to take her turn at the microphone. Most of the other contestants had talked about their lives as models, students and so forth, but she had said that she was a proud member of a study of children born in 1958. The scientists had scrambled to invite Miss Hammersmith West to cut the cake. Unfortunately, the van carrying the cake met with an accident on the way to the party and there was not much of it left to cut when it arrived. After a few moments' panic, someone dashed around the corner to the nearest bakery and bought a replacement, which had fewer frills but still served the purpose.

The crushed cake was a perfect metaphor for the state of the cohort study itself, which was one mishap away from collapse. Money was the recurring problem; this cohort was in an even more precarious state than its predecessor. As Britain struggled through economic difficulties in the 1970s, the government was cutting back on funding for research. The cohort was still passing round a begging bowl for every sweep and finding that the bowl was getting harder to fill. The birthday party itself was as much a celebration as it was a desperate publicity exercise to try to drum up more attention from politicians and the press. At the same time, Kellmer Pringle was leaning on her political connections to the full, and going directly to government departments to convince them that another survey of the cohort in their twenties could provide useful information about young people as they entered their adult life. 'Mia was moving heaven and earth,' one colleague recalls. 'She just went around being a pain in the ass.'

Kellmer Pringle secured verbal agreements with five departments to cover the nearly £2 million the sweep was estimated to cost. On 3 May 1979, however, the political winds abruptly changed when a Conservative landslide brought Margaret Thatcher to power. The Bureau scientists found that the money that they had been promised was suddenly in the lurch. Kellmer Pringle, however, had already ensured that Thatcher was a personal friend, and eventually the hard-won reprieve came through. Kellmer Pringle immediately took everyone out for a slap-up lunch – then the work of designing and sending out the survey began. But that time round it was a nightmare.

Striking a financial deal with the Conservative government had come at a heavy cost. Thatcher was, in general, extremely sceptical about the value of social sciences, and not just because she had studied chemistry – a rigorous experimental science – at the University of Oxford and worked briefly in research. She also viewed the discipline as a hotbed of left-wing ideals to which she was politically opposed. This came to the fore a couple of years later when her government commissioned Lord Rothschild to investigate the work of the Social Sciences Research Council, and rumours swirled that the aim was to abolish the SSRC entirely and thereby stifle research in the area even before the investigation had begun. The Rothschild Report didn't go that far, but it did deliver a massive shake-up to the field by saying that it had to incorporate more observation and experimentation and so become more empirical in its approach.*
The 1958 cohort study actually was a prime example of empirical social science: it was all about careful observation and the collection of data with which to test ideas. But this distinction wasn't always recognized by politicians, and the growing antipathy towards social science meant that the cohort was facing an increasing battle for survival and autonomy.

At one point, Keith Joseph – by then Thatcher's Secretary

---

* The report also led to a symbolic move to expunge the word 'science' from the name of the research council and rename it as the Economic and Social Research Council – thus explicitly including economics, which was one of the more empirical sciences that the government favoured. The leader of the SSRC at the time said that it could have been called the White Fish Authority for all he cared, as long as it was allowed to continue funding good social science research.

of State for Industry – sat in on a meeting and said, 'Well, I'll start funding your research when you start telling me things I want to hear.' The scientists' jaws dropped. One of the central beliefs of researchers is that they should have academic freedom, meaning that they can pursue research into any subject without undue interference from the state or any other group. In Britain, this idea is often traced back to the Haldane Report, an influential document published in 1918 that recommended the creation of research councils of scientists to distribute government money. The idea that researchers, rather than politicians, should decide how funds are spent is now known as the 'Haldane Principle'. But the cohort scientists weren't getting money from a research council; they were getting it straight from the government, and the government wanted to call the shots. What's more, the policy-makers were interested only in questions about what was happening to people now, in that sweep, when they were twenty-three – as a snapshot survey of the population – which completely defeated the point of having a cohort study at all, with its ability to make links to events in the past. The cohort scientists were very uncomfortable at having to bow to government paymasters, but if they wanted the money, they had little choice.

The scientists held their tongues as a big squabble ensued about each government department getting its fair share of questions into the survey. The questionnaires ballooned, rambling through every aspect of people's lives, including health, employment, income, housing, marriage, children, leisure, voting behaviour, trade union membership and more. (Do you live in a house/bungalow/self-contained flat/maisonette/room/caravan/mobile home/houseboat/other? Have you ever played bingo/done the pools/gambled/placed bets of any kind? Have you used the sheath/cap/pill/coil/jelly/ vasectomy/withdrawal? In the last seven days, how many glasses of martini/vermouth/similar drinks have you had?) Even after three previous sweeps, no one had kept tabs on where the cohort members lived, and the tracing exercise had only become more complicated now that many of them had left their parents' homes. Sometimes the interviewers had to play detective, and just keep knocking on doors until they found someone who knew a family's whereabouts.

The situation worsened when the data came in, because it was so copious that the scientists got completely bogged down in producing their reports. It was impossible to wrestle the data into shape. The government departments started to get angry that the results were taking an age, and the scientists were getting angry that the government was in the driver's seat. They knew that the delays were a threat to the cohort study, because none of their work was being published or recognized by academics and the press. As remarkable and irreplaceable as this study of a British generation was, it was dangerously close to slipping out of sight.

This problem was compounded by an even larger one: the cohort was losing its driving force. In 1980, while on holiday, Kellmer Pringle's second husband suddenly died, and she visibly fell apart. She was also suffering from arthritis and taking strong drugs for the pain. In 1981 she announced that she would step down as director of the Bureau and, without her as its advocate, the cohort really lost its way. Soon the London office was hosting one redundancy party after another, as money for the cohort dried up. The government was disgusted with the whole set-up and wanted to pull the plug. It had had enough of everlasting studies that never seemed to deliver anything concrete in the way of results.

*

Meanwhile, the 1970 cohort was treading a parallel path of its own difficulties. It suffered from being a third child, overshadowed by its older siblings and left to get on by itself. The results from the 1970 birth survey had never had much impact on the field of obstetrics, perhaps because radical changes were already under way by the time it came out. In many people's eyes, the whole thing had ended up being rather an expensive disappointment, and all the good intentions to follow up the children came unstuck.

If the 1970 survey was going to be turned into a long-term cohort study, it needed a home and a champion. It found one in Neville Butler, the paediatrician who had started the second cohort and carried out the pioneering work on its data on smoking and pregnancy. In the mid 1960s Butler had taken up a position as a professor of child health in Bristol. He had remained a co-director of the second cohort with Kellmer Pringle, and had never lost his boundless enthusiasm for it. But with so much physical distance between him and the study in London, it became clear over time that it was Kellmer Pringle who was really in control. Now, with the 1970 cohort, Butler had an opportunity to have a longitudinal study of his very own. So when the children in it were three, Butler packed up the cohort and took it with him to Bristol, where it entered Butler's idiosyncratic world.

Anyone who knew Butler from those days remembers the old laboratory in the Bristol Children's Hospital where he worked, conducted staff meetings and sometimes slept. The back of the office consisted of a bench top, a Bunsen burner and a square sink fed by a swan-necked tap. The front of it housed a desk, radio and bed, all suffocating under a blanket of Butler's books, files, folders and papers and adorned with tins of mouldy condensed milk. Some mornings Butler was seen appearing from the hospital washrooms, where he had performed his ablutions, strolling down the corridor to his office and later emerging, tie knotted, ready for his clinic. At other times the daily tasks of life seemed altogether too much for him. One night Butler called his administrator, Christine Porter, telling her that something terrible had happened, and that she must come to help. Porter arrived to find the walls and ceiling of his office spattered with baked beans from an exploded tin. Butler had carefully followed the instructions to heat the beans in a saucepan, which he had perched atop the Bunsen burner. What it hadn't said, and he hadn't realized, was that he needed to take the lid off the tin first.*

The cohort records, however, were unscathed. Butler had installed those in a solid Georgian house halfway up a hill near the hospital and recruited a small team of researchers and coders to follow up the children at the ages of five and ten. It's something of a mystery how he managed to pull off these sweeps, given that the other cohorts were, financially, hanging on by a thread. But the answer probably lies in Butler himself and his unswerving belief in the wonder of the birth cohort and its power to improve child health. As the ten-year-old survey approached, Butler would load up his white Volkswagen Beetle with a suitcase leaking academic papers and underpants. Then he would speed off to give impassioned talks about the birth cohort in order to convince health visitors and educational authorities to help him trace the children – yes, these children too had to be traced from scratch – and to deliver his questionnaires for free.

---

* The story goes that the bang was heard at the bottom of St Michael's Hill, and that Butler's office subsequently had to be redecorated.

Butler's passion for the cohort may have been keeping it going, but his idiosyncrasies were simultaneously holding it back. Butler was a perfectionist and just couldn't convince himself that a research paper, or anything that he wrote for that matter, was finished until he had scrawled correction after correction over it, and his secretaries were worn out. (He had such trouble completing research papers that a widespread conspiracy went into operation that involved fellow scientists handing Butler a draft of the paper, telling him it was the final version, allowing him to fiddle with it, and then taking it away to finish off themselves.) His behaviour presented the cohort with difficulties, because it meant that there was relatively little science coming out: Butler didn't publish the results of the five-year-old sweep until the children were sixteen. When Wadsworth was moving to Bristol in 1979, Douglas gave him one sterling piece of advice: 'Don't get mixed up with Neville, whatever you do.'

Running in tandem with these problems were financial ones. In November 1981 Butler decided to take the dire money problems into his own hands. He announced to his administrator that they were leaving on a last-minute trip to London. 'We're going to talk to Mrs Thatcher,' he said.

Porter objected: she was unhappy with Thatcher's politics. 'Politics aside, Chris,' said Butler, 'she has the key to the money, so we are going.'

Thatcher was due to talk that day at a London prize-giving event, to which Butler and Porter hadn't been invited. But such trivialities didn't faze Butler, who announced at the door that he was Professor Butler from Bristol University and so was waved in. The pair waited in the tea and coffee reception until Thatcher arrived and swept along a corridor of attendees, to which Butler attached himself at the end. Then, as Thatcher neared, Butler deliberately dropped his cup and saucer on the floor and stooped down to mop up the spill. (According to one account, some of the coffee splashed on Thatcher.) As Butler stood up, he said to her, 'Mrs Thatcher, I'm Professor Butler, we're doing a national study looking at thousands of children. We need more funding!' Then he kept right on talking and wouldn't let her go. Thatcher turned coolly to one of the men in her entourage. 'Please, will you talk to this gentleman?' she said, and then sashayed on to deliver her speech.

The Thatcher incident was just one of Butler's increasingly energetic attempts to secure a future for the 1970 cohort as his own retirement loomed and money became scarce. He wanted to organize a sweep of the cohort when they became teenagers, but the prospect of finding support from government sources seemed remote.

It wasn't just the money that was looking stretched. As time went on, Butler was too. He was running his paediatric clinic, while working flat out to keep his treasured cohort alive. Colleagues saw his moods grow more unpredictable; when one of his senior scientists left on a trip one winter, she left a long 'What To Do If' document, spelling out the steps that should be taken if Butler came off the rails. Other scientists in the team felt that they were running the academic side of the study and producing the papers that Butler couldn't finish. From a distance, it all looked like some mad romp for the sake of science, but inside the office relationships were strained. Things just couldn't carry on in this way. The university was getting frustrated with Butler, and he was worried that it would abandon the cohort when he retired in 1985. But Butler would do anything for the study – so, at some point, he decided to go it alone.

In the early 1980s he set up a charitable foundation called the

International Centre for Child Studies, or the ICCS, and started making incredible plans. He wanted to raise over £3 million to build a centre that would become a world-leading authority on child development and form a home for the cohort. He spent nights reading *Who's Who* and selecting influential people to ask to be patrons of the charity. Some he wrote to; others, like Thatcher, he tried to seduce face to face. He lunched with the actor James Mason at the Dorchester, and had an armchair meeting with the politician Norman Lamont. Butler sold the cohort on the heartstring-tugging idea that it would help sick children – and it seemed to work. Within a year, Butler's list of patrons included dames, viscounts, barons, MPs, lords, knights, countesses, marquesses, princesses and bishops, not to mention the pop stars Cliff Richard and Twiggy. In fact, with a list mounting to 600 and more, it was hard to think of anyone who was anyone who was *not* a patron. Despite the coffee incident – or perhaps because of it – even Thatcher agreed to join the list of patrons and to host the charity's launch party. A local primary school sang a song especially composed for the centre, and Butler shook hands with the guests under a big rainbow, the charity's logo. Butler's plans for the charity were so ambitious that some people started calling it the Intergalactic Centre behind his back.

Butler didn't manage to raise £3 million, but he did raise enough to buy an old orphanage office on the cheap, a broad-shouldered building with columns guarding the door. So, in 1985, when he retired from the university, he cleared out his office-cum-bedroom at the Bristol Children's Hospital and moved everything there. What Butler couldn't take with him, however, were some of his key staff. They were employees of the university and wanted to stay where they were. For all the patrons and glossy brochures, the 'Intergalactic Centre' at that stage pretty much *was* Butler – he was its driving force and he was determined to keep the cohort study on the road.

Butler pressed on, and planned a survey of the sixteen-year-olds that scientists still talk about with awe today. (According to cohort legend, the survey finally secured enough to push ahead when Butler collected a £50,000 cheque from media tycoon and Mirror Group owner Robert Maxwell.) Whatever the size of Wadsworth's and Kellmer Pringle's last surveys, the one that Butler and his colleagues carried out on these teenagers in 1986 was in a league of its own. Butler designed a sixteen-page questionnaire inquiring about the adolescents' friends and relationships (I have done it once/I have done it several times/I wish I had done it/I expect I shall do it soon); a nineteen-page questionnaire for parents about the family, finances and household (Is the house over-tidy/very tidy/average/untidy/chaotic?); a thirteen-page form for doctors (What is the teenager's weight in underclothes? How intelligible have you found the teenager's speech?) and another for the head teachers (What percentage of pupils come from 'large houses set in their own ground', as opposed to 'closely packed houses in a poor state of repair'?). Altogether, Butler deployed nineteen separate survey documents, including manuals, tests, self-completion questionnaires, interviews, diaries and the medical examination. He may not have had much money, but that wasn't going to stop him asking everything he could think of.

At some point, in the midst of designing this survey, Butler decided to ask his British sixteen-year-olds, nearly 17,000 of them, to do something unprecedented in the history of the cohorts. He wanted them to send him a detailed diary showing absolutely everything – 'the interesting bits and boring bits' – about their lives during a four-day spell from Friday to Monday. This was a lot to ask: teenagers typically have more pressing concerns than contributing to the nation's scientific enterprise through detailed documentation of their daily activities. So he decided to send his teenagers two pages of detailed instructions in small, 10-point type and – just to be sure the adolescents knew the type of thing he wanted – a complete example of a sixteen-year-old's diary. And it read like this:

LEISURE DIARY

SATURDAY

a.m.

07.30   Woke up. Raining!

07.40   Had cup of coffee with milk.

07.45   Walked to paper shop.

07.55   Began paper round. Walked 3 miles.

08.55   Walked back home (1 mile), got very wet.

09.05   Had a shower.

09.30   Cooked my own breakfast (scrambled egg on toast, cup of tea with milk).

10.05   Tidied my room – boring!

10.25   Wrote letter to French penfriend and posted it.

11.15   Watched TV *Saturday Superstore*.

p.m.

1.00   Had 3 sandwiches, 2 biscuits, 2 cups of coffee.

1.20   Got ready to go out.

1.40   Walked to bus stop (½ mile).

1.50   Took bus into town. Cost 30p.

2.10   Visited shops. Bought 1 cassette £3.

3.20   Met friends and went for snack and coffee. They smoked and I coughed!

4.15   More shopping – bought pair of shoes. Cost £7.

5.05   Took bus to friend's house.

5.30   Watched TV at friend's house *The Dukes of Hazzard*.

6.30   Had supper at friend's house (fish and chips, ice cream).

7.15   Got ready to go out with friend. Decided on Youth Club instead of Cinema.

7.50   We walked to Youth Club (¾ mile).

8.00   Attended live gig/disco at Youth Club – met lots of friends there. Had 2 drinks (small glass of lager each time).

10.00   Got involved in argument outside Youth Club and got a black eye.

10.30   Got a lift home with friend's dad.

10.45   Argued with my parents about how I got black eye!

11.00   Watched video recording – 2 episodes of *Spitting Image*.

a.m.

12.00   Had small mug of coffee and 3 biscuits.

12.15   Went to bed and read *Smash Hits*.

12.40   Went to sleep. A mixed sort of day!

Butler's idea of a teenager's life seems distantly removed from the real world when compared with the weekend activities of an actual cohort teenager in 1986. Take Gail Gleave, who liked going up to the top of the 'muckies' near her hometown in Cheshire, and speeding around on the back of her boyfriend's motorbike. It was around the time of the survey that he had braked suddenly, and Gail had come off the bike and torn up her knee. So the weekend she kept the diary was probably one she spent on crutches. But this didn't stop her from spending most of her time round at her boyfriend's house – and the rest of what she was up to became apparent some months later, when Gleave went to the doctor because she was being sick. She found out that she was six months pregnant, even though she was still skinny as anything and her periods had never stopped. By then, she was seventeen.

Administering such a colossal survey was never going to be easy, and when Butler finally sent out the leisure diaries and the rest of his instruments, the 1980s themselves presented a major stumbling block. The country's teachers had gone on strike, protesting against paltry pay increases, and were refusing to do extra-curricular activities such as football clubs, let alone questionnaires that took hours to complete. Butler had to redesign some of his forms and tests, and the entire survey eventually stretched out over two years. Even then, the data was thin and spotty. Only around 40% of the kids took a stab at filling in the leisure diary with their Saturday shopping trips, TV shows, discos and brawls, and a measly 20% of teachers returned questionnaires. It was a poor response rate – and Butler was struggling to write up the results. He was finding that 1986 was an altogether different world from 1958, when he had pulled off his very first survey of births. Then, one man with lots of passion and energy could achieve a lot. Now, a cohort study required a dedicated team and millions of pounds to sustain it, and it had to be continually producing credible results or it would go down.

On 8 April 1989, to mark the cohort's nineteenth birthday, Butler threw one of the biggest birthday parties in the world, inviting all the cohort members to Alton Towers, what was then considered to be the country's best theme park. Butler used his contacts to get free entry to the park as well as discount travel on British Rail. The teenagers queued for entrance to the Black Hole – the must-do rollercoaster of the day – and Butler rode an elephant wearing a mortar board and gown, to the amusement of everyone there. Gleave remembers him as a nutty professor, with his hair blowing wildly in the wind.

And then the 1970 cohort fell out of sight. Some scientists concluded that the study had been so damaged by the survey that it was no longer worth following up. Without Butler, the cohort would never have got so far; but it would need more than Butler to go any further than this.

The difficulties being faced by the first three birth cohorts were nothing in comparison with those faced by the fourth. The fourth, you say? Well, it was, after all, a tradition by this stage to carry out a massive survey of British births every twelve years – and you probably worked out long ago that the next one would come due in 1982. No other country in the world was tracking generations of children in this way, and there was a widespread expectation both at home and abroad that a fourth perinatal mortality survey would take place and that this too would turn into a cohort study. Some people in the obstetrics community were interested in establishing an entire research centre – called the National Perinatal Epidemiology

Unit – to cement Britain's place as a world leader in the epidemiology of birth. The unit got under way in Oxford in 1978, under the direction of a young doctor called Iain Chalmers, and part of its remit was to work out whether it was feasible and desirable to carry out a fourth perinatal mortality survey in 1982, as many expected. The survey was not a given, but it had become a very urgent concern, because the planning took years and time was slipping past.

Early in his career Chalmers had become frustrated with the way that evidence was being used in medicine, and he would eventually help to bring in sweeping changes to how this was done. When he was training, he had spent two years in the Gaza Strip, where he learnt that some of what he'd been taught about medicine was lethally wrong. As a student Chalmers had been told that he should never treat measles, a viral infection, with antibiotics, which kill bacteria. He later found out that there were several clinical trials showing that antibiotics can prevent the bacterial infections that cause pneumonia in children with measles, and that children in his care had probably died as a result of the poor teaching he had received. Later, when Chalmers was training in obstetrics in the city of Cardiff, he realized that medical practice there also wasn't being guided by evidence. Different obstetricians would follow different procedures to treat the same condition – so much so, that when he was called in the night to care for a woman in labour, the first question he would ask was 'What's wrong?' and the second one was 'Which consultant is she booked under?' This didn't seem right – shouldn't evidence, rather than opinion, be used to work out the best way to treat women?

Chalmers had become curious about some of the dramatic new approaches in obstetrics care. The way that women delivered their babies had been changing radically, as more women gave birth in hospital, with an accompanying rise in caesarean sections, inductions and other tests and procedures. Some of this could be traced to the 1958 perinatal mortality survey: its high-profile condemnation of home births had helped drive more births into hospitals and promote the use of inductions for women who were overdue. Now, in the early 1970s, a growing number of women's and consumer groups were questioning the increased medical intervention in pregnancy and birth, fuelled by the idea that women were being instructed in this uniquely female experience by men.

Chalmers wanted to try to work out whether the increase in medical procedures at birth was saving more babies' lives. To answer this question, he turned to a data set called the Cardiff Birth Survey, which had collected very detailed information on women who bore children in the city of Cardiff between 1965 and 1973 – nearly 40,000 cases altogether. Chalmers' analysis confirmed that hospital delivery had become almost universal over this period; that it was commonplace to induce and accelerate labour with drugs; and that it was also standard practice to monitor the baby's heartbeat during labour. But, despite this, Chalmers couldn't find any statistically significant change in the number of babies that died perinatally or the way in which they died. A woman giving birth in 1973 was just as likely to see her child die as one in 1965, regardless of everything that modern medical care could throw at her. This was 'depressing', Chalmers wrote candidly in a paper published in the *British Medical Journal* in 1976. Chalmers also looked at the problem in another way: by comparing a group of some 5,000 women who were treated by doctors who freely used induction, caesarean sections and all the other medical procedures around birth with a group of women who were treated by doctors who took a more conservative, hands-off approach.

Again, there was no clear advantage to either type of treatment. These studies caused quite a stir, because they suggested that the major medicalization of childbirth that had occurred since the war appeared to be having no beneficial effect. And they played right into the by-now-red-hot debate about the best way to give birth.

At the same time, Chalmers was troubled by the limitations of his studies, which, like the birth cohorts, were based on passively observing and collecting data on birth. It could be that changes in medical practice really were rescuing more babies in Cardiff but that the drop was being masked by some confounding factor that he wasn't controlling for; or it could be that the numbers in the sample were too small to detect a significant difference between the groups of women; or perhaps the result was just a statistical fluke. He found himself butting his head against the constraints of observational studies – against the inherent difficulty in eliminating confounding factors in order to pinpoint an association and a cause. Were these medical procedures causing better outcomes for women and babies, or weren't they? The evidence just wasn't clear cut. The same day that Chalmers published his Cardiff study, a scientist called Jean Golding published a paper in the same issue of the *BMJ* that reached the opposite conclusion. She had examined records from over 100,000 births in the Oxford area and concluded that the rate of stillbirth was falling fastest among those women who had been induced. It was a nice illustration of how science can sometimes point in different directions at the same time.

Chalmers was frustrated; he felt that simple observation couldn't provide the definitive answers that doctors and women needed. There had to be a better way to test whether medical techniques worked – and there was, through a type of experiment called a randomized controlled trial.

It was Austin Bradford Hill – the same medical statistician who had carried out the pioneering cohort study of smoking and lung cancer – who put this type of clinical trial on the map. In the 1940s, as the age of antibiotics dawned, doctors were just getting their hands on a new drug called streptomycin, and they wanted to know whether it was effective in combating tuberculosis. It was already standard in medicine to test a drug by comparing one group that receives it with a control group that does not. But this only works if the two groups are identical on every other count – and bias can easily creep in. The doctors who allocate patients to the two groups may inadvertently choose certain types of patient – maybe the sickest ones, or those most likely to benefit – to receive the drug, distorting the groups and making it impossible to work out the drug's true effects.

To avoid this, Hill realized that patients must be randomly allocated to the treatment group and the control group. He subsequently designed a study in which this randomness was guaranteed, because even the doctors entering patients into the trial didn't know in which group a patient would end up. (This information was hidden in sealed envelopes that were opened only after a patient had been enrolled.) Hill's trial, which was published in 1948, quickly showed that the tuberculosis patients who received streptomycin recovered faster than those who did not. The study became a landmark for establishing the randomized controlled trial as a 'gold standard' in medicine – the most rigorous way of testing the efficacy of a new treatment. Still, long after this had taken place, doctors didn't necessarily pay much attention to such trials when they were working out how to treat a patient in front of them. That really started to change in 1972, when a Scottish doctor and epidemiologist called Archie Cochrane published an influential book that emphasized the importance of randomized controlled trials as the most reliable form of evidence for identifying medical practices that really worked. A few years later he gave thought to which specialities in medicine had shown the best use of randomized controlled trials. The trophy went to the study of tuberculosis, thanks to Hill's landmark trial. The wooden spoon went to the field of obstetrics and gynaecology for its failure to rigorously evaluate its practices using such trials.

Chalmers was deeply influenced by Cochrane's work and much taken with the power of randomized controlled trials. It chimed with his own experience, in which observational studies were not providing him with solid answers about how best to help women and children at birth. He became convinced that if doctors really wanted to know the safest procedures, they had to carry out randomized controlled trials in which pregnant women were randomly assigned to receive a particular medical procedure – induction, say – or not, and then followed up to assess any differences in their health or that of their babies.*

In 1975 Chalmers's research led to a big break. After presenting his results at a conference in Warwick, he was approached by a couple of senior obstetricians. Would he be interested in establishing the new National Perinatal Epidemiology Unit, dedicated to exploring best practices in the field? The debate about childbirth had attracted the attention of politicians, and the

---

* Chalmers later became a highly influential figure by championing the idea that medical treatment decisions should be guided by randomized controlled trials and other solid evidence. He established a group called the Cochrane Collaboration, which became the definitive source of evidence in all medical fields.

Department of Health and Social Security agreed to fund the centre, which became quite a high-profile venture. Chalmers knew that, at thirty-two, he was still a bit wet around the ears, but this seemed like too exciting a proposition to pass up. He began to set up the unit in a few rooms of a research building in Oxford. Randomized controlled trials were not his first order of business, however; of much greater urgency was the question of whether a fourth perinatal mortality survey should be conducted in 1982. Chalmers needed help, and he brought in Jean Golding as one of his first recruits.

Golding was an expert in mathematics, births and, perhaps more than anything, in succeeding against the odds. She had had an early lesson in the lasting impact of disease. As the lower-middle-class daughter of an oil company worker, she had been flying through grammar school when she was struck by polio at the age of thirteen, a few years before the vaccination was introduced. It left her paralysed for a time – she wore callipers and lost a year's schooling – and it meant that she couldn't study zoology at university as she had hoped, because field trips and laboratory work would have been too physically demanding for her. Mathematics, on the other hand, required only mental strength, and she had plenty of that. She won a place at Oxford – one of about ten women taking the subject along with of several hundred men.

After graduating, Golding started teaching, married a PhD student and bore two babies within thirteen months. She was left holding both of them when, a few months later, her husband ran off to America when she was twenty-four. Golding took a cheap flat in London and started to look for any work she could find that involved numbers and could be done when the children were asleep. At just that time, scientists working with the 1958 perinatal mortality survey advertised for someone who could do some calculations for them. They wanted to find out if there were patterns in conditions such as anencephaly, spina bifida and other defects in the neural tube, the delicate roll of nervous tissue in the growing embryo that balloons and branches into the brain and nervous system. Golding was more than qualified to do the calculations, and she didn't need a tabulating machine either; she used a hole punch to make her own punch cards and then knitting needles to thread through the holes and sort them into piles on her living-room floor. So, during her children's early mornings, afternoon naps and bedtimes, she punched and sorted her cards as if she were playing some kind of macabre parlour game with death and disability cards.

Golding's work was mundane and the tools she was using could hardly have been more primitive, but the picture that emerged was profound. Her sums showed that the rate of neural tube defects was far higher in the lowest social classes than in the higher ones; and that it was substantially higher in the north and west than in the south and east – a finding that strikingly mirrored the regional patterns in the rate of babies' deaths. The results were stark, depressing and, to Golding, thrilling. She desperately wanted to know what had caused the patterns that her needles were picking out. She embarked on a career in the epidemiology of pregnancy and birth, and catapulted from her living room to academic positions in London and Oxford. With her background, Golding was very well placed to look into the idea of a fourth perinatal mortality survey, and, as the new epidemiology unit was starting up, she landed a job and started to sketch out a plan.

In an imaginary world, the ideal way to launch a birth cohort study would be to write out the near-term and long-term aims, work out how to enrol the children and plan how to follow them up over the next few decades. Then the proposal would be scrutinized to make sure it passed muster and, with any luck, it would win a whopping research grant and off everyone would go. In the real world, this is not the way things work.

The first problem that cohort scientists run up against is articulating their aims. All scientists learn that the scientific method proceeds by the formulation of hypotheses, which are then tested through observation and experimentation to work out if the hypothesis is correct or should be abandoned in favour of something else. Scientists and funders usually like to see a hypothesis that is crisp, easy to explain and will be tested by the experiment that is being proposed. For example, if you have a hypothesis that smoking causes lung cancer, you can ask people questions about their smoking habits and then measure the number that develop cancer. The experiment looks like it should test the hypothesis, as indeed it did.

But what if, like Golding, you are broadly interested in the influences on infant and child health, but you don't know in advance what they are – what do you ask? One solution to the problem is to hedge your bets – devise lots of hypotheses and ask lots of questions in the hope that nothing of importance is missed and that something useful will emerge. This scatter-gun approach is sometimes described as exploratory science, because when scientists set out they don't know quite what they are going to find. A more dismissive way to describe exploratory science is as a 'fishing expedition', to which Golding likes to respond that 'if you don't go fishing, you won't catch any fish'. Fans of birth cohort studies argue that if you keep your hypotheses and data collection broad at the outset, you can pull out connections that no one anticipated – just as the 1958 cohort found itself able to find the association between smoking in pregnancy, reduced birth weight and perinatal mortality.

Most scientists recognize that exploratory science can potentially bring up all kinds of fish, and that it is very useful for generating new hypotheses that can be tested in the future. But this type of science comes with no guarantee of success. The hard-nosed question that scientists and funders have to ask themselves is whether the cost of the exploration is likely to be justified by worthwhile discoveries. This question is a very high-stakes one when it comes to a birth cohort study, because it is big, expensive and can take years, decades or even an entire human lifetime to produce major discoveries. The cost and time involved are huge deterrents to politicians and policy-makers, who are operating on political cycles of four or five years and are unlikely to see any results during their time in office. From their point of view, birth cohorts are overpriced, high-risk, protracted gambles from which, if by some miracle there are winnings, they will never see a penny. Birth cohort studies also pose a practical problem for funding organizations, whose budgets allow them to hand out money in chunks of only a few years. That is why birth cohorts always face a battle to get off the ground. The previous British birth cohort studies had sidestepped all this by starting out as one-off surveys; there was no expectation at the outset that they would continue. They were kind of smuggled into existence.

The second problem scientists encounter in launching such an exploration is deciding what to ask. It is almost paralysingly difficult to devise a study that will only come to full fruition in twenty, fifty or even a hundred years' time, when the instigators of the study will be old or dead and when scientific topics and techniques that they could never have imagined have emerged. Look at Douglas: he didn't know he should ask pregnant mothers if they smoked, because the idea that smoking in pregnancy was harmful had not yet gained currency. Scientists can only make decisions based on history, the present and their inevitably flawed predictions of the future.

Golding's answer to all this was to make bold, sweeping plans

– she planned a fishing expedition on a grand scale. She spent about a year travelling around the country, talking to scientists and doctors and working out the logistics of a fourth birth survey. It wasn't that Golding lacked hypotheses; she collected a legion of them and saw no reason to whittle them down. She proposed that the new birth survey should explore the causes of premature delivery, growth retardation, perinatal death, most other problems at birth, as well as the quality of antenatal care and the impact of interactions between mother and child. It should also test a slew of hypotheses about the causes of congenital defects, including whether they were linked to stress, saunas, mothers' occupation and consumption of tea, potatoes, corned beef and processed peas.* Golding suggested that scientists could advertise in top medical and science journals for hypotheses to be tested by the study, as well as scour women's magazines for old wives' tales about pregnancy that could be put to the test. And if Golding were to address all these hypotheses, the amount of information that would need to be collected on the parents, children and home must be correspondingly vast. The information that she proposed to gather on the parents, for example, extended to their shoe size and whether they owned a telephone, bicycle, fridge or car.**

The logistics of the proposed study were phenomenal.

---

* These may sound surprising today, but at the time there were links in the medical literature between all these elements of diet and anencephaly, a major birth defect in which parts of a baby's brain and skull are missing. The link to maternal tea-drinking, for example, emerged from the observation that anencephaly was higher in parts of Britain and Ireland – two tea-loving nations – than anywhere else in the world. Later studies have not always supported the link.

** The argument was that each of these measures had a use. Shoe size could be an easy measure of bone length and growth; a telephone measured whether a family could easily communicate or get help; a fridge showed whether a family could store food safely; a bicycle or car indicated a family's economic status.

Golding decided that she should start the study in pregnancy, so that she could monitor the health of mothers before the actual birth and avoid the inaccuracies introduced by asking them to recall events after the fact. But she still wanted to capture all the births that took place within a short time period – she proposed one month, rather than one week. The way to reconcile these two aims, she proposed, was to enrol and monitor *every* woman who fell pregnant in Britain over the space of about a year – which would be a staggering 800,000 women – and then, once the babies started to arrive, continue to follow the 50,000 or so who actually delivered during the chosen month. Golding also wanted to collect details on an estimated 5,000 women who would suffer miscarriages in a month, as well as 4,000 babies who would die at birth and 6,000 low-birth-weight babies over an extra six-month period. 'Jean's ideas just grew and grew and grew,' lamented one colleague at the time.

There was more. Golding wanted to take on board a hard-learnt lesson from the earlier cohorts, which had all scrambled to add the follow-up sweeps later on. She would incorporate them into the plan from the start. Although this was extremely sensible, it was also her biggest mistake. The costs of the birth survey alone would have been steep, at about £850,000, but the additional sweeps pushed the price beyond £2 million or so. By the time Golding had finished her plans, they took up ninety, neatly typed pages and outlined a study that would be by far the biggest and most ambitious so far. And, unfortunately for her, she proposed this monster of a study in the wrong place, at the wrong time and to the wrong people.

In light of the leading characters involved, the prospect for the 1982 cohort never looked good. Golding had cut her scientific teeth on the 1958 birth survey; Chalmers shared the opinion of some doctors that, in driving up the rate of induction without sufficient proof that this was the right thing to do, it had backfired. Chalmers viewed the idea of a fourth survey as a loose possibility; Golding behaved as if it were a done deal. Chalmers was also a male medic who was by his own admission still very green; Golding was a driven, ambitious female academic who had been working in the field for longer than Chalmers and often reminded him of this fact. Golding loved cohort studies; Chalmers was frustrated by their limitations, and a growing advocate of randomized controlled trials. And Golding's plans were now running up against a growing preference in the scientific world for the methodology of the randomized controlled trial.

Unsurprisingly, the relationship between Chalmers and Golding quickly soured – soon there was no relationship at all. Golding organized workshops about the new cohort, but did not invite Chalmers. At one point they were only communicating through letters, which Chalmers would prefer to remain buried for ever in the archives of the research unit. It was, says Chalmers now, the worst year of his life and one in which he could easily have tried to end it all.

On 20 April 1979 Golding stood up and presented her plan at a make-or-break meeting of the unit's advisory group, held in a room at Oxford's Hertford College, with its imposing courtyards and unblemished lawns. Chalmers was there. So were scientists who had worked on the earlier birth cohorts, as well as representatives from the Department of Health and Social Security, which was going to decide whether to fund the survey. It was a grand setting for a meeting that couldn't have happened at a worse time.

The country had recently pulled out of one recession and was on the verge of plunging into another; government departments were under pressure to cut costs. Thatcher would be in office within a matter of days, leading to great uncertainty about what Britain would look like with a new leader in charge. That same month, the MRC was a whisper away from pulling the plug on the first cohort, and Wadsworth was begging for a reprieve. Kellmer Pringle was pleading with government departments – including the very same Department of Health and Social Security – to throw the second cohort a lifeline. Butler was speeding around the country in his VW trying to drum up enthusiasm for the third.

All the objections to sprawling, expensive cohort studies were coming to a head – and here was Golding, standing in front of the meeting and asking for £2 million to start up the most ambitious, expensive, sprawling cohort of all. The scientists called in to examine her plans had already expressed concern about its expense, its lack of focus and its overabundance of hypotheses.

It's hard to say precisely when, in that meeting, the 1982 cohort died. The way Golding remembers it, Chalmers stood up and, with 'a knife-in-the-back-type blow', said that the money would be better spent elsewhere. Chalmers just recalls that, by the end of the meeting, the verdict on her proposal was unambiguous. As the exhausted committee members filed out, they were surrounded by ivory-coloured towers. Hertford College opens into a stunning square lined by Brasenose College, All Souls College and the Radcliffe Camera, a famous outpost of Oxford's world-renowned Bodleian Library. Their elaborate limestone façades were an embodiment of what scholarly enterprise could achieve.

At that point, one of the committee members dropped her keys and split the air with a strident curse. It perfectly summed up the mood. The entire birth cohort enterprise had spiralled out of control and now it had to stop. Three months later, the government formally decided not to support a fourth perinatal mortality survey. Golding's overarching ambition would not be realized, and the astonishing achievement that was the series of British birth cohorts appeared to have reached a bitter end.

On 29 March 1982 Douglas, Kellmer Pringle and Butler were all sitting in a small studio owned by the audio-visual department at Bristol University in order to shoot a video. It was probably the first time that they had ever been in a room together. Douglas, who was by then retired, wore a beige flared suit and sat looking relaxed on the left. Butler, in a wide purple tie and thick-paned glasses, sat amiably on the right. Kellmer Pringle cut the space between them in a brown floral skirt, smartly crossed legs and a lipsticked smile that looked excruciating to maintain.

Wadsworth and Goldstein had organized the shoot because they believed that the three would not be around for much longer. Douglas was getting on; Kellmer Pringle was suffering badly from her arthritis; and Butler, well, one just didn't know with him. They'd had great difficulty in getting the three cohort leaders together; Kellmer Pringle, in particular, wasn't keen on recording a discussion with Douglas, whom she viewed as a rival, or with Butler, with whom she found it impossible to get anything done. On the day, Kellmer Pringle was furious at Butler because he hadn't slept for two days and kept nodding off.

Wadsworth introduced the three of them to camera. 'This film is a piece of social history in two senses,' he said. 'First, it is a record of three British national birth cohort studies – that is to say, three studies of all babies born over a period of a week. But it is also social history in another sense,' he added.

'They span twenty-four years of British history, during which time major changes in social welfare, education and medical care have taken place.' After the introduction, an interviewer started by asking Douglas about the origins of the 1946 cohort. 'I was rather attracted by a short-term project that we had to complete in two years,' Douglas began. 'It seemed that by continuing for a mere four or five years – and we didn't think of more than that – we might be able to answer some questions, such as the relation of ill-health in the different social classes to the mortality levels.'

Wadsworth and Goldstein shot about two hours of footage and then spent two days editing out the parts of it in which Butler had fallen asleep. The video is the only recording of the three cohort leaders talking about the studies that they loved best, and it was shot in their darkest hour. The three scientists spoke about the impact that the studies had had on academia and policy, even though it was often difficult to draw direct lines between the two. Whenever politicians identified a problem, Douglas noted drily, they would think that they'd be able to find an answer if they only had a long-term study of people's lives. Then they'd realize 'Oh, but we have three!'

And what of the future, the interviewer asked Kellmer Pringle; what do you think should happen next? 'Well, I would like to see – it's dreaming, you know – but I would like to see longitudinal cohort studies regularly mounted every say ten or twelve years, become part of a pattern of things in this country,' she replied – which would mean establishing an institution to mount and compare them. 'That's hoping for something which at the moment I have no grounds of hoping for,' she said. Everyone there knew that plans for a fourth cohort had already died by this point.

Now the interviewer turned to Butler: what do you think

the future holds? 'Well, all three have survived, and it seems to me that they will go on surviving,' Butler replied amiably, even though all the studies were hanging by a thread.

The next year Wadsworth and Goldstein's presentiments came true when Kellmer Pringle died, at the age of sixty-two. Most people believe that she took an overdose because of her physical or emotional pain. One cohort leader had passed away, and one cohort study had failed to quicken into life. The fate of the rest now remained to be seen.

5

Older and Wiser

Cohorts Come into Their Own

There are some things about the night of 23 July 1991 that Diane Iles will always remember, and there are some things that will always be a blank.

The memorable part was the birth of her first child, Alex, who was a healthy 7 lbs 6 oz when he arrived at 5 a.m. that morning. Iles had had a busy time leading up to the birth. She worked full time at a NatWest bank in Bristol, and three weeks before Alex was born she had sat exams for a diploma in computing. That July night, when her waters broke, she went straight to hospital for the birth, just as 98% of British women did by that time. But her contractions didn't accelerate, and she spent so long wandering the corridors waiting for things to speed up that the staff sent her husband home. An hour or so after he left, when doctors examined Iles, they realized that her cervix was fully dilated and told her to start pushing. 'No, I can't,' she said, 'because my husband wants to cut the cord and he's not here.' We've rung him and he's on his way, they replied.

Like Gertrude Palmer, some forty-five years earlier, Iles didn't receive the pain relief that she wanted for the birth, even though an array of drugs was widely available and free on the NHS. By the time she decided she would like an epidural anaesthetic – which is routinely administered into the spine to

numb pain – her labour was too far advanced for it to be done.
Still, Iles doesn't recall too much about the pain from the next
hour and a half of pushing, or from the 3 cm incision that the
medical team eventually made to widen the baby's exit and get
him safely out. She does know that after her baby arrived and
the doctors were pulling on the umbilical cord to ease out the
placenta, the cord snapped. At that point, the doctors offered
her either an epidural or a general anaesthetic so that they
could extract the placenta and stitch her up. 'I thought, "I'm
not having an epidural – I didn't have an epidural as pain relief,
I'm certainly not having one for the placenta",' Iles says. She
opted for a general anaesthetic, which is why the rest of the
night remains a blank and she was out cold when her placenta
– a circular mass of tissue that typically weighs about 1.5 lb, is
the size of a dinner plate and resembles a gelatinous bag of raw
offal – slipped out.

Iles also isn't sure if her placenta was shipped off to the hospital incinerator, as many are – or washed and tenderly lowered
into a bucket by scientists who had asked if they could take it
for a study of children that they were launching in the city.
'They could have taken it,' Iles says. 'They may have, in the
operating theatre. I wouldn't have asked for it back. I wasn't
cooking it or anything, you know. I weren't overly bothered
where that went.'

The most likely place that placenta went was into an extraordinary collection of human tissues that scientists were
gathering as part of the fourth British birth cohort study, which
finally got going some twenty-one years after the last. The placentas – around 9,000 of them – can today be found in a secure
storage shed on the outskirts of Bristol. Each placenta floats in
a white bucket full of formalin, a chemical that preserves the

tissue, and together the buckets line rows of shelves like a collection of very peculiar, pallid seaside pails.

The placentas are a tiny fraction of the tissues that scientists have amassed during the nearly twenty-five years that this cohort has been alive. Most of them can be found behind locked doors that read BIOHAZARD and HUMAN TISSUE AUTHORITY, which open into two dark basements beneath the headquarters of the study in the city centre and then a walk-in freezer wired with 24-hour alarms. In here, cardboard boxes that once contained bananas and bell peppers have been emptied of produce and carefully stacked with bottles of mothers' serum, the transparent liquid that sweeps blood cells and nutrients through the body. A few steps further on, a parade of freezers is crammed with vials holding blood, urine and saliva. Blue metal boxes are stacked with microscope slides featuring a paper-thin cross-section of umbilical cord. Held to the light, they show the two arteries and one vein that once carried blood to and from the babies of the fourth cohort.

Over the years, Iles has contributed plenty of her tissues and Alex's to this store. She particularly remembers the time the scientists asked her to send in his baby teeth. She didn't mind making the donation. 'I would've just thrown them in the bin,' she says. She did discover that Alex, who was by then seven years old, was terrified by the idea of a tooth fairy coming into his room at night to leave money under his pillow in exchange for the tooth, and she had to tell him that no such fairy existed. Alex's teeth, along with those from another 4,000 children, are all collected in transparent plastic bags in the scientists' deep freeze. Next door are boxes holding 15,000 nail clippings and 20,000 locks of hair. The basements also hold four boxes filled with blood spots on pieces of cardboard and three boxes filled with vials of freeze-dried blood plasma. Altogether, this study has amassed nearly 1.5 million biological samples – and there are plans to collect many, many more.

To find the origin of this remarkable tissue store, we must return to Jean Golding, nursing her wounds after her failed attempt to bring a fourth cohort to life in 1982. Golding bided her time: she worked with Butler on the 1970 cohort and helped to write some of the papers that he didn't complete. But she still stubbornly believed that her birth cohort was a good idea – and, before long, life threw her a second chance.

In 1985 Golding flew to Moscow to attend a meeting organized by the World Health Organization, which had the somewhat vague remit of improving the health of children in Europe. Golding was the only native English speaker there, so she was appointed to write up the proceedings every night and present them the next day. After a couple of days, it became clear that no one really knew what was affecting the health of children in Europe, nor did anyone seem to be reaching much of a conclusion about how to find out. So Golding decided to write what she thought they *ought* to have decided. She dusted off her design for the 1982 cohort and inserted that into the report. She suggested that lots of countries should launch birth cohorts, and then compare their results afterwards.

It's hard to say exactly why her proposal for a huge birth cohort got a friendlier reception in Moscow in 1985 than it had in Oxford in 1979. One probable difference was that the World Health Organization wasn't looking at having to foot the bill. The WHO did commission some small pilot studies, and then it wrote to all the ministries of health in Europe saying that a birth cohort study would be well worth pursuing if each country could find its own funding. This ruled out almost every nation from the start.* Golding, however, was determined to make it work. The WHO had given her a formal mandate to build her cohort. All she needed now was money and several thousand pregnant women willing to take part.

Having been so badly burnt by her overambitious plans for the 1982 cohort, Golding made some radical changes this time around. To start with, she threw out much of the baggage that history had attached to the first three cohort studies. She would no longer try to record all the births in a single week or month, opting instead to collect as many births as she could across a year or more. And this study was not going to span the entire country; it would concentrate on the county of Avon, which includes Bristol and is named after the river that rolls through it.** Her sample would not capture and represent children across the nation, but it did have the advantage of allowing her to drastically cut down on the number of pregnant women she enrolled. And having everything close at hand would give Golding more control over the interviews and examinations, rather than having to coordinate a nationwide troupe of data-collectors, as Douglas, Wadsworth and Butler had. The location also endowed the cohort with its name – the Avon Longitudinal Study of Parents and

* Some countries did, with Golding, participate in a study called the European Longitudinal Study of Pregnancy and Childbirth, which followed over 40,000 children.

** The county was officially abolished in 1996 and its components redistributed into the city of Bristol and the counties of Gloucestershire and Somerset. Golding chose the location mostly because that was where she lived, but it also included children distributed across a city, several towns and more rural locations, which made for a good mix.

Children – and the truly nasty acronym by which it is known, ALSPAC. All of the participants know it by a friendlier title, 'Children of the 90s'.

Changes were now taking place on the world stage that would cast birth cohort studies into a much more favourable light. The biggest of these was the growth of genetic research, which was accelerating at an astonishing pace. For decades, biologists had been focused on breaking down the body into its component parts – cells, which together make up our tissues and, zooming in closer, the molecules that make up cells. They had become especially fixated on DNA, a stringy molecule that is balled up at the centre of human cells and that contains sections along its length called genes. In 1953 scientists in Britain – most famously James Watson, Francis Crick, Maurice Wilkins and Rosalind Franklin – changed the face of biology with the discovery that DNA has the structure of a double helix, like a twisted ladder, revealing how this molecule could store and pass on biological information from cell to cell. DNA is built from a sequence of chemical letters, and cells are able to read the sequence within a gene and use it to build proteins, the molecules that make up the structure and machinery of cells. DNA is able to split into two strands – a half-ladder each – and then reconstruct the other half of each ladder to produce two identical copies, which are passed on to daughter cells. It is a stunning molecule, and it has captivated biologists ever since.

The rapid developments in genetics were important for epidemiologists trying to understand the causes of human disease. It meant that they were able to broaden their gaze beyond the influences that we encounter in our environment, in the form of infectious microbes, as well as pollution, smoking, diet, social class and all the other factors mentioned so far in this book. Now a new field of inquiry opened up – genetic epidemiology – in which researchers tried to understand how the DNA that we inherit from our parents influences our susceptibility to disease. In some cases this involved finding just one gene that, when mutated, caused a disease. But chronic diseases such as heart disease or diabetes involve many genes, so the task of identifying them was much more complex.

By 1990 the fixation with DNA reached a pinnacle when scientists announced the formal start of the Human Genome Project, an international, muscle-flexing, high-profile, expensive effort by scientists to sequence 3 billion letters in a person's DNA. Call it a code, call it a blueprint, call it a book of life, call it what you will – the hope was that the human genome sequence would reveal how this remarkable molecule builds a healthy human body and what aberrations in that sequence make bodies break down during disease.

This was an interesting backdrop for Golding as she tried to build support for her birth cohort. For one thing, it meant that arguments over the value of exploratory science – 'fishing expeditions' – were playing out internationally. The Human Genome Project was an exploratory study on a grand scale – a highly priced exploration of the genome sequence, even though no one really knew what they were going to find. And some scientists didn't agree with the idea. They pointed out that genes themselves are only a tiny fraction of the human genome (the vast stretches of DNA in between were considered so unimportant that they were called junk); that ordering all the letters in DNA was mindless and repetitive (it involved cranking DNA through sequencing machines); and that the money would be better spent on more focused experiments to test hypotheses about the working of specific genes. But these arguments were drowned out by supporters of the Genome Project, who countered that it was impossible to know what was in the genome unless they ploughed in and sequenced the entire thing. Today scientists agree that the Human Genome Project was worthwhile, because it offered enormous insights into the way in which genes and cells work, insights whose potential scientists have only begun to tap in the interests of human health.

When Golding restarted her campaign for a new cohort in the mid 1980s she found that the objections to expensive, exploratory birth cohorts remained iron-strong. It didn't seem to matter that the country was heading into an economic boom and research funding was picking up — the big funding bodies such as the MRC still showed little interest in a protracted data collection exercise with no overarching hypothesis or any guarantee of results. Everyone thought that if they started paying for a cohort study, they would be forever throwing money into a bottomless pit. So Golding had to take a different tack. If one organization wouldn't foot the bill, it was possible that lots of organizations might each throw in a little bit and together the bits would make up the whole. She identified lots of specific hypotheses that the cohort study could answer and started furiously writing applications to government departments, charities, companies and anyone else she could think of to try to persuade them to pitch in. Over the next sixteen years she and her collaborators wrote about 670 applications for grants. For every three that they wrote, one was successful and the other two were bounced. But at least the money began to trickle in.

The Human Genome Project had other repercussions for Golding, because some farsighted scientists realized that cohort studies offered a way to understand what the sequence means. A single genome – a catalogue of letters in DNA – was actually fairly meaningless in terms of understanding human health. The bigger challenge lay in working out how each person's genome differs from that of the next person's and how these differences influence our development and health. This was never going to be an easy task, when every human genome is more than 99% identical to the next. Where are the differences, and what do they mean?

One way to tackle the problem is to collect detailed medical information on a large cohort of people alongside samples of their DNA. Then it may be possible to link up variations in their genetic code with particular characteristics, such as their height, weight, pattern of growth or the onset of disease. This type of genetic epidemiology is just like conventional epidemiology but with a few tweaks. Rather than looking for an association between smoking and lung cancer, for example, the aim is to look for an association between a particular genetic sequence and cancer (or another condition) instead. The ultimate goal – the epidemiologist's dream – is to understand how both genetic sequence and environmental factors such as smoking combine together to produce disease.

Golding wasn't a geneticist, but she quickly teamed up with one called Marcus Pembrey, who convinced her that collecting DNA was just as important as collecting detailed questionnaire information on the children as they grew up. They decided to collect samples of the mother's blood, from which they would extract DNA, and the very first sample of the baby's blood it is possible to obtain, drained from the umbilical cord after the birth. And DNA was just the start. From the point of view of biologists, birth is a once-in-a-lifetime opportunity for collecting human tissue, because it generates so much unwanted debris in the form of the placenta, umbilical cord and cord blood; at no other point in life are we so carelessly willing and able to give up several pounds of blood and flesh as we are at the time of birth. Golding added the placenta and umbilical cord to her list of tissues to collect. What with the bloods, placentas and so on, the plan for this cohort was beginning to look pretty big. If there was one lesson that Golding had failed to learn from the 1982 cohort débâcle, it was to keep the data collection focused and tight. The four final questionnaires administered during the pregnancy alone spanned over 110 pages. Do you have use of a working telephone in your home / pay phone in the building / pay phone in the street / neighbour's phone / none within five minutes' walk? Do rats / mice / pigeons / cats / cockroaches / ants / dogs / other invade your home or garden? How often do you eat sausages / burgers / pies / pasties / poultry / liver / kidney / heart?

There was another scientific development this cohort had to grapple with that the earlier cohorts had not: medical ethics, the idea that doctors and researchers should give great consideration to the way that they treat people who are taking part in research. During the first three birth surveys, no one told the mothers much about how their information would be used, and, as long as they agreed to answer questions, this was taken as consent. That's not to say they were unethical; it was just standard procedure at the time. But by the time the fourth cohort was being planned, the expectations in science had changed. The new awareness of research ethics grew from the Nuremberg trials after the Second World War, in which German doctors were convicted of sickening acts of human experimentation in concentration camps. In 1964 the World Medical Association, which represents doctors worldwide, adopted the Declaration of Helsinki, a set of ethical principles stating that individuals should have the right to make informed decisions about their participation in research and that their welfare always comes first. It slowly became standard practice for human research projects to have to pass ethical review boards and for participants to sign consent forms before they entered into studies. But even by the 1980s the procedures were still haphazard, and sometimes scientists felt that they were locked in battle with overzealous ethicists who just wanted to get in the way of their research.

For the new cohort, Golding and her team did something that was quite ground-breaking at the time: rather than submit reluctantly to ethical scrutiny, they welcomed it. They did this by establishing their own ethics committee, which tried to balance the desire to do the best science – which generally involves collecting as much information as possible – with the damage that might inadvertently be done to the people involved in the study. The group included lawyers, scientists, ethicists and, in an innovative step, study-mothers themselves. (The committee would sometimes grill Golding about her plans until she squirmed.) One question that it debated was whether to enrol and collect DNA from fathers, something that sounds evidently worthwhile but that eventually the committee decided against. Around that time, DNA testing studies were exposing the uncomfortable fact that as many as 10% of children had been fathered by a man other than the one who considered himself to be the dad, and this was being reported in the news. The committee was worried that parents wouldn't sign up to the study for fear that they would end up undergoing a paternity test that they didn't want.* The ethics

---

* Golding came to regret having missed out on the fathers' information and DNA, and in the last few years the scientists have asked the dads to come back in and belatedly enrol in the study. (The fears about non-paternity have faded and the ethics committee gave it the all-clear.)

committee was considered so successful that when, nearly twenty years later, the UK launched a massive effort to collect health information and biological samples from half a million British adults, it borrowed and fine-tuned the rubric that the 1991 cohort committee had devised.

By the summer of 1990 the placenta buckets were readied and almost everything was in place – but Golding still didn't have quite enough in the bank to feel comfortable about kicking off – until, that is, she received a call from an administrator at the Department of the Environment. The department had contributed a hefty sum to the cohort so that it could ask mothers to take air-pollution measures indoors, and now it had taken on staff to handle the results. Why hadn't the study started, the administrator wanted to know. At that moment, Golding realized that she had to launch the cohort, even though she had only about a year and a half's worth of money. 'We were kick-started,' she later said.

Golding still needed a few thousand pregnant mothers, and she began to drum up interest by talking on television and radio, leafleting doctors' surgeries and paying staff to loiter in ultrasound clinics where pregnant women were going to have their scans. (Iles was recruited at her twenty-week scan.) The team distributed posters titled EXPECTING A BABY?, which explained the study in Hindi, Urdu, Punjabi, Gujarati, Bengali, Chinese and Vietnamese. None of the other cohorts had put much effort into recruiting ethnic minorities, because Britain was predominantly white. But the proportion of the population with origins outside the United Kingdom had been slowly edging upwards, and scientists were keen that this time they should be included in the count. In April 1991 the cohort babies started to arrive en masse.

The babies weren't the problem. What the team hadn't realized was how difficult it would be to collect thousands of placentas and umbilical cords, especially in the emotion-sodden minutes after a birth. While the baby was rightly taking centre stage, the cord blood had to be siphoned off into a special tube, a sample of umbilical cord trimmed off, and the placenta placed in a bucket and put to one side. The procedure was so rushed and complicated that Golding's team asked midwives in Bristol to save the placentas from *every* birth, regardless of whether the mother had even signed up to the study. They would sort it out later, and keep and analyse only those samples for which they had written permission, a process that took at least a year. Golding also had to do a little greasing of the wheels to make sure that she got the placentas at all. It's a little-known fact that some hospitals used to sell placentas to pharmaceutical manufacturers that used extracts from the tissue in anti-ageing creams, and midwives viewed the money as a perk of the job. Golding agreed to pay 50p per placenta collected, to compensate them for the lost revenue.

The placenta paybacks were the least of Golding's financial woes. She knew the figures weren't adding up. She trained herself to sleep three hours a night; most of the rest she was writing grant applications or last-ditch plans. Extreme scenario number one was to stop everything now, but that would mean paying back the money she'd already spent before there were any results. Extreme scenario number two was to carry on collecting data and to hope desperately that the money would eventually come in. Number two was the route she took. Every month, Golding's forty to fifty staff would receive a letter from the university saying that their job was coming to an end; the next week Golding would secure an extension and they would receive a letter saying they had one more month's pay. Golding pressed on, in the blind belief that everything would somehow work out. She signed 3,000 Christmas cards to all the mothers who had enrolled so far. All she had to do, she thought, was to tell everyone not to worry and that she had it all in hand. There was no way this study could go down.

The façade eventually slipped in December 1991, when the cohort plunged into the red by some £50,000. There was no hiding it now: a note went to staff in the Department of Child Health saying that the finance department was going to freeze all the academics' discretionary funds to pay for the cohort study. Senior colleagues exploded from their offices, furious that their money was about to be squandered to pay for Golding's irresponsible debt. It was 'a major ruction', as one staff member recalls. Soon the university was threatening to close her down.

Golding cancelled her Christmas holiday and wrote a letter to the university vice chancellor, pleading with him to allow her to borrow funds to keep the study alive. She delivered the letter to his house by hand one bitterly cold night. The study couldn't stop now, at this most critical of times. Almost all the pregnant women had agreed to take part, but only half of the babies had been born. And those study-babies that had arrived were furiously growing, babbling and crawling through the months in which human beings change more quickly and dramatically than any other. Time had become Golding's enemy: if she didn't collect information on the children at one-year-old, she too would miss this decisive time of their lives.

Golding's letter must have struck a chord. The university agreed to carry the debt and to extend the study's life by a few months, and then a few more. True, Golding had to go back and beg each time, but she always won an extension. By New Year's Eve in 1992, when the last cohort babies were born, she had recruited 14,541 pregnancies – 70% of those that were eligible in the region – and 14,062 children who were born alive.*

Golding did have to jettison the one-year questionnaire, however. The team sent one at fifteen months instead, and went back to the children at least every year from then on. At first the scientists just quizzed the parents. (Do you ever have a battle of wills with your toddler? How often during the week is the TV switched on when he is in the room?) Later, the questionnaires were also posted direct to the children themselves. (I think I'm very clever/quite clever/not very clever/not clever at all. Do you have no pubic hair/a little light-coloured hair/dark, coarse hair like an adult? Have you ever tried cocaine/crack/amphetamines/inhalants/sedatives/hallucinogens/opioids/other?) As well as more than a hundred questionnaires, the scientists also invited them to regular clinical examinations and continued to stock the tissue bank with whatever they could get. Meanwhile, the cohort eventually ran up a debt of some £1.5 million.

While the fourth cohort had been coming to life, the first one had been nearing middle age. In 1984 a team of MRC reviewers had stepped off the London-to-Bristol train to assess what Wadsworth had been doing with the 1946 cohort during his time in charge. Wadsworth was exhausted and on edge. He

---

* Although the babies in Golding's cohort were born through 1991 and 1992, for simplicity I will refer to it from here on as the 1991 cohort.

and his team had been working flat out, collecting thousands of measurements of blood pressure, weight, diet, lung function and mental health in his 36-year-olds and now he needed to show that tracking young adults in the prime of their lives had been worthwhile. Luckily, he had a good lead.

Wadsworth was interested in high blood pressure, which was by now a well-established risk factor for cardiovascular disease, and he plotted all the thousands of blood pressure measurements to see what he could find. The first thing he could see was that reams of the cohort members had dangerously high blood pressure that had not been spotted before. (This was akin to Butterfield's urine survey, which had shown how many people were on the road to diabetes before it was actually diagnosed.) But then Wadsworth did what only a birth cohort scientist could do: he began to look across the lifetime of data that had been previously collected on the cohort for factors that might explain the differences between people's blood pressure scores. When he did this, social class leapt out: people born into a lower social class tended to have higher blood pressure as adults, which suggested that the impact of class on health had certainly not gone away. Wadsworth also found that people with higher body weights tended to have higher blood pressure, which fitted with the accepted idea that being overweight or obese puts people at greater risk of cardiovascular disease. Then Wadsworth wondered whether the influence of body weight started much earlier in life – and, with the weight of every child in the cohort having been recorded over the years, he had an exceptional opportunity to find out.

What Wadsworth actually discovered, however, came as a total surprise. The correlation between weight and blood pressure could be traced back to life's start: babies with a low birth weight tended to have higher blood pressure as 36-year-old adults. It seemed extraordinary to think that the weight of a baby could be linked to blood pressure three and a half decades down the line, particularly because it countered the dominant idea in epidemiology that adult behaviour and lifestyle – smoking, lack of exercise, diet and so on – were what established our risks of chronic disease. It was so extraordinary, in fact, that Wadsworth assumed at first that the association must be a mistake, and that a confounding factor must be responsible for the link. He kept on torturing the data, adjusting for this confounder or that to see if the association was a false one – but it wasn't. He published the paper in the *British Medical Journal* in November 1985. By that point Wadsworth's data had already persuaded the MRC reviewers to fund the cohort for another five years. After a day of discussion, the chair called Wadsworth into the room. 'When we were coming down I decided to shut you down because we've had enough of this,' he told him. 'But you convinced us.'

The day the blood pressure paper came out, an epidemiologist called David Barker rang Wadsworth from the University of Southampton, where he worked. 'You scooped me,' Barker told Wadsworth. Barker was also reaching the conclusion that birth weight influences our risks of chronic disease, and his work was just months from being published. 'This is exactly the way science is going to go,' he said. At the time, neither had any idea how far that would be – that Barker would become famous and that epidemiology was heading towards a much richer understanding about the origins of chronic disease, with cohort studies at its very heart.

Barker's ideas germinated from a heavy book that contains brightly coloured maps of England and Wales. The book is a death atlas, and it was published by Barker and fellow epidemiologists in 1984. Each page charts the number of people who died between 1968 and 1978 from various common causes. But the two maps that most interested Barker show deaths from heart disease in men and women: regions with low rates are green; those with high rates are red. Most of southern England, which is the most affluent part of the country, is a healthy sheet of green, but many of the poorer regions in Wales and northern England are splattered with red. After studying these maps, Barker and his colleague Clive Osmond puzzled over what set the red-coloured regions apart.

To Barker, the conventional idea that heart disease could be blamed on a poor adult lifestyle didn't make sense, because there was no obvious reason why people in the poor, red areas should be leading a worse lifestyle than people in the affluent, green ones. This made Barker look for a different explanation, and he found it when he overlaid the heart disease map with another map showing the rates of infant mortality from 1921 to 1925, the period when many of the adults dying of heart disease had been born. He found that the two maps married up: the regions with high heart disease were generally those with high infant mortality too. In a paper reporting the results in the *Lancet* in 1986, Barker and Osmond proposed that babies in those regions had suffered from poor nutrition before and shortly after birth. These tough conditions killed many babies – hence the high infant mortality – but they also left those that survived susceptible to heart disease decades down the line.

This was a curious idea, but it was going to take a lot more to convince people that it was true than a loose correlation based on maps. Barker needed a stronger link between the growth of babies in the womb and their risk of adult disease

– and he found one when he realized that the first good indicator of foetal growth is a baby's weight at birth. He set out to locate a group of people whose birth weights had been recorded long ago and who would already have died or fallen sick in significant numbers.* Barker dispatched letters to health officials all over the country looking for old birth weight records, and eventually arrived at the desk of an archivist who had the medical records of babies born across the county of Hertfordshire between 1911 and 1948, all handwritten in heavy books. The archivist told Barker that he couldn't have them, because for reasons of medical confidentiality they couldn't be released for fifty years. At this stage, luck offered Barker a hand. He could see that some of the records were from the village of Much Hadham – where his own family had moved during the war and where his sister had been born. That meant his sister's birth weight was written somewhere in those ledgers. 'I don't think there's a better person to look after them than me,' Barker said. The official relented, and Barker piled the books into the boot of his car and drove off.

One of the reasons why epidemiologists had been ignoring the influence of early life on adult health is because it is laborious and expensive to follow a group of people from birth until death. So Barker did something very smart: he cheated. Once he'd dug up the historical birth records, he spent at least two years tracing the men those babies had become and found out if they were alive or dead and, if the latter, how they had died. (He concentrated on men because women tended to

---

* Barker couldn't use the records of the 1946 cohort because its members, by then in their thirties, were not old enough to have developed heart disease in large numbers. ('It's not big enough and not enough of them are dead,' as he put it.)

change their names after getting married and so were harder to trace.) He created a birth cohort – which is now known as the Hertfordshire Cohort Study – from scratch, by collecting information on the start and end of their lives and skipping over the decades in between.

When Barker connected the dots between birth weights and deaths, a fascinating pattern emerged, which supported his earlier idea. He found that the babies who had weighed the least at birth, and who were light at age one, had the highest death rates from heart disease when they were men. The findings perfectly mirrored those Wadsworth had pulled from the 1946 cohort linking low birth weight and high blood pressure, which is also an indicator of a cardiovascular system starting to go bad. But, once again, the 1946 study was overshadowed by another cohort – just as it had been by the massive adult cohorts, such as Framingham, in the past. That's because Wadsworth hadn't made too much of a song and dance about the connection in his paper; it seemed far-fetched and he didn't really know of a mechanism that could link foetal growth and adult health. But Barker did. He went on to propose that a foetus that is deprived of nutrients in the womb is 'programmed' in a way that increases its vulnerability to future heart disease. It ends up building its heart on the cheap, and the shoddy construction leaves hairline cracks and tiny chips. You'd never know the flaws were there until the wear and tear of adult life slowly takes its toll and, one day, the weakened heart gives out. This idea that conditions in the womb leave a lasting impression on the developing baby is now known as 'foetal programming'.

Long before Barker came along, there had been other signs that events we experience *in utero* and as infants can have a life-long impact on our health. In 1934 a chemist called William

Kermack was led to this conclusion when he carried out a simple but powerful analysis in which he divided people up into the different years in which they were born in England, Wales, Scotland and Sweden, and then examined the rate at which they died. (He effectively broke them up into a series of birth cohorts born into successive generations.) He saw that the death rate was gradually falling for cohorts born in later years, and ascribed this to the gradually improving living conditions into which children were being born and spending their first year. 'The health of the man is determined preponderantly by the physical constitution which the child has built up,' he wrote.

Over forty years later, the idea surfaced again in a study of another famous cohort that, like Barker's, was constructed long after the births themselves. In October 1944 the German military blocked food supplies into occupied parts of the Netherlands and people were forced to live on paltry rations of bread and potatoes that amounted to as few as 500 calories per day. This caused widespread starvation until food supplies were resumed when the country was liberated in May 1945. During the famine – called the 'Dutch Hunger Winter' – pregnant women couldn't get enough to eat and their foetuses suffered from very poor nutrition. This created what scientists call a natural experiment, in which life steps in to manipulate people and then scientists examine the results. In the 1970s scientists examined whether starvation *in utero* had consequences for adult health by analysing the medical records of over 400,000 men that had been collected during their conscription into military service. They found that children whose mothers had starved during the first half of pregnancy had twice the level of obesity as those whose mothers had got enough to eat. Later follow-ups showed that children conceived during the worst of the famine had an increased risk of schizophrenia and other measures of poor health too.

But, as we know, science goes through cycles of discovery and rediscovery, and when Barker first published his findings in the *Lancet* in 1989 they grabbed the imagination of scientists in a new way. That was partly down to his clever work at creating the Hertfordshire Cohort Study and partly due to the evangelical zeal with which he promoted his ideas. And, at first, not all the attention paid to his work was good. In fact, some epidemiologists ripped it to shreds. After all, the work was a direct challenge to the established idea that chronic disease could be blamed on adult lifestyle. And epidemiologists are also a particularly self-critical group of scientists, always picking holes in each other's work in their efforts to find confounding factors that others have missed. In the case of Barker's studies, one glaringly obvious confounder he hadn't accounted for was socioeconomic position: it could be that the children who were born small were also more likely to be born into a lower social class, or to suffer social disadvantage during their lives and, as a result, be more likely to have adopted unhealthy behaviours such as smoking as adults. So it could be that disadvantage was the real cause both of low birth weight *and* of later ill-health – creating a spurious association between the two.

There were other reasons that Barker's work raised hackles. One was Barker himself, who pushed his ideas with such supreme self-confidence that it rubbed other scientists up the wrong way. And some people were just uncomfortable with the implications of studies such as his, which said that events completely outside our control – such as our time *in utero* – could have a major role in determining our susceptibility to health problems decades down the line. One advantage of the adult lifestyle model is that it offers an escape route for us all, because avoiding the cigarettes, excess food or other risky behaviours can lower the chances of disease. But there seemed to be no such escape route on offer in the Barker school of thought, where disease risks are already imprinted on the body at birth. The whole concept smacked of determinism, the idea that our paths have been dictated by events over which we have no control.

But worry slowly gave way to acceptance as studies came through that supported the link between poor foetal growth and adult disease, even when confounding factors were taken into account. Barker extended his findings by showing that the people most at risk of heart disease, high blood pressure or type 2 diabetes have a particular pattern of growth, in which they are small at birth and for the first two years, but gain weight very quickly thereafter. The idea that poor nutrition during foetal development increases risks of such chronic diseases became synonymous with his name: it was called the 'Barker Hypothesis' (or sometimes the 'Foetal Origins Hypothesis'). Many scientists now view Barker's work as pivotal in epidemiology, because it shifted the focus away from adult lifestyle towards the importance of early life. And they are still working to understand exactly how experiences in the womb can alter a foetus in ways that last for the rest of our lives.

Barker became fascinated by the role of the placenta, which channels oxygen and nutrients to the growing foetus and so has a role in regulating its growth.* He also followed the foetal

---

* Just as his ideas were developing, he ran into Golding at a meeting and heard of her plans for the 1991 birth cohort. 'Whatever else you do, Jean, get the placentas,' he urged her. He didn't yet know how he might use them, but he had a sense that, one day, he would.

programming idea to its inescapable and radical conclusion, which is that the best way to rescue the next generation from chronic disease is to act before children are even born to ensure that the foetus gets the nutrition it needs. Barker argued forcefully that by the time pregnancy happens, it's too late to make much of a difference, and that it is important to improve the health of women and girls long before they even conceive so that their bodies have the reserves they need to support pregnancy. Not everyone agrees with this, but the work helped to build the consensus that good nutrition is important during pregnancy and early life. Meanwhile, Barker's original idea, which focused on the growth of the foetus, has been stretched into a broader concept that development from the moment of conception through birth and early childhood is important in shaping our lifetime health, an idea sometimes called the 'developmental origins of adult disease'. In short, early life matters – a lot.

This shift in the winds of epidemiology was wonderful news for anyone who happened to be running a birth cohort study. What better way to tease out the links between early and adult life than a study that already had detailed information on birth, infancy, childhood and adult health? The spread of Barker's ideas gave the 1946 cohort a new lease of life – some scientists say today that Barker rescued it.

Soon Wadsworth and his team were starting to uncover a tangle of connections between infant and child development and adult traits. They confirmed that small babies were more likely to have higher blood pressure in their forties, even when the effects of social class were taken into account. Big babies tended to have better cognition and educational qualifications as young adults. Children who stood, walked and passed other developmental milestones relatively later were more likely to develop schizophrenia as adults – strong evidence for the idea that the origins of mental illness are found early in life. In one curious collision between Barker's ideas and the cohort databanks, Wadsworth's team showed that heavier babies had a stronger hand grip when they reached their fifties. (The scientists had asked cohort members to squeeze as hard as they could on a little electronic device that measures grip strength, and is a standard and easily collected measure of muscle strength overall.) The idea here is that bigger babies are born with more muscle fibres, and that this advantage affects strength for the rest of their lives. But being born large isn't correlated with everything good. Women in the cohort who had been big babies were more likely to develop breast cancer, perhaps because they had a greater stock of potentially cancerous cells. The stream of associations continues to gush out of the birth cohorts, and sometimes the links are very hard to explain. The connections are there, but, like the intricate strands of a spider's web, it's difficult to see how they were spun.

While evidence was stacking up in support of the childhood origins idea, however, the competing concept – that adulthood is what matters – was hardly going away. It was blossoming right next door to Wadsworth's office. In the mid 1980s Wadsworth had taken the cohort study from Bristol back to the capital, where he joined the new department of epidemiology at University College London run by Michael Marmot, who went on to achieve god-like status in British epidemiology and public health. (When Wadsworth moved, the university didn't have space for the punch cards, so he sold them for scrap and used the money for a lunch with Douglas – the last time he saw him before he died, in 1991.)

Marmot had heard of this cast of eccentric Englishmen doing world-shaking studies, and he was happy to take one of them in. But he and others at the UCL department were working on two major adult cohort studies of their own. In 1967 researchers had started signing up middle-aged male civil servants to a cohort study looking for risk factors involved in cardiovascular disease, respiratory disease and diabetes. This was the Whitehall Study, which eventually recruited over 18,000 members. The civil service was divided into clear grades, with people doing the least skilled jobs – such as messengers and porters – in the bottom grade and senior officials in the highest. According to one idea, the stressed, rich officials at the top of the tree were most likely to be dying from heart disease, but the Whitehall Study showed that the opposite was true. Those in the lower grades suffered higher rates of mortality than those in the highest ranks.

As Wadsworth joined the department, Marmot was starting a follow-on cohort called Whitehall II, which recruited over 10,000 civil servants – this time, both men and women – and tried to find reasons for this social gradient of health. It showed that the expected risk factors, such as smoking and other unhealthy behaviours, were only partly to blame and that a major explanation for the elevated death rate lay in the psychological and social disadvantages suffered by those in the menial positions, such as increased work stress, a lack of support from supervisors and the struggle to hold down a job. So, although Marmot took in the 1946 birth cohort, he was focused on the Whitehall cohorts and middle-aged adults; he didn't pay early childhood much mind. (At one point, says Wadsworth, Marmot took him aside after a meeting and thanked him for looking after the cohort until the real interest set in, when people got seriously ill or died.) This didn't make for a particularly comfortable academic home for the 1946 cohort, and visitors to the department remember a less than friendly atmosphere – it seemed like every door was shut.

Further afield, epidemiologists found themselves stuck between the two competing schools of thought about the causes of chronic disease. One said that smoking, diet and aspects of adult lifestyle mattered most. The other, led by Barker, said that foetal growth and childhood were what counted. For scientists, this was a battle over money as well as ideas, because they were fighting for funding from the same limited pot. The answer was also important because the stakes were so high – knowing the causes of chronic disease could reveal how best to intervene and stem the tide of ill-health. So which mattered more: the way in which we had spent our early years, or the way we lived our lives as adults? Girl or woman? Boy or man? It would take some very smart thinking to sort this one out.

When Diana Kuh took the train from Exeter to London to interview for a research position with the 1946 cohort, there were three reasons why she couldn't possibly take the job. One was the extortionate London house prices, and another was the unfriendly department. The third was that she knew nothing about epidemiology. She convinced herself that at the interview she'd done a terrible job.

It was true – she had. But Wadsworth knew that she had a good track record and offered her the job nonetheless. Kuh spent a lonely six months commuting from her family home in Devon up to London every week and wondering if she'd made a dreadful mistake. Until one day Wadsworth told her that he was going to meet somebody called David Barker – perhaps she'd like to come along? When Barker got up and talked about his ideas on foetal programming, Kuh thought it was the best thing she'd ever heard. The idea that early development can have lifelong consequences spoke to her personally as well as intellectually. Her father, who had suffered from respiratory illness as a child and smoked as an adult, had died of emphysema, aged forty-eight. Barker's idea resonated and seemed to matter to Kuh, and she gradually realized that with the cohort she'd landed on her feet.

Kuh sometimes describes herself as 'one of those who got through', meaning that Beveridge's post-war reforms helped her to escape working-class roots. Her father was employed as a sailor in the war, but Kuh passed her 11-plus exam and then the entry exam for Cambridge. When she arrived there to study economics, she suddenly found herself invited to sherry parties and was completely out of her depth. It was while she was in her first year at university that she heard her father had died, something that helped to convince her for evermore that chance events can kick life on to a new path. The next summer she applied blindly for a job as an au pair in the United States. Her employer, it turned out, was Joseph Stiglitz, who would go on to win the Nobel Prize in economics, and his wife Charlotte, an influential economist in her own right. The job was at their house in Martha's Vineyard, a vacation retreat of America's intellectual, political and celebrity elite, and Kuh spent a life-changing six weeks bouncing the couple's newborn baby on the beach while debating neoclassical economics with the Stiglitzes and their high-powered friends. She gained confidence, and fell in love: Charlotte's brother Peter is now her husband of some forty years. Back in England, after graduating, Kuh got to know Wadsworth and his wife through her work assessing aspects of care in the NHS, and when she started looking around for her next job, she called Wadsworth, who encouraged her to apply for a spot that had just come up with the 1946 cohort.

Whatever wobbles Kuh had about working in London soon faded as she plunged her hands into the birthday cards, questionnaires, coding and general business of interrogating a birth cohort. She carried out an intensive study of the menopause by sending out detailed annual health surveys to women in their forties and fifties. At the end of her questionnaires she always left a blank page where the women could write any comments they wanted – and, when they did, Kuh read and replied to them all. She felt as if she were having a correspondence with thousands of women. From that work, one of the more mysterious connections between child and adult health emerged: women who had performed well on Douglas's childhood intelligence tests tended to reach menopause several years later than those who had performed poorly. This was very hard to explain, and the scientists threw everything that they could at the association to see if they could make it go away. But it was solid, and once they stopped to think about it, it began to make sense. The brain controls production of some of the reproductive hormones that drive the menstrual cycle. The theory is that the intelligence tests offered a readout on the overall health of the developing brain. High scores were the sign of a brain that was well developed all round and so was able, through control of hormones, to sustain reproduction for longer when those girls reached middle age.

Meanwhile, Kuh found herself thrust into the increasingly polarized debate about the cause of chronic disease. Was adult lifestyle more important? Or was it, as Barker said, all about foetal origins? In 1995 Kuh was in a meeting with a group of epidemiologists who were discussing whether to carry out a critique of Barker's work. She thought it was ridiculous that people were fighting over their different ideas, and suggested a different route. 'Why don't we actually review the evidence across life about what is important?' she said. That would make a change from tearing pieces out of each other. Kuh teamed up with another bright young epidemiologist called Yoav Ben-Shlomo and that's what they did.

The idea that grew out of that discussion is beautifully simple and helps a part of the world make a little more sense. What Kuh and Ben-Shlomo realized was that disease risk doesn't have to be an either/or, a fight between our childhood experiences and our adult ones. It's both – and more. As Philip Cheetham's story showed, our state of health is a consequence of *everything* that has happened to us through life: on the biological side, that includes the genes we inherit from our parents, our development in the womb, growth in childhood, maturation during adolescence and our behaviour as adults; on the social side, it encompasses our social class at birth, our parents, homes, schools, jobs and socioeconomic status as adults. One thing influences the next, which influences the next, and so on in a chain reaction until all the benefits and risks have accumulated to produce the state of health that we have today. These chains can play out in very different ways. Sometimes one bad thing leads to another: a child born into poor socioeconomic circumstances might be more likely to be of lower birth weight, eat a poor diet, be exposed to passive smoke and conflict at home and have fewer educational opportunities, all of which add up to poor health. Sometimes it's the other way around and a good experience sets people off on a healthy trajectory for life. Kuh and Ben-Shlomo called their approach 'life course epidemiology', and the idea took off. They later realized that the concept wasn't limited to chronic disease; it had a wide reach that encompassed the development of pretty much any state of health or disease ranging through cancer, mental health, strength and ageing.

The first thing that most people say to Kuh and Ben-Shlomo when they hear about the idea of life course epidemiology is: well, that's bloody obvious, isn't it? The pair acknowledge this with grace. It *is* obvious that the events and experiences we encounter in our lives affect how it later plays out, and other scientists had reached this conclusion long ago. The field of psychology, in particular, was streets ahead. The old Jesuit maxim says 'Give me a child until he is seven, and I will show you the man' – the implication being that the best time to shape our minds is as children. Since the 1960s, developmental psychologists had been building on this idea, drawing on longitudinal studies to show that our minds are shaped and moulded by experiences throughout our lives. If anything, epidemiology was rather slow to catch on to the life course view, and Kuh and Ben-Shlomo freely confess that they borrowed ideas from elsewhere. Even so, when Kuh and Ben-Shlomo articulated the life course concept in epidemiology, it helped a lot of things fall into place. It was, as one scientist describes it, 'a transformative way of looking at the world'.

The life course idea is also a hopeful one, because it dispenses with any thought that life is deterministic and that babies born at low birth weight, for example, are doomed to die from heart disease in middle age. Cohort scientists generally accept that we have the best opportunity to shape life's trajectory in the first few years, but they are also quick to say that our fates are not set in stone at that point. The life course model allows for the interpretation that life is malleable and that it is possible to break the chain of events and improve our chances of good health along the way. Take, for example, the association that the 1946 cohort revealed between reduced birth weight and weaker muscles in middle age. That's hardly fixed: a person born with fewer muscle cells could make up for any innate disadvantage by strength training to build the muscles that they have. So it is with other conditions too. Whatever risks you have accumulated this far can often be somewhat ameliorated by the familiar guidelines of not smoking, not drinking too much, eating lots of fruit and vegetables, keeping weight under control and taking exercise.

But although the life course model was clarifying, on its own it did not take epidemiologists any closer to bringing down the rates of chronic disease – if anything, it showed how far they had to go. Once you start thinking about *all* the biological and social factors in life that could be contributing to disease, the task of identifying these factors and the relationship between them begins to sound even more horrendous than it did before. Epidemiologists had identified some of the big risk factors, such as smoking – the hard work now lay in identifying all the other myriad contributors and there would probably be a different list for each disease. And if you're a policy-maker with a limited purse to spend on public health, it's important to know not just what the risk factors are but which are the most important, so that you can get the most bang for your buck. Should you spend more on supporting the health of pregnant mothers or more on anti-smoking campaigns, or more on redesigning cities to get people walking?

Clearly epidemiology had made progress since the end of the war, but it had also become tremendously complicated along the way. From the point of view of birth cohorts, however, complexity kept them in a job. If you want to understand how everything in life affects our health, it really helps to already have a study that has logged almost everything about life and health. And that is just what Golding had managed to create.

In deciding to collect the baby teeth of her cohort children, Golding took some advice from afar. She had heard of a cohort study in New Zealand that had collected baby teeth in the 1980s and rewarded each child for their sacrifice with a 50 cents piece. But soon the scientists realized they had made a blunder. They started receiving phone calls from irate parents pointing out that the going rate for a tooth was only 20 cents and that the study had managed to inflate the rate – and therefore the expectations of children across New Zealand – by 150%. What with that, and having no money anyway, Golding decided to send children a badge in return for their teeth, which she collected from the time they were five until they were seven. She also recognized a publicity opportunity: she designated one of her team as tooth fairy and got her to pose with a wand and a cute child.

By this point, in the late 1990s, Golding's fishing expedition was starting to get a few bites. Researchers now point to a handful of results for which the cohort is famous and that have had an impact on public health. One such finding helped to settle a debate about how babies should be laid down to sleep. In the 1980s the UK and other countries started to see evidence that babies who were put to sleep on their backs were at lower risk of cot death – also known as sudden infant death syndrome (SIDS) – than those who went to sleep on their fronts. But there was concern among paediatricians and policy-makers that children who slept too much on their backs might be more likely to choke or suffer colic, or that the practice would slow the normal development of their muscles and lungs. The Bristol cohort study found itself in a position to test these claims. In 1991, just as Golding was about halfway through enrolling babies into the cohort, the British medical authorities launched a campaign encouraging parents to put children on their backs to sleep, and cohort parents started to follow the advice. Golding had asked parents in what position their children went to sleep, and she later looked for associations with any kind of illness or developmental problem as the babies grew up. The result was encouraging: babies who went to sleep on their backs suffered nothing more than a touch more nappy rash at the bottom and cradle cap at the top. This helped to reassure doctors in Britain that the practice was safe and encouraged the medical community in the US to launch a back-to-sleep campaign of its own. The advice stands to this day.

Golding's cohort also helped to shape advice about women's diet during pregnancy. In the late 1990s health experts were trying to balance the idea that eating fish was beneficial to foetal development with the knowledge that tuna, swordfish and other species near the top of the food chain contained high levels of mercury and other toxic pollutants. Golding had this covered, because she had asked pregnant women about their diets in great depth. The team pulled out an association between pregnant mothers who had eaten more fish and improved IQ, as well as better eye and brain development, in their children. In one study they were able to use their bank of umbilical cord blood samples to show that most pregnant women also had very low levels of mercury in their tissues and that the levels were not linked to developmental problems. This suggested that the benefits of eating at least some fish largely outweighed the harm. Health advice in the UK and the United States today suggests that women balance the benefits and risks by eating fish but avoiding or limiting the types of fish known to have high toxin levels.

Meanwhile, genetic epidemiology was slowly coming of age. On 26 June 2000 scientists announced that they had completed a draft of the human genome sequence after ten years and at a cost of some $3 billion. It was a scientific achievement so momentous that it was announced at a White House press conference with President Bill Clinton on the stage and Prime Minister Tony Blair patched in by video link. The achievement 'represents a pinnacle of human self-knowledge', crowed an article in the *New York Times*. In truth, there was a long way yet to climb. Although scientists had one human genome in hand, no one yet had the technology to analyse the several thousand unsequenced human genomes that Golding had stocked in her DNA banks. 'All these high-powered alpha-male geneticists were talking the big talk about genetics – when you actually gave them DNA for a thousand individuals it was too much,' Golding remembers.

A few years later, technology was starting to catch up. Researchers still couldn't work out the entire genome sequence of all the cohort members, but they could do cruder analyses that compared a limited amount of sequences from lots of human genomes in one swoop. Suddenly everyone wanted banks of DNA linked to people's medical data, just as Golding and Pembrey had predicted, and the 1991 cohort was perfectly placed to catch the wave. In 2007 data from the cohort and several other large human tissue banks were used to scour the human genome for sequences associated with obesity, another of those chronic diseases that has been gradually overwhelming Western countries in the last few decades. The work turned up a gene called FTO* and found that one version of this gene is more common in people who are

---

* The full name is fat mass and obesity-associated gene.

overweight. Adults who carry two of these 'risk' copies are about 3 kg heavier, on average, than those with no risk copies – a discovery that began to make sense when it was found that people with the risk copies tended to eat several extra calories per day. It's not that having the risk copy makes you fat. As one scientist explains it, 'The FTO effect doesn't move you from one end of the BMI distribution to another, it just shifts the whole distribution a little bit. So the super-skinny people are just a little bit less super-skinny and the super-big people are just a bit more super-big.'

Genetic studies using the 1991 cohort have taken off from there. They have recently helped to identify DNA sequences associated with foetal growth, bone density, eczema, childhood growth and tooth development. They have even been used to find DNA that is associated with how many years people spend in education and whether they obtain a college degree. The ability of scientists to sequence an entire human genome has advanced at lightning speed, so that it can now be done in less than a day and for under a thousand dollars. The full genomes of more than 2,000 of Golding's cohort have already been fully sequenced and, in a few years, it's likely that all of them will have been. Most of the time scientists around the world who want to study the cohort's DNA don't need to touch the actual samples; once they get the necessary permission, they can simply download genetic information that has been deposited in computer databases. For Golding, all these advances meant that she could get a little more sleep. Since 2001 the cohort has had the backing of several heavyweight funders, including the MRC and the Wellcome Trust, the latter the biggest charitable supporter of biomedical science in the world.

At the same time, the other cohorts were tentatively entering the world of DNA. In 1999 Wadsworth secured funding to collect DNA samples from all members of the 1946 cohort. In 2002 the 1958 cohort banked theirs, as part of a massive sweep of the cohort that centred on health. (The 1970 cohort is making plans to collect DNA in its next sweep, in 2016.) And, in one glorious piece of cross-cohort fertilization, the findings on obesity from the fourth cohort threw the first cohort an investigative lead.

The body weight of the 1946 cohort has followed an intriguing path. Hardly any members of this post-war generation were fat as children because food was rationed, and they stayed trim as young adults too. But in the 1980s, as the cohort entered their mid-thirties, the line plotting the proportion who were obese edged upwards – in their late thirties, it soared. Although those in lower socioeconomic brackets did get fatter faster, no social class was immune. The picture became more puzzling when scientists compared the first two birth cohorts and found that both had started to get fat at around the same time, in the 1980s, even though they were of course different ages at the time. Genes cannot explain this, because human genes do not change fast enough to make large swathes of the population suddenly and rapidly gain weight. The answer has to lie in our environment and lifestyle, which changed enormously in the 1980s, when incomes in the UK were climbing, eating out was more affordable, and cars were the way to get around. Scientists think that people with genes that make them more susceptible to weight gain started to pile on the pounds when our lifestyle and diet underwent a radical change.

In 2010 a statistician called Rebecca Hardy, who works with the 1946 cohort team, led an elegant analysis to show how the genetic and environmental influences on obesity interact. She examined which members of the 1946 cohort had the version of the FTO gene that puts them at risk of weight gain, as well as another obesity-associated gene called MC4R. Then she matched this up with the body weight of the cohort members, which had been measured twelve times since birth. She found that the association between excess weight and the high-risk versions of the genes increased in childhood and adolescence, reached a peak at twenty, and then weakened as the cohort grew older. This suggested that genes were having a strong influence on appetite and body weight in the early part of people's lives but that later on the risk genes had less sway and environmental forces took over. The overwhelming onslaught of fattening influences from the 1980s onwards meant that genes weren't having much effect any more. Other cohort scientists rave about this study, because it showed so neatly the ability of a cohort study to filter out the relative impacts of genetics and environment on our health.

But studies such as this are still the exception rather than the rule, and genetic epidemiology has not produced the simple answers about disease that many people initially had hoped for. Scientists have found it quite difficult to find individual genes that have a big impact on common conditions such as heart disease and obesity. This is probably because many genes are involved and each one makes a small contribution to our risk of illness. This makes the scientific analyses very tough, because if a gene is causing only a tiny increased incidence of disease, it is very hard to detect that signal in a population while making certain that it's not just noise. Everything becomes even more complicated when you realize that the genes are interacting with environmental factors, just as Hardy's obesity gene study showed. Now consider that you've got thousands of genes, and thousands of environmental factors, and they're all interacting in unknown ways, and you'll understand why scientists sometimes come a cropper trying to tease all this apart like a knotted ball of string.

To some extent, epidemiology had become a victim of its own success. It had found the big hitters, the major contributors to chronic diseases such as smoking and cholesterol levels that dramatically increase risks and were relatively easy to spot. Now they were looking for more subtle influences, such as components of our diet, which have a smaller impact on disease risks and are that much harder to isolate. It was true that epidemiologists had Austin Bradford Hill's criteria to help them work out if an association was causal, but knowing this didn't always help, because controlling for confounding factors was hard to do. Some scientists thought that observational studies were reaching their limits. 'Unless you do a trial, you're buggered,' one epidemiologist told me – and unfortunately, that was too often true. In many cases the associations could not be put to the gold standard test of a randomized controlled clinical trial, because the trials were unfeasible or unethical or would take decades. It's very difficult to get people to stick in a clinical trial of drinking (or not drinking) alcohol or eating red meat for the years it might take to see an increase in cancer, for example, and you can't ask people to breathe pollutants for years on end. So, observational studies were often the best that science had to offer, and some epidemiologists saw new ways that cohort studies could help.

By 2005, when Golding reached retirement age, she thought her cohort study was on safe ground. It had grants, tissues, databases and a couple of hundred scientific papers under its belt. Now she was hoping to find a successor whom she could gradually train up before handing over the reins. So she was dismayed when she heard mutters from above about closing the cohort down. Golding remembers one meeting when she just laughed at the idea that the study would come to an end. 'Which was stupid,' she says, considering all the battles she'd endured in the past. 'I didn't see those knives.'

From the university's point of view, the arguments for continuing the cohort weren't so cut and dried. It was still carrying about £1 million in debt, and it could be seen that a vast amount of information and tissue samples (including the placentas) had barely been touched. The arguments that had nearly ended the 1946 cohort also surfaced all over again: the cohort members would soon be entering that young, healthy stage of adulthood and it would be ages until they did something of interest to epidemiologists, like died. After some deliberation, however, the university didn't close the study down, but it did bring in someone fresh to take the lead. (Although Golding officially retired, she is still to be found working in her Bristol office on most days.)

George Davey Smith has very long legs, an earring and a leather jacket, and his apprenticeship in cohort studies was just as bizarre as that of everyone else. In 1987 he threw open the door of a shed in Scotland where agricultural researchers were burning the carcasses of sheep and waved away clouds of noxious smoke. Then he walked through the haze to a long row of cupboards at the back, where he unearthed a set of forgotten files on 4,999 children living in Britain that had been collected by Scottish doctor and biologist Sir John Boyd Orr between 1937 and 1939, just before the start of the war.* The pages

---

* The shed was part of the Rowett Institute for Nutrition and Health, an acclaimed research centre in Aberdeen that was responsible for carrying out chemical analyses of experimental animals by burning the carcasses. Boyd Orr established the institute, which is how the files ended up in a cupboard there.

recorded what each family had eaten for seven days – sorted into milk, meat, vegetables and condiments – as well as detailed physical examinations of many of the children, including height, weight and leg length. Boyd Orr's study, which was a pioneering survey of diet and health, revealed how many poor children were undernourished and he went on to devise the national food policy that sustained Britain through the war.

Fifty years later, after collecting the files, Davey Smith and his colleague Stephen Frankel rented a van, loaded it up with the files and Frankel drove them the nine hours or so to London. Then the pair launched a monumental effort to computerize the records and trace the study members, who were by then in their fifties and sixties. The Boyd Orr Cohort Study, as it became known, showed that children who had consumed the most calories were more likely to have developed cancer, reinforcing messages that early life influenced later health in unexpected ways. And for Davey Smith, it seeded a deep affection for cohort studies that lasts to this day.

Even so, Davey Smith wasn't looking to take over the 1991 cohort, and one of his conditions for the job was that the university write off Golding's lingering debt. He thought it was a fantastic study, a great thing for Bristol and a personal challenge. He views the cohort and its bank of tissues as a tool to tackle some intellectually fascinating problems – and he is particularly caught up with finding smarter ways for epidemiologists to filter out causes from misleading correlations.

One way to do this is to compare one cohort with another, something Davey Smith did recently to find causal associations with breastfeeding. In the 1991 cohort, breastfeeding is correlated with less obesity, lower blood pressure, higher intelligence and many other good things in children. But in the United

Kingdom, breastfeeding mothers are also more likely to be in the higher socioeconomic brackets. So is it breastfeeding that helps children, or some other aspect of a comfortable middle-class life? Davey Smith and his team found a way to solve the problem by turning to a birth cohort based in Pelotas, Brazil, where the social structure is different and breastfeeding is not linked to socioeconomic status. When he used this to strip out the effects of class, the links with obesity and blood pressure fell apart, but the link with IQ held up.

Davey Smith's biggest insight was to see how the explosion of genetic knowledge could be used to exclude the confounding factors bedevilling the search for causation in epidemiology. In 1999, on vacation in Goa, India, he sat outside the small room where his baby son was resting, started reading a first-year undergraduate genetics textbook and moved from book to book until he had a handle on the field. ('I didn't want to embarrass myself,' he says.) He is now known for introducing epidemiology to a technique called Mendelian randomization, which is named after Gregor Mendel, a nineteenth-century monk who posthumously became famous for deducing the basic laws of inheritance by crossing pea plants. Mendel obviously knew nothing about DNA because it was discovered after his time, but what we now understand he showed is that parents pass on a random selection of genes to the next generation and that each gene is inherited independent of the rest. Armed with a bank of cohort DNA, Davey Smith saw in Mendel's laws a way to extract causal associations.

Let's say, for example, that you want to unpick the contentious issue of whether drinking alcohol during pregnancy does any damage to children's cognitive development – something that Davey Smith took on in 2013. The epidemiological studies have been confusing, to say the least. They have variously suggested that moderate alcohol consumption during pregnancy is bad, or that it's hard to say, or that it might even do some good. But women who drink alcohol during pregnancy also tend to be of higher socioeconomic status. (This might sound counterintuitive, but studies in Britain consistently show that people in higher socioeconomic brackets drink more than those in lower ones, and this spills over into pregnancy too.) So the challenge here is to filter the effects of alcohol on a baby's developing brain from the confounding effects of higher social class, which is strongly associated with better cognitive development.

To do this, Davey Smith took the banked DNA data of the 1991 cohort mothers and divided them up into groups on the basis of the make-up of a gene called alcohol dehydrogenase. It is well established that people with a particular version of this gene – let's call it the 'don't-drink' version – feel the toxic side effects of alcohol more quickly than others and so they drink less, and this holds during pregnancy too. Mendel's laws of inheritance ensure that the 'do-drink' and 'don't-drink' versions of this gene are shuffled and randomly delivered to offspring. (It makes no difference what social class you are born into – you will inherit a random selection of the gene versions carried by your parents.) So scientists could examine this gene in the mothers' DNA and use it to identify a group of pregnant mothers who were very likely not to have drunk in pregnancy – irrespective of the confounding factor of social class. When the scientists removed the misleading associations of class from the equation in this way, they found that children whose mothers drank less while pregnant performed better on school tests at age eleven than those whose mothers were more likely to have indulged. Davey Smith says that years ago he had told his pregnant sister that a glass or two would be fine, but that now he has changed his mind.

Davey Smith is already moving beyond genetics. He is driving the 1991 cohort into one of the most advanced frontiers of epidemiology today: the science of epigenetics. Epigenetic marks are chemical changes to DNA that alter the way in which genes behave by dialling up or down the production of protein, and sometimes switching production off altogether. (One way to think about it portrays a gene as a volume switch, and the things we encounter in our lives can turn it from loud to silent and everything in between.) Both social scientists and medical researchers are enormously excited by epigenetics, because it could reveal how environmental influences – ranging from pollution through to diet, exercise, smoking, stress, disadvantage and so on – adjust the volume of genes, and therefore influence our bodies, behaviour and health.

That's why, upstairs in the Bristol headquarters of the 1991 cohort study, a grey £300,000 machine has been mapping the epigenetic marks on the DNA of the cohort members. The plan is to build up a bank of data that shows the epigenetic marks scattered across the genome of each child at birth, how that pattern was established and how it changed as the child grew up.

This is cutting-edge stuff, and the studies are only just starting to trickle through. In 2012 researchers at the universities of Bristol and Newcastle teamed up to look at epigenetic marks on DNA collected from the 1991 cohort's umbilical cord bloods at birth. They found that a handful of genes had characteristic patterns stamped on them that were linked to the children's height and fattiness at age nine. Some of them might have arisen spontaneously as the baby developed; others might be linked to the mother's behaviour, such as her diet, whether she smoked, or the amount of weight that she gained. But the key to the future lies in whatever it was that etched those marks.

A few years ago, Barker wanted to find out how the placentas in Bristol were doing, so he gave Davey Smith a call. The placentas had been a bit of a pain since they were collected. For many years they had been stacked up in the basement of the general hospital, but then the hospital had closed down and they had to be moved. One day, a convoy of trucks stuffed with the organs sailed calmly through central Bristol, ferrying them to their new home, the secure storage shed just outside the city where they have been ever since. But hardly anyone had actually used the placentas for anything, and it was costing the university an arm and a leg to store them. When Barker spoke to Davey Smith, the university was starting to question if the costs were worthwhile.

Barker thought the placentas were priceless. His interest in foetal programming had grown into an obsession with the placenta's role in regulating foetal growth, and now he was being channelled money by two American philanthropists to explore some of his ideas. Barker had shown that the size and shape of the placenta is associated with the risk of heart disease, high blood pressure and even lifespan. He even liked to say that studies of the placenta are likely to be of more importance to human health than the human genome sequence – so if anyone could find a use for 9,000 buckets of placentas, Barker could.

'I'll fix it, George,' Barker said to Davey Smith on the phone.

Barker was friends with the University of Bristol vice chancellor, so he rang him up and told him not to throw the placentas out. Shortly afterwards, Barker hired a young woman to start prising open the buckets, rinsing the placentas and carefully photographing them. She took snaps of about 1,400 of them before the contract came to an end, but by then Barker had more than enough. He used the pictures to count up the number of placental cotyledons, which are lobes of tissue where the all-important exchange of gases and nutrients occurs between the mother's blood and the foetus'. Then he matched these up with the extensive health records of the child who had once been attached to each of the placentas.

The results, published in 2013, showed that having a placenta with a greater number of cotyledons is associated with higher blood pressure in the children at the age of nine. The reasons for this are still obscure. It could be that the extra cotyledons are signs of a placenta that is not working efficiently, one that is struggling to supply a foetus with the nutrition it needs. This could programme the foetus in a way that leads to changes in blood pressure years later. Barker had planned to carry on the work by rifling through the cohort databanks for factors in the mother that might determine the number of cotyledons in her placenta. 'Don't ask me about our hypothesis, I'll tell you that when I've got the results,' he said. But sadly, Barker died in the summer of 2013 before he got that far.

Golding, too, recently put some of her old samples to a new use. Now well over seventy, she has grey hair pulled back from her face and speaks from a motorized wheelchair, a legacy of her childhood polio. A few years ago Golding and her collaborators threw open the freezers and thawed out over a thousand urine samples taken from pregnant women in their first trimester of pregnancy. They showed that many women were mildly or moderately deficient in iodine – which we get from seafood and dairy products – and that the children of these women had lower IQs at age eight and were worse at reading at age nine. This was a shock, because iodine deficiency wasn't thought to be a big problem in the UK – but now this study suggested it could be having a major, unrecognized impact on the brain development of the country's children. (This might also go some way towards explaining those earlier studies that pointed to the benefits of eating fish in pregnancy, because a diet rich in fish could have helped to increase the mothers' iodine levels and so raised their children's IQ.) The study is yet another vindication of Golding's decision to gather up every sample from pregnancy that she could. The only way the link could have been found was with a cohort study that had started in pregnancy, because you can't go back and collect those urine samples retrospectively.

And that is why the 1991 cohort team is taking things one step further down the line. In 2013 they entered a massive new phase in which they started to recruit the children of the cohort members and to collect all the samples and tissues that accompany pregnancy and birth. The idea of tracing a third generation makes biologists salivate with excitement because of a quirk of human reproduction. Men make their contribution to the next generation – sperm – throughout their lives, but that is not the case for a woman's eggs. All the eggs she has were formed in the developing ovary when she was still a foetus; once she is born, she will never make any more. This means that events that affected the grandmother's pregnancy – such as her diet, smoking and so on – could have left biological marks on those developing eggs and that this could influence the health of the grandchildren once they are born. Whatever your grand-mother was doing when she was pregnant could have affected you in many ways – and the cohort scientists, by looking for associations between events in the lives of grand-parents and the streams of data that they plan to collect about the grandchildren, may yet be able to determine exactly what those are.

The lab workers are ready to go. They have a 'placenta hot-line' – a mobile phone that the local hospitals can call to say that a birth has happened, so that someone can rush out and collect the tissues. A stack of shiny white plastic buckets sits ready on the floor and an instruction sheet explains how to distinguish the foetal side of a placenta – grey, wrinkly with visible blood vessels – from the side that was attached to the mother, which is bobbly and dark maroon. It says how to take grape-sized samples of placental tissue, preserve them in for-malin and extract DNA. As I write this, the team has already followed this procedure to preserve thirty-one fresh placentas from third-generation babies and by the time this book has been published, there will be many more.

The information stacks up in every form. The scientists in Bristol have sent out more than a hundred different question-naires and their data has led to over 1,200 papers from scientists all over the world. They have also collected well over 1.5 mil-lion biological samples. Terrified by the thought of a sample muddle, they long ago started labelling the vials with barcodes and employing robots to handle them in the lab. For over 7,000 children, they have created immortal cell lines – samples of cells that will survive and be experimented on long after the cohort members themselves have died. These are preserved in the Bristol basement, in steel vats of freezing liquid nitrogen, near the nails, hair and teeth.

Golding's 'fishing' approach is being put to use in ways that could never have been foreseen at the time her cohort was established; and it may yet be put to use in ways that we are totally unable to predict.

6.

Opening Up
Cohorts Yield Their Treasures

To find the unlikely salvation of the second and third British birth cohorts, you must go down, once again, into a basement – this time at the University of Essex. You certainly won't have an easy time of it.

The university, which is on the outskirts of Colchester, was born in 1964, during a great expansion of the higher education system and amidst optimism that scholarship could forge a new future for the country. It quickly achieved notoriety for student protests, and demonstrations there often made the national news. Another legacy from the 1960s is its architecture: brutal concrete structures that some might say lacked soul. The campus consists of grey tower blocks much like disappointed skyscrapers and a series of interconnected courtyards that do nothing so much as suck in cold winds and channel them through the desolate quads.

Once you have navigated your way through this grim landscape, you must cross a concrete walkway, enter one of the buildings, go down some steps and walk along a dark corridor, until you arrive at a steel door in a brick wall that has been reinforced with the type of wire used to strengthen prison walls. After navigating your way through the three lock systems, you emerge into a small vestibule that smells of new vinyl and is scrutinized carefully by security cameras. Here you can see thermometers carefully monitoring for any sign of

overheating and tiny ceiling sensors that will set phones ringing across the campus at the first sniff of smoke. If you pass
muster and get through the vestibule and the next door, you
will arrive in the basement room, only to be hit by a wall of
noise. The roar comes from the racks of sleek, black, computer servers that are lined up like rows of humming
refrigerators and together can store some 40 terabytes of
digital information – the equivalent of around 10.5 million
King James bibles. These machines in Essex hold one of the
the largest collections of social science data in the world,
which is why they are so carefully protected by walls, locks
and sensors. It is here – at the UK Data Archive – that most of
the data on the 1958 and 1970 British birth cohorts is now
stored and it is from here that scientists around the world can
now access it.

Most people who want to use the cohort data have no need
to visit the basement in person, of course. They can log on to
the website of the archive, request permission and, if they
receive it, simply search for the data that they need.* A user
searching for SOCIAL CLASS, for example, would bring up the
files of data on the 1958 perinatal mortality survey, as they
would if they were searching for BLOOD, HOSPITALIZATION,
HOUSEWORK, SMOKING or any one of another sixty terms.
Almost any search will bring up Butler's mammoth survey of
the 1970-born children when they were sixteen, which is filed
under more than 350 keywords, including PREMARITAL SEX,
VIDEO RECORDINGS, LAVATORIES, TRUANCY and EMO-
TIONAL STATES. The cohort data altogether takes up just

---

* Users include academics, government workers, members of charities and non-
governmental organizations as well as commercial users, but permission to access
the data is given only on the condition that it will not be used for profit.

under 2 gigabytes in the store – a piffling trifle in today's world – and lives cheek-by-jowl with another 7,200 or so data sets ranging from the national census to crime surveys to more obscure information, such as a survey of British carpet-buying behaviour in 1968. The carpet survey has been used only once. The British birth cohorts, by contrast, had 1318 users, from 37 different countries, between April 2012 and September 2015, and are in the top-ten most-used data sets in this store.

People are often rude about Essex and its university, but one thing that can be said for it is that it's safe. The student protests are long over, the university seems an unlikely target for terrorists, and it is also secure from natural disasters: it sits on no fault lines and is far enough from rivers and seas to escape flooding. Even so, all the data stored in the archive is copied to three separate back-up servers on site, and another one resides at a confidential location several miles away. (One downside of all the back-ups is that on the rare occasions when someone wants to drop out of one of the cohorts, erasing them from the system is a chore.) And the reinforced walls and locks, which provide physical protection for the servers, are in reality far less important than the sophisticated firewall and encryption systems that protect the data from possible hackers in the virtual world.

It's not natural disasters or even hackers that keep cohort directors awake at night: it's the thought of confidential data on the cohort members escaping after a scientist has downloaded the data, through a mislaid laptop or other inadvertent security breach. If such an accident should happen, they worry that the negative publicity could foul the reputation of the cohorts and alienate the study members – in which case, without willing participants, the cohorts would immediately collapse. That's why data security and confidentiality have become top priorities for the study leaders. The data is anonymized – stripped of information which could identify individuals – before it is given to researchers, and anything that is particularly sensitive, such as medical data, cannot be downloaded and can be accessed only via a secure data link. Aside from that, the biggest challenge at the archive lies in keeping the data in a form in which it can be used, a hamster wheel of a process that involves constantly migrating data to a new format as the old one becomes obsolete. Over its life-time the cohort data has moved from paper questionnaires and punched cards, to reels of half-inch-wide magnetic tape, to optical disks and hard disks, and finally to these black machines, which are stacks of disk drives just like those that form the backbone of modern computer storage around the world.

This being Britain, not everything about this data centre is cutting edge; when the archive received a large sum a couple of years ago to create a new secure data centre, rushed government budget deadlines meant that the money had to be spent in just a few months – too short a time in which to build anything really fancy. So the university quickly converted part of an old storeroom into this sleek, humming space with hundreds of international users. It is a world away from the destitute state of affairs that the second and third cohorts found themselves in during the 1980s, when both were broke, shambolic and drowning in data that they were unable to manage.

In the 1960s, when the social sciences as a discipline were still struggling to build recognition and esteem in Britain, there were concerns that although the country was carrying out a wealth of social surveys, the information collected then went adrift because there was nowhere to store it. This meant that other scientists were wasting their time repeating work that had been done before – and there were even accusations that some data was being sold to the United States.

The Social Sciences Research Council* was still a fledgling organization at the time, but its leaders had the foresight to realize that it needed a central archive where researchers could deposit and share data. To host the archive, it chose the University of Essex, which had just opened its doors and was strong in social science, but also because it offered to do the work at a rock-bottom price. When the archive opened in 1967, it was little more than a battery of steel filing cabinets packed with punch cards. The first collection of data to land there was a survey of village life in Hampshire, in which residents were asked whether the village was friendly, what they thought of the bus service and if the respondents frequented a church or a public house. The next year, however, the seven-year-old sweep from the 1958 cohort became one of the first major surveys to join the archive, and the cohort scientists had diligently deposited data from every sweep after that. By the early 1980s the archive had taken in data from all kinds of major studies, including national opinion polls and surveys of voting behaviour and family spending. At this stage the data usually arrived on reels of magnetic tape or, occasionally, new-fangled floppy disks.

But here, then, was the puzzle: although researchers were

---

* The name was changed to the Economic and Science Research Council (ESRC) in 1983.

taking advantage of many other data sets in the archive for their research, the cohort data was barely touched. By 1984 the archive had received only eighty-three inquiries about using that wealth of data in *fourteen years*. In less than half of these cases had data actually ended up exchanging hands, and in only a quarter of them had the data led to any results solid enough to be published in a paper or book. It was truly pitiful that this national treasure chest of data was moulder-ing away at Essex, and it wasn't clear why. So the ESRC decided to investigate. It turned to a lean, energetic scientist called John Bynner, who would eventually rescue the second and third cohorts and get them the recognition that they deserved.

Bynner was already neck-deep in surveys of the British population. He had started out his research career working on a ground-breaking survey of teenage sexual behaviour in the 1960s (not as many of them were doing it as you might expect) and moved from there to a major survey of smoking in schoolboys that was carried out to inform anti-smoking efforts at the Ministry of Health. This survey took place well over a decade after Doll and Hill's seminal epidemiological work linking smoking with lung cancer, and most of the boys had heard of the risks, but Bynner found that about a third of them smoked and that they did it because they thought it looked tough and wanted to fit in with their friends. His survey also showed that smoking was associated with poor performance at school and parents who turned a blind eye. This seeded a lasting interest for Bynner in the origins of problem behaviours, and it meant he was com-fortable carrying out research relevant to government policy; both of these skills would eventually prove useful for getting the British birth cohorts on to solid ground. But in 1984 Bynner knew virtually nothing about the 1958 cohort and wasn't quite sure why the ESRC was asking him to investigate why it wasn't being used. Still, he accepted the task and then did what he knew best, which was to carry out a survey. He telephoned or visited about forty people who had tried to use the cohort data and talked to them about what had happened. It quickly became clear why most people left the cohort well alone.

The first and most obvious problem was that most people had little idea that the cohort existed until they stumbled on some publication from scientists at the National Children's Bureau and rang them up. Compounding this was the fact that computing was still in its early days and most social scientists had no training in how to handle data at all. In fact, there was a longstanding tension between social scientists over the methodology that they used. Some scientists gathered their data using qualitative methods, such as interviewing or observing a group of people, and then looking for themes or patterns. These approaches were often used in fields such as sociology, anthropology and psychology; they were also used, for example, when market researchers observed and interviewed focus groups. Quantitative methods, by contrast, involved the collection of numerical data and statistical analyses, and had always been the bread and butter of disciplines such as economics and experimental psychology. Most of the work on the cohort studies, with their wealth of numerical data, fell into the quantitative camp. Scientists often had their preferred method and sometimes regarded the other with a dubious eye: those using qualitative methods were unfamiliar with the mathematical skills necessary to carry out quantitative ones and thought that complexities of human behaviour couldn't be understood through impersonal statistics. Those pursuing quantitative methods viewed qualitative ones as less rigorous and open to bias. Today many social scientists still tend to classify themselves as quantitative or qualitative, although they have reached an appreciation that each method has its place.

The second problem was that the cohort dataset was now immense, with some 4,000 measures (such as answers to questions) recorded on each of the thousands of cohort members. And the data was a mess, with few documents that explained what measures were included or how they were gathered – the type of information that today we call metadata and that helps people to navigate through the figures and facts. About the only metadata the cohort had was a set of typed notes written by Kellmer Pringle and a complicated book of codes. It was not a surprise that the cohort had only rudimentary metadata, because the scientists at the Bureau had been collecting the data for their own use and they knew the study inside out, but it did make it impenetrable for anyone else.

Any quantitative social scientist competent and brave enough to try to use the cohort data despite all this would then run up against a third problem. In order to actually lay their hands on it, they had to go through a Kafkaesque process that involved rounds of letters, phone calls and permission requests exchanged between the scientists, the Bureau and the data archive. Then, to crown it all, the researcher would have to drive to the Essex campus with their own reel of magnetic tape, which was about the size of a long-play vinyl record but much heavier, make copies of what they needed and then drive it directly to a first-class computing centre, which would be the only place with the wherewithal to carry out the analysis. This entire rigmarole would take weeks or months. In fact, one pair of researchers had spent two years trying to interpret the data and still failed to wring anything useful from it. It was all very sad. Everyone at the Bureau had been desperately squirrelling away all this valuable information about Britain but the rest of the world either didn't know it was there or, if they did know, found it far too unwieldy to use.

However, recognizing a problem is the first step towards solving it, and Bynner wrote everything he found into a report that he submitted to the ESRC in October 1984, along with some recommendations on how to turn things around. The report was long, dull and yet it was probably the biggest turning point in the cohort's life. Bynner recommended that the cohort must undergo a makeover. It had to advertise its existence to scientists and then make sure that the data was user-friendly so they weren't scared off any longer. Bynner's insight was to see that data could be the cohort's salvation. Up to this point, the data was like a locked library to which only a handful of scientists had a key. If only he could throw open the library door, Bynner was convinced, a new generation of scientists and their computers would find ways to craft discoveries from the contents in imaginative ways. (He felt strongly that scientists were also under an obligation to open up the data, because if taxpayers were paying for the cohorts, the results should be made available for anyone to use.)

Bynner's suggestion fell on receptive ears, because the social sciences as a whole were embracing the use of numerical data. By the mid 1980s the field had weathered the worst of the Thatcher years, in which social science was too often considered a dirty word, and had emerged leaner and wiser. (Thatcher eventually resigned in 1990, after eleven years as prime minister.) It had also learnt lessons from the Rothschild Report, which had recommended that the SSRC focus on more rigorous research and on studies that were of public concern – in other words, there was a move towards applied science, which could be put to use, rather than science for science's sake. Leading social scientists realized that the field had to adapt to survive and this meant turning to quantitative methods, and to the rapid advances in computing in particular. It had to breed contemporary scientists who were comfortable with mathematical and computational techniques. So when Bynner suggested a move to open up the cohort data, he was pushing on an open door.

What Bynner didn't realize was that, in the course of investigating the cohort data, he would become bewitched by the study. The person who would come to implement Bynner's proposals was Bynner himself.

The 1958 cohort had been in trouble ever since its leader, Mia Kellmer Pringle, had retired, and eventually a search began to find someone willing to take it on. John Fox, a statistician at City University in London, seemed a good fit. One day, in 1984, he opened up a letter asking if he would be interested in adopting a national birth cohort. It had come out of the blue. 'I didn't know anything about it,' he says. 'It arrived from three secretaries of state and the head of the ESRC asking, "Please would you take over this study?"' He may not have known too much about the 1958 cohort, but he was building up a world-leading research unit at City University that specialized in sifting and sorting massive data sets. So Fox agreed to take in the destitute cohort study and try to get it back on its feet.

Scientists who work with the British birth cohorts tend to develop a dogged devotion to the studies, and Fox was no exception. He fell quickly, deeply under the cohort's spell. For the few years that the cohort was his, he fought for it as if it were his own, becoming so intent on finding the cohort financial support that he even considered mortgaging his own home. But before that was necessary he flew to the United States and visited scientists at the National Institutes of Health (NIH), an organization that is the chief source of government funding for biomedical research in the US – something like a bigger, richer MRC. Fox had never had a more positive conversation in his life. The researchers there loved the idea that these Brits had been following a generation of children and they could see a great opportunity to compare the British cohort with an American cohort of about the same age.* One lunch later, Fox had a promise from NIH that it would provide half a million pounds for the cohort, a big sum at the time. When Fox returned to the UK with the good news, all hell broke loose. That the prestigious American NIH was willing to pump money into the cohort appeared to shock the British into realizing that perhaps their study was worth something – and, if it was, what the hell was Fox doing selling our precious study to the States? Shortly after, the ESRC matched and bettered the US funds.

In 1988, when Fox moved on,** Bynner took control of the cohort and was determined to address its deepest problem: that the data wasn't being *used*. It had built up all this incredible information on a generation of children but hardly

---

* The study, which took place a while later, looked at the cohort members and their children. It found that British children were more advanced in reading and maths tests when they were young (roughly five to nine), probably because British children start formal schooling a year earlier than American children. But by the time the children were teenagers, these differences had disappeared.
** Dedicated though he was to the cohort study, Fox left to take up his dream job as the United Kingdom's Chief Medical Statistician.

anyone was accessing it outside the close circle of scientists who were keeping it alive. So Bynner put his rescue plan into action. He and his team spent several years patching up the data, making it easier to handle, advertising that it was there to the international research community and helping them to use it. The team dispatched cohort scientists to evangelize about the data and guide people in; they built a data dictionary (ranging from N515 – BIRTH WEIGHT – to N509722 – HOW SATISFIED ARE YOU WITH YOUR LIFE SO FAR) so that researchers could find what they needed; and they promoted small, digestible data sets that scientists and students could play with. The aim was to give them a little taste of the cohort's riches, and then, with any luck, get them hooked. At the same time Bynner was making plans for the next sweep of the cohort, in 1991, when its members would be aged thirty-three. All the upheaval and lack of funding meant that a full decade of the cohort members' lives had flown by, undocumented, since the last sweep.

Then, just as those questionnaires were going out, the birth cohorts shifted course once more. Neville Butler, the tireless leader of the 1970 cohort, turned up at Bynner's office in London. Will you help with my cohort? he asked.

The sensible answer to this question would have been no. The 1970 cohort had been in a pathetic state ever since the sixteen-year-old mega-sweep in 1986, from which hardly anything in the way of results had emerged. The new data wasn't being deposited in the Essex archive, thus depriving everyone else of the study as well.

Butler, however, was pushing blithely on. To process the results of the 1986 sweep, he had filled his Bristol orphanage building with some thirty or forty coders and other staff, many of whom he had hired on the cheap through the Youth Opportunities programme, the government scheme for helping school leavers into work. He had employed day secretaries and night secretaries because there was so much to type up, and he was organizing fundraising events for the cohort and his children's charity, the International Centre for Child Studies, on an increasingly spectacular scale. In 1989, he hosted an elaborate charity luncheon at Hickstead, one of the country's premier horse-jumping venues, featuring a champagne reception, charity auction, afternoon tea and strawberries and a celebrity appearance by Prince Edward. But, while patrons of the cohort may have thought that they were helping sick children, scientists suspected that the cohort was an academic shambles that Butler was smearing with a gloss of success. And whatever cheques Butler was winning from his donors just weren't enough to support a national cohort study in an era when costs were running into millions of pounds. The numbers of coders and typists in the Bristol orphanage soon dwindled until the charity was down to Butler and one loyal secretary. Later, the pair moved out altogether, into the downstairs of Butler's house. Butler was getting on, and eventually he realized that his beloved cohort needed help.

When Butler went to London to find it, his first call was to Wadsworth, who was busy keeping the 1946 cohort on the road. But Wadsworth's mother was taken ill, and he had to miss the appointment – something he now calls a narrow escape, because taking over another cohort would have led to physical, mental and scientific ruin. Bynner, however, leapt at the chance. 'I thought I would move heaven and earth to do it,' he says now.

Ever since Bynner had first learnt about the cohorts, he thought it was heart-breaking how little they had worked together up to that point. Each was so deeply engaged in its personal battle to stay alive that there just wasn't much time and energy left over for collaboration with its siblings. It didn't help that the cohorts were competing for funding and that the cohort leaders had never got on. Bynner thought this was a terrible shame because, while one cohort said something about one generation, with two cohorts scientists could start to compare the generations and understand how they differed and how they were the same. Take social class, for example. It was clear from the early work on the cohorts that the lives of children born in 1946 and in 1958 were dramatically shaped by their social background, such that those born into disadvantage were more likely to fall behind at school. But was that true of the 1970 generation too and, if it was, had the country changed in ways that made the boundaries of social class easier to transcend? Only comparing the cohorts could answer questions like this; then scientists could see how the country was changing around them and how this affected the way that the cohort members' lives played out. So, when Butler asked if Bynner would take in the 1970 cohort, Bynner immediately said yes. If one cohort was illuminating, he thought, two together could be a beacon.

And so, in the 1990s, reams of data from the 1970 cohort landed with a metaphorical thud in the Essex databases, where it was united with its sibling study. Now Bynner just needed scientists to use it.

And they did: his strategy became a roaring success. Scientists in all kinds of fields started hearing mutters about a remarkable database on Britain and its people. Apparently, some mad scientists had decided to record the births of every child born in one week in 1958 and in 1970, and had recorded their lives in painstaking detail ever since. Imagine that! The number of phone calls to the Essex data archive started to pick up, and throughout the 1990s and 2000s there was a veritable explosion of research using cohort data, as scientists in Britain and abroad started mining it to understand every complex social issue of modern life, ranging from family, to education, to work. Does a short period of unemployment affect our earnings after that? (Yes, dramatically.) Is taking educational qualifications financially worthwhile? (Yes.) Are women who pursue education and careers having children later? (Again, yes.) Today when you ask a cohort scientist to point you to the big discoveries, their brows tend to furrow, and they start to mumble and squirm. It's not that there's nothing to say; it's that there's so much to say that they don't know where to start. The bibliography kept by the cohort scientists lists over 2,500 papers and books on the 1958 cohort and over 770 on the 1970 cohort, and everyone cheerily admits that it is hopelessly incomplete. It's hard to find an aspect of social science research that the cohorts *haven't* reached.

The work that drew the most attention, however, emerged from a small group of economists in London, who started to play with the cohort data. That wasn't just because of Bynner – it was also because the cohort members were now old enough to find jobs and earn money, matters that economists like to study. And when they began dabbling with the cohorts, these economists had no idea that their work would go on to cause the stir that it eventually did.

The economists may have been new to the cohort studies, but they quickly found themselves grappling with all the old issues that had dominated the studies' early days: in particular, the impacts of poverty and social class. The discussion over inequality had never gone away, but through the Thatcher years it had reached a new heat. The number of families living in poverty surged to historic levels during the 1980s, and the difference between the incomes of the richest and poorest sections of society widened dramatically. At the same time, many people were growing fatigued with Conservative Party rule, which stretched on for another seven years after Margaret Thatcher resigned in 1990 and John Major became prime minister. In 1997 Tony Blair won a landslide election for the Labour Party with the promise of change. Part of Blair's brand of New Labour politics was a pledge to create a more equal society, one in which merit would come before privilege. He famously promised that his top three priorities in office would be 'education, education, education' – he would iron out inequalities in the education system and ensure that every child was able to fulfil his or her potential.

The Labour government also promised that it would be guided in its strategies by evidence, rather than by opinion – part of a wider, burgeoning movement known as evidence-based policy-making. The idea was that politicians would move away from policies based on theory and ideology, and instead use data and facts to work out how best to improve the country. The concept grew directly out of evidence-based medicine, the effort driven by Iain Chalmers and many others, which demands that doctors make decisions about how to treat patients based on randomized controlled trials and other rigorous, objective studies, rather than on opinion. The new focus on evidence-based policy was good news from the point of view of the British birth cohorts. It meant that just as economists and others were starting to exploit the cohort data to understand society, Labour policy-makers were receptive to data that suggested what needed to be done. But evidence-based policy is rather different from evidence-based medicine, because in social science, researchers rarely have the option of performing randomized controlled trials, the gold standard method that medical researchers use to distinguish a cause from a correlation. You cannot, for example, randomize people to different social classes, or different school types, or to wealth and poverty, or to married or divorced parents, in order to test their impact, as you can when testing a drug or medical technique. Very often observational studies, such as cohorts, are the best source of evidence that researchers have.

Into this milieu stepped a sharp economist called Leon Feinstein, who in the late 1990s was starting to use the cohort data as part of his PhD studies. Feinstein became interested in Blair's pledge that improving the education system would reduce inequalities. But would it? Feinstein was curious to know whether the gaps in educational performance between social classes emerge even before children start school – in which case, any attempt at tackling inequality would need to start earlier than the school years. To answer this, he needed a measure of children's early intellectual development as well as their social class, and he found precisely what he needed in the cohort databanks, and records collected on the 1970-born children that most people had forgotten were there.

Back in 1972, when the cohort children were nearly two, doctors had started a small study to investigate whether malnutrition of the foetus during pregnancy has a lasting impact on the development of a child. The survey traced about 20% of the children and put them through a battery of tests. Can he say 'Ma-ma'? Can he point to his eyes, nose, hands or feet? Can he build a tower of blocks? Can he take off his pants or shoes? Then, when the children reached three and a half, they were put through a more taxing set of tasks. Can he count ten cubes? Can he name the picture of a car, cup, apple, fish or chair? The study showed that babies who may have been malnourished tend to grow fast enough to catch up with their heavier peers – but the information had barely been touched since. When Feinstein dug out the data, he found the measures a little ad hoc, but he thought that they were close enough to standard-ized cognitive tests to give a readout on the children's intellectual ability at that very young age. He loaded all the data on to his computer, along with the results of cognitive tests that the children had completed when they were five and ten, as well as their families' social class. Then he combined them all into a graph that has since become so famous in cohort circles that it is known simply as the 'Feinstein Graph'.

Along the horizontal axis, Feinstein plotted children's age; on the vertical axis, he put their performance in the cognitive tests. Then he selected four groups: children from the highest-class families who scored the best marks on the tests at 22 months (rich, clever); children from the lowest classes who scored equally well (poor, clever); and children from the high-est and lowest classes who scored particularly badly on the tests (rich, dim; and poor, dim).* The question that Feinstein asked, using the exceptional richness of data collected on the 1970 cohort, was how these different groups performed on cognitive tests over time.

---

* These are my shorthand labels for simplicity. Feinstein argues that the children should be labelled as high-scoring and low-scoring, because they cannot be classed as innately clever or stupid based on tests at twenty-two months.

The Feinstein graph

Average test scores of 1970 cohort children at 22, 42, 60 and 120 months by socioeconomic status (SES) of parents and rank position on tests taken at 22 months.

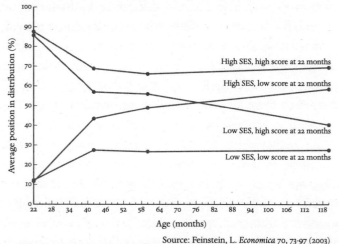

Source: Feinstein, L. *Economica* 70, 73-97 (2003)

The Feinstein Graph

Average test scores of 1970 cohort children at 22, 42, 60 and 120 months by socioeconomic status (SES) of parents and rank position on tests taken at 22 months.

Credit: Leon Feinstein

Feinstein found that the rich, clever children and the poor, dim children more or less flatline – in educational terms they didn't get much better or worse as they grew from three and a half to ten. By contrast, the performance of the poor, clever children on the cognitive tests slowly declined, so that the line plotting their progress drifts down. At the same time, the scores of the rich, dim children slowly rise, until, somewhere between the ages of five and ten, the lines on the graph cross, and the scores of the rich, dim children overtake those of the poor, clever ones. It was a very simple and striking picture. These two lines appeared to show that the brightest working-class children in Britain were quickly and unavoidably surpassed by the stupidest middle- and upper-class kids.

This would have come as no big surprise to anyone who had thumbed through the last fifty years of birth cohort results. In the 1960s Douglas had shown how middle-class schoolchildren in the group accelerated away from their equally bright, working-class peers. And studies from the second cohort had shown that children from disadvantaged backgrounds also tend to perform worse at school than the rest. Now, over thirty years later, Feinstein had evidence that class seemed to have a major influence on the educational performance of the third cohort too. But he had also gone further, to show that the performance gaps between rich and poor emerged at a shockingly young age and then quickly widened over time. That's why this new illustration of the impact of class got people worked up all over again.

Feinstein published the graph in a chapter of his PhD thesis, and in a paper in the academic journal *Economica* in 2003 – but soon the graph was getting a far wider airing than that. It started to feature in academic seminars, then commentaries, blogs, newspaper articles, government policy documents and talks around the world. It simply took off. It was, as one commentator wrote, 'something to get angry about' because it showed the class divide in such a simple, vivid way, and just as New Labour was promising to even out inequalities and make class count for less. Often, the birth cohorts hold a mirror up to Britain – and sometimes we don't like what we see.

The Feinstein graph didn't just show that class mattered; it showed that the performance gaps between children of different classes emerged at a very young age, and therefore suggested that the best way to close the gaps is by supporting children before they reach school. This was just the type of evidence that the Labour government needed. Since 1998 it had been introducing a major national programme called Sure Start, which was designed to support disadvantaged children before they reached school through programmes targeted at health, early education and family support. (The programme mirrored the Head Start Program that was introduced in the United States in the 1960s.) When Feinstein's graph emerged, it was used by policy-makers to support the argument that the programme was exactly the right thing to do and should be expanded; in 2000, the government more than doubled the funding for Sure Start. In fact, Feinstein had not produced evidence that this type of early-years programme would close the gaps and redraw the lines of his graph – that would have required an experiment in which children were followed through such an intervention programme and compared with those who did not participate, something that social scientists later attempted to do. But Feinstein agreed that efforts like Sure Start were worth a try. If you waited until children got to school, it looked like it would be too late.

While politicians were embracing the graph with open arms however, in academic circles there were soon questions about whether it was even right. In April 2011 two researchers published a high-profile paper arguing that the graph and the way it was being interpreted were a matter of concern. John Jerrim and Anna Vignoles, at the Institute of Education in London, claimed that it was difficult to accurately classify children's level of ability based on a set of relatively crude tests the children had taken at just twenty-two months of age. Some children would be assigned to the 'clever' group just because of blind luck on the day of the tests – their tower of blocks happened to balance; they accidentally pointed to their nose when asked – and on later tests, many would perform less well. The researchers said that Feinstein's findings could be clouded by this type of statistical noise and when they tried to correct for it using what they considered to be better data and methods, they generated a different-looking graph. In this analysis, the scores of poor, clever children did not slope down as steeply as Feinstein had observed – and there was no crossing of lines with the rich, dim group. One blogger labelled the saga as the 'rise and fall of the killer chart'.

Vignoles and Jerrim did not undermine the main thrust of the Feinstein graph. They agreed that disadvantaged children as a group tend to score worse on educational tests than those from wealthier backgrounds and that this gap is apparent at a very young age. But they argued that poor children did not necessarily lose their talent as they developed – and they warned that policy-makers should not place too much emphasis on one single result. Feinstein, meanwhile, has welcomed the debate. He argues that some of the finer points of his work have been misinterpreted – but that the graph has done a lot of good by capturing the public and political imagination and bringing attention to the roots of the class divide.

Just at the point Feinstein was showing that class mattered in the early lives of the 1970-born generation, other economists were working on social mobility: the measure of how much people move between one social position and another. And they were plumbing the depths of the birth cohorts for data that could test their ideas. The topic was all too familiar, but the results would cause the biggest ruckus experienced by any of the birth cohorts to date. Studies of social mobility in Britain stretch back several decades and have been dominated by sociologists, who assign people to social class groups based on their occupation. Broadly speaking, the aim in most social mobility studies is to look at the social class of parents, and then look at the social class of their children and see if there has been any change. If all the working-class children are now working-class adults, and the upper-class children are still upper class, then there is zero social mobility – no one is going up or down the class ladder. But if the working-class children and upper-class children, when grown up, are spread evenly across the class spectrum, there is plenty of social mobility – everyone is climbing up and down the ladder with ease. In Britain, the truth is somewhere in between.

When sociologists have examined how social mobility has changed across time, they have described it in two ways: absolute social mobility and relative social mobility. Absolute social mobility considers the actual numbers of people who move from one class into another. Through the middle decades of the twentieth century, sociologists found that absolute social mobility had gradually increased – more people had migrated from one class to another – mainly because more professional and managerial jobs were being created to draw people upwards. In other words, there was more room at the top, and people moved upwards to fill the space. By the end of the century, however, this upwards movement – sometimes called the Golden Age of social mobility – was levelling out for men (but not women) as the growth of professional positions stalled.

The picture looked different when researchers described it using relative social mobility, which examines the chances of children in one social class moving up or down the ladder in comparison with children from other backgrounds, after these wider changes in class structure have been taken into account. For example, during the Golden Age, lots of children may have moved from working class to middle class, but if most people were moving upwards at the same time, the relative mobility of a working-class child is no greater than that of anyone else. So sociologists have concluded that *relative* social mobility had remained pretty constant during most of the twentieth century in Britain, even though *absolute* social mobility had increased. That this distinction can be hard to explain and hard to grasp helps to show why studies of social mobility were mostly an academic pursuit – until, that is, the economists and the British birth cohorts turned things around.

In the 1990s, amidst the growing debate about inequality in Britain, a few economists decided to estimate social mobility in a different way. Instead of looking to see if people had moved up or down the ladder of social class, they looked to see if people had moved up or down the financial ladder. Their aim was to examine the income of parents, and then the income of their children, to find out if the same families were still at the bottom of the heap. At the time, the best data around for doing this was from the 1958 birth cohort, which had recorded the income of families when the cohort children were sixteen, and that of the cohort members themselves when they were aged thirty-three. The economists Lorraine Dearden, Stephen Machin and Howard Reed mined the cohort data and used it to generate a new estimate of relative social mobility – the chances of a child going on to earn substantially more or less than his or her parents.

The study showed that the earnings of children were fairly tightly correlated with those of their parents: some had seen their income go up, some had seen it go down, but a large part of a child's income could be explained by the size of their parents' income. This supported the idea that there were barriers that prevented poor children from becoming rich adults, or rich children from becoming poor ones – no big surprise. The next part of the work, however, was. In 2000 data started to roll in on the income of the 1970 cohort as it hit thirty, and the economists saw that they had a rare opportunity to repeat the analysis and compare social mobility across two generations to assess how it had changed. This was precisely what Bynner had hoped that researchers would do when he pooled data from the 1958 and 1970 cohorts in the Essex archive, and tried to entice scientists to use it; now his strategy was paying off. To do their comparison, the economists had to extract data that Butler had collected in his dazzlingly detailed 1986 survey, which asked parents of sixteen-year-olds to indicate their income. They also drew on data showing the income of the cohort members at age thirty.

This study was handed to Jo Blanden, who was just cutting her teeth as a researcher, pursuing her PhD at the London School of Economics. When Blanden first pulled up the cohort data on her computer, her reaction was one of complete horror. The data set was huge, and there seemed to be all this irrelevant stuff about how many times a week people ate dripping. But, once the shock had passed and she'd crunched the numbers, what she saw falling out of the data was very striking. In fact, given what happened afterwards, she wonders now if everyone got a little bit overexcited at that point.

Blanden and her colleagues found that social mobility had got worse: the income of children born in 1970 was tied more tightly to the income of their parents than it was for those born in 1958. The economists illustrated this by imagining a relatively poor boy born in 1958 alongside a richer one whose parents earned twice as much. When those 1958 boys had grown up, the richer boy would earn on average 17.5% more than the poorer one – so poor children were at a disadvantage. But when the researchers repeated the imaginary exercise for a rich and poor boy born in 1970 they found that the rich boy would now earn 25% more than the poor boy when both had grown up. It had become harder for children born in 1970 to escape their background: poverty, it seems, had become a stickier glue. This was startling, because it contradicted the sociologists' idea that relative social mobility had been pretty constant in Britain, and it was also dismal because it suggested that people here were increasingly constrained by the financial situation into which they were born. The picture looked worse when the economists compared Britain to other countries and found that it had about the lowest social mobility of all European countries, and was equalled only by the United States.

If social mobility had fallen, what was driving it down? The economists could see one obvious answer in education, which had changed a lot between the two generations. Between the time that the 1958 cohort and the 1970 cohort had passed through school, a major expansion of higher education had got under way, so that many more children were staying on in school after the age of sixteen and then progressing to university. When Blanden and her colleagues looked into this using the cohort data, they found that well-off families were benefiting from that expansion the most. It was true that more children as a whole were progressing into higher education, but a disproportionate number of those were the richer ones. This, they concluded, was a major reason for the decline that they had observed in social mobility: well-off children born in 1970 were now more likely to get higher qualifications and so were more likely to land the well-paid jobs and leave the poorer children behind.*

The first sign that this work would cause a fuss came in March 2002, when Blanden presented her results at the annual conference of the Royal Economic Society, held that year at Warwick University near Coventry. The talk itself was no big deal, and as she spoke the shoulders of academics in the audience looked pretty relaxed. But after the session, a press officer bundled her into a taxi to the BBC's Pebble Mill studio in Birmingham to do an interview. Blanden was twenty-five at the time, and was about to go on live national radio to talk about her first major piece of research. 'I was absolutely petrified,' she says. It was not the last interview that she did.

As Blanden and her colleagues published and discussed their work over the next few years, it sparked some very high-profile debate. The ideas resonated with a whole group of people in political and journalistic circles who had come from relatively deprived backgrounds, such as the 1958-born Labour politician Alan Milburn, who had grown up on a council estate, and John Major, who had risen from working-class roots – his father was a music hall performer and seller of garden gnomes – to become prime minister. What they

---

* The idea that you have to be rich to get ahead was cemented in place by a 2007 survey of leading figures in law, politics, medicine, journalism and business. It showed that more than half had attended independent schools – which are generally the domain of rich families – even though these schools educate only 7% of all children. When you put it all together – poor social mobility in comparison with other countries, worsening social mobility overall, and Britain's elite stemming from a privileged part of the social spectrum – the work pointed to a land that is increasingly divided by money.

saw around them mirrored perfectly what the studies showed: they had climbed upwards from relatively poor circumstances, but they were conscious that politicians born ten or fifteen years after them were from privileged backgrounds. The most prominent examples were soon-to-be Prime Minister David Cameron and Deputy Prime Minister Nick Clegg, who both attended private schools. Cameron, born in 1966, had attended Eton, while Clegg, born in 1967, went to Caldicott and Westminster. 'In every single sphere of British influence, the upper echelons of power in 2013 are held overwhelmingly by the privately educated or the affluent middle class. To me from my background, I find that truly shocking,' Major said in a speech.

Another young researcher called Lindsey Macmillan stirred the pot when she compared data from the 1958 and 1970 cohorts, and found that not only were those in the top professions – such as doctors, lawyers and accountants – more likely to originate from higher-income families if they were born in 1970, but that they were also, on average, declining in IQ. This supports the idea that rich children are securing more of the top jobs, even if they are not as bright, on average, as their predecessors were. Or, as one economist puts it bluntly, 'They are coming from more affluent families, but they are thicker.'

The economists' work caused ripples for the same reasons that Feinstein's had. The idea that social mobility is declining was very easy to digest and it landed at an opportune time, right in the middle of a growing debate about inequality. Some of the research was sponsored by the Sutton Trust, a charitable organization whose goal is to improve social mobility, and that issued press releases to draw attention to the work. Pretty soon, the results were being picked up by the media and used by politicians of all stripes. When New Labour was still in power, the study served a purpose because it supported its pre-existing drive to increase social mobility and prioritize education. On the other side, the Conservatives found it useful for arguing that New Labour's strategies were failing to equalize opportunities. Blanden's results were like a scatter gun that could be fired at anyone around. 'It just went a bit ridiculous, really,' says Blanden, who was spending long hours in select committees and policy briefings.

And yet Blanden, like Feinstein, found her work under vigorous attack even as it was being fêted. The critique has been led by John Goldthorpe, a sociologist who has studied social mobility between classes, rather than between incomes, for the last few decades and has found no evidence for the type of decline that the economists have seen. Goldthorpe says the economists' analysis is wrong because the income measures in the cohorts are not very reliable. They are one-shot measures – taken at one moment in time – that fail to take into account the fluctuations that occur as people move in and out of employment or switch jobs. Goldthorpe argues that this fluctuation is greater in the family income of the 1958 cohort than in the 1970 cohort, because there were more manual workers being paid per garment sewn, for example, or pound of fruit picked – from which income can vary week to week. By the 1970s many of these jobs had vanished and workers were more likely to be paid a steady monthly wage. If this is correct, the income data for 1958 parents is less accurate than that of the 1970 data, and this could explain away the economists' result. The weaker correlation between the earnings of parents and children in 1958, compared with 1970, could simply be a result of more 'noisy' data in the first generation compared with the second. Goldthorpe was so irritated by the economists' work and what he saw as the widespread misunderstanding of social mobility that he has aired his grievances widely in papers, talks and interviews.

The economists struck back, by combing over their calculations and, after six years' work, publishing a paper in 2013 saying that their conclusion held up all the same – because they were using one way of measuring social mobility and sociologists were using another. The reason for the discrepancy, they argue, is that the incomes of the rich have soared away from those of the poor since the 1970s, so the range of incomes earned by people within each social class has stretched out. The upshot is that children born in 1970 may be tethered more tightly to the income of their parents than children born in 1958, even if they are not tethered more tightly to their social class. Goldthorpe disagrees* – and the two sides are presently barely talking and somewhat fatigued. (One of the cohort leaders today uses the debate about social mobility as a lesson for her social science students, who assume that crunching numbers will produce definitive answers, when nothing could be further from the truth.) Meanwhile, in the wider world, the ping-pong doesn't make much difference, because the complexities of the debate have been eclipsed by the now-unassailable idea that social mobility in Britain is in long-term decline.

Even the economists, however, say that idea is too much of a stretch. Blanden and her colleagues are well aware that their early studies had only two data points, from the two

---

* In 2015 Goldthorpe, Erzsébet Bukodi and their colleagues again found no change in social mobility from a study comparing four birth cohorts: the ones started in 1946, 1958 and 1970, and a cohort born in the early 1980s that the scientists constructed from other data sets.

cohorts, and their work said nothing about whether the fall in social mobility that they observed was the start of a longer-term trend. To find out, they needed a third cohort – one born in the early 1980s would have been best. These children would have been coming of age as the millennium turned, providing an opportunity to see if New Labour's policies were making it easier for the disadvantaged to get ahead. But of course the decision was taken long ago not to create a 1982 cohort, something that the economists bitterly regret.

The academic debate may still be raging, but the impact of Blanden's original study continues to be felt. In April 2011 the work got another high-profile airing, and so too did that of Feinstein and his famous graph in which the rich, dim 1970-born children overtook the poor, clever ones. The coalition government published its social mobility strategy, and both economists' work on the British birth cohorts had a prominent place. (Deputy Prime Minister Nick Clegg referenced the Feinstein graph directly in his speech to the House of Commons marking the strategy's launch. 'By the age of five, bright children from poorer backgrounds have been overtaken by less bright children from richer ones – and from this point on, the gaps tend to widen still further.') The report argued that the income and social class of parents has a huge impact on children's life chances. It contained a commitment to keep social mobility at the heart of the government's policy agenda, and shortly afterwards the government introduced a set of 'trackers' that it said it would use to show whether its policies were improving life chances for the disadvantaged. The trackers include figures on the number of poor children achieving preschool developmental targets and the numbers of poor sixteen-year-olds achieving a good grade in their maths and English GCSEs. Blanden's and Feinstein's work has been popping up in policy and academic documents ever since. One professor says that he has shown the Feinstein graph at least 200 times in the talks that he gives all around the world.

All this commotion has left Feinstein and Blanden with mixed feelings. The birth cohort work had helped to make their names, but it also left them feeling uncomfortable and exposed because their results were being bandied about by all and sundry and used to justify policies that went far beyond the conclusions of their work. Neither is under any illusion as to why. Their studies had a simple message and their timing was perfect, arriving just as a national conversation about class and inequality was taking off. Over sixty years earlier, James Douglas had learnt from his wartime reports that politicians could use data in any way that they wanted; now these two young economists were learning exactly the same thing.

It can be seen from all this that the relatively arbitrary decision to track the lives of thousands of babies born twelve years apart has had repercussions that its instigators could never have imagined. Butler would not have had computer-savvy economists in mind when, in his 1986 survey, he asked parents of his sixteen-year-olds to indicate their income. And when doctors were assessing whether thousands of obstreperous 1970-born toddlers could put on their shoes and pants, they probably weren't thinking that this information could end up as the foundation of a graph that would drive government policy and academic debate forty years on.

But that's the thing about birth cohorts: you may know where they start, but you never know where they're going to end up. And this is exactly what happened to Bynner, who had set out to study one thing and then found himself passionately engaging with innumerable others.

★

Back in 1991, when Bynner inherited the third cohort, he had made a promise to Neville Butler that he had to honour. Butler had successfully secured some money to test the reading and maths ability of 10% of the cohort members that year, when they were aged twenty-one. A few years later Bynner did a similar survey of 10% of the 1958 cohort too. The cohort members were asked directly about their skills. (Can you read aloud from a children's storybook? Can you fill in a form from the council? In the past six months, have you read a cook-book / the Bible / a self-help book e.g. keep-fit?) It's well established that most people are very bad at recognizing their own difficulties with reading and writing – not necessarily because of a conscious effort to hide them, but because they are so used to coping with them that they may not see that a problem exists. So the surveys also put their skills directly to the test. (On what page of the *Yellow Pages* are the plumbers listed? How much change will you have from £2 if you buy a 68p loaf of bread and two tins of soup for 45p each? What is the floor area of a room that is 21 × 14 feet?) Bynner didn't realize it then, but the answers to these somewhat arbitrary-sounding questions would reveal another uncomfortable truth about modern Britain, which would dominate much of the rest of his career.

The results of the two surveys exposed the shockingly large proportion of adults in Britain who struggle with basic reading and maths. They showed that about 19% of adults in both cohorts had a reading level lower than that expected of an eleven-year-old child even though most of them had finished school. In practical terms, someone reading at this level probably cannot locate the page reference for plumbers in the *Yellow Pages* and may be classed as functionally illiterate. When it came to numbers, things looked even worse: nearly half of all adults had skills below those expected of an eleven-year-old (they could not calculate the area of the room, even with a calculator) and a quarter had skills at or below the expected level of a seven-to-nine-year-old (they could not work out the change from the £2 problem). A comparison of Britain's basic skills with those in other countries in the OECD showed that Britain was loitering near the bottom of the league. This widespread lack of basic skills had gone largely unnoticed until the cohorts brought it to light.

At the time, no one was giving too much thought to adult reading and writing – but that complacency soon vanished. For an individual, struggling with reading and maths can be an embarrassment and limit his or her ability to find a job. For the country, it comes at a major financial cost, because it means that employers cannot find appropriately skilled people for the positions they need to fill. Lack of basic skills came to be seen as a brake on the economy; work from the cohorts later showed that a small improvement in adult literacy and numeracy would save about £3 billion. The idea that our collective ignorance was costing the country billions of pounds was one that politicians immediately got. And, once again, the cohort results were well timed because they hit just as New Labour was coming to power, with its emphasis on evidence-based policy. Bynner made sure that the right people knew about them. He had long ago realized that if the cohorts wanted to survive, they had to pump out the type of evidence that policy-makers found relevant and useful, a quality that undoubtedly kept the funding coming in during his time in charge and that caused him to be described by other scientists – and in the nicest possible way – as a political animal. Many scientists have fallen for the studies over the years, but wiry, white-haired Bynner radiates enthusiasm for them like a physical force.

In 1998 the Labour government commissioned an investigation into the problem of basic skills from statistician Sir Claus Moser, and Bynner was on the committee. The report, which leant heavily on cohort results, called for a national strategy to halve the number of functionally illiterate people of working age, and in 2001 the Labour government followed up by launching Skills for Life, a raft of measures to boost adult literacy and numeracy, including free adult courses to those without the equivalent of a satisfactory grade at GCSE English or maths. Anyone who was watching TV in the mid 2000s may remember one consequence of this initiative, which was a series of advertisements featuring gremlins – grey, pointy-eared creatures that mocked people about their lack of basic skills. The ads encouraged people to get rid of their gremlins by signing up for an adult education course, and several million people eventually did so.

The Skills for Life programme, which stretched over several years and eventually ate up billions of pounds, is another case where it is possible to draw a direct line between cohort evidence and policy change, but it is less clear how much of an impact the strategy had on the country's basic skills. Unfortunately, there was no evidence that people who had already passed through primary and secondary school without learning to read were going to be helped by a few weeks of adult education – and when the effects of the programme were evaluated, there was little evidence after a year or two that those who had taken one of the adult education courses had improved their wages or their employment compared with those who did not. But it did have positive effects: they often emerged with higher self-esteem, and a new determination to get qualifications and a good job. Another consequence of the new focus on basic skills was the introduction in primary schools of an hour each day dedicated to literacy and numeracy, in the hope that today's children wouldn't emerge as ill-equipped as those born in 1970. The issue of basic skills has never gone off the boil, and Bynner's findings have bled into various national and international policy documents, Commons debates and committee hearings ever since.

For Bynner and the cohorts, the high-profile attention to basic skills also produced hard cash. As part of the Skills for Life campaign, the government generously funded Bynner's team to establish a national research centre on adult literacy and numeracy. One rather awkward question that had to be addressed was how a substantial proportion of the population had passed through at least eleven years of compulsory schooling without ever having learnt how to read or add up well. This was hardly ancient history: the 1970 children had been in secondary school in the 1980s and belong to the same generation as those who now govern the country. What had gone wrong? To find out, Bynner and his team went back and tested the reading and maths skills of the entire 1970 cohort at the age of thirty-four. Then the scientists looked back through the data to compare the lives of those cohort members who now struggled to read and write (they focused on those with the reading and maths skills of seven-to-nine-year-olds) with those who could read and write well (they had progressed to the standard expected of sixteen-year-olds who got a reasonable grade in their GCSEs).

It was this exercise that brought Bynner face to face with disadvantage all over again. The first signs that the non-readers were in trouble had been emerging when the children were only five, when Butler had asked them to point to pictures corresponding to the words 'drum' or 'insect', and to copy a series of shapes including a circle, a cross and a square. The ones who had struggled to master such skills were far more likely to end up in the non-reading group nearly thirty years on, and in many cases these problems had gone unnoticed by parents and teachers. And you've probably already guessed that these children often faced disadvantages in their early years. They were more likely to have grown up with very little money, with working-class or unemployed parents, in overcrowded homes and with parents who did not read to them and were not interested in their education – in other words they had massive challenges right from the start.

The picture worsened as Bynner worked his way through the lives of the non-readers and found that they were more likely to have fallen behind at every step. They were more likely to have left school with no qualifications, more likely to think education was a waste of time, more likely to have low-paid, low-skilled work and periods of unemployment, more likely to end up in poverty and in poor housing or homeless. The men were more likely to be living alone in their mid thirties, whereas the women were more likely to have been teenage mothers or to have had four or more children. Both were less likely to own or use a computer, which was very worrying in a world in which an increasing number of jobs involve computer skills. Sadly, the consequences of all this could be seen ricocheting into the next generation, because Bynner surveyed some of the children of the cohort members too. The parents with poor maths and reading skills were less likely to read to their children and the children themselves were less interested in school.

This was sad, but not surprising, because it mirrored over fifty years of discoveries from the cohort studies that had gone before. Study after study on the first and second cohorts had taken children who start out in difficult circumstances and followed them forwards to show that their lives often tracked a difficult course and that they were more likely to struggle or fail. Bynner had come at it with the third cohort, and from the opposite direction. He'd started with those who were failing on a certain measure – reading and maths – then he'd traced them backwards and arrived at precisely the same conclusion as all the earlier studies, which was that they had very often experienced a difficult start. From this work, Bynner formulated a way to describe these troubled lives, which he called a 'trajectory of disadvantage'. Children who had had a tough start, and then struggled to learn to read or write, would tend to encounter one bad event after another, which pushed them slowly down a troubled life path.

This chimed with research emerging all over the world, and in different disciplines, about the trajectory of people's lives. In epidemiology, scientists had moved towards the idea of the life course – that everything we encounter in our lives, through birth, childhood and adulthood, contributes to our state of health. In sociology, researchers had long ago reached a parallel idea that events and experiences throughout our lives contribute to our eventual destination, which they also called a life course approach. It's another of those concepts that may sound very obvious, but this still doesn't negate its worth.

One of the most influential life course studies in sociology emerged from two cohort studies of children in California. The first study started when researchers recruited 167 schoolchildren who were born in 1920–21 and studied them intensively through the 1930s in order to chart their normal physical and intellectual development. The second study involved nearly 250 children born a few years later, in 1928–9. It wasn't until a few decades later that a sociologist called Glen Elder resurrected some of the old records and used them for a different purpose, which was to examine the impacts of the Great

Depression, the worldwide economic crisis that started in the late 1920s and caused widespread hardship through the next decade. Elder found that many children in the first cohort escaped their disadvantages, perhaps because their earliest childhood years had passed before the Depression really started to bite and because they left home after some of its worst years had passed. The second cohort, by contrast, showed a different pattern in which disadvantage often took a steep and lasting toll. This group was born just as the Great Depression hit, which means that many experienced major difficulties at home during their formative years. Then, as adolescents, they were hit by more troubles during the Second World War, when many parents were again working extremely hard.

Elder used all this to help build a framework with which to understand the various influences on people's lives. He proposed that a person's life course is shaped by the moment in history at which they are born and by the events – such as the Great Depression – which they encounter as a result. He also proposed that the impact of such events depends on the time during our lives at which they occur, just as he'd seen the very different impacts that the Depression had had on the lives of the two cohorts, depending on when they felt its effects.

Yet there was another crucial element to the life course idea. It is true that people are constrained by the moment in history in which they are born and by the social circumstances in which they find themselves. But within those confines, they do have opportunities to shape their life course by making choices or taking actions that can alter their path. Elder called this 'human agency', which is the term used in sociology, psychology and philosophy to describe the capacity of human beings to make their own choices in the world. This idea is exactly the same as the one that permeates life course epidemiology, which says that our health in adulthood is influenced but not determined by our health and circumstances at birth and in early life, and that we have opportunities to better ourselves through exercise and other lifestyle choices.

Bynner had followed Elder's work with great interest, and he was fully signed up to the life course idea. So when Bynner was following the troubled trajectories of the 1970 cohort members, he didn't become discouraged – if anything, he emerged as one of the most optimistic cohort scientists of the lot. It was undeniably true that people born into tough circumstances were more likely to follow a trajectory of disadvantage, but this was a statistical tendency rather than an inescapable destiny. He became convinced that life is malleable, and that it is possible for people to transcend their difficulties if they can find the right motivation, opportunities and support.

Bynner, like Douglas, concluded that parents offer the first and strongest buffer against disadvantage, and he was hardly alone. By this point, there was a stack of evidence from the cohorts and elsewhere that pointed to the enormous value of parental interest and involvement in children, particularly in the first few years.* The challenge for cohort scientists lies in separating out the impact of parental interest from the confounding effect of socioeconomic class, because better-off parents often appear to be the most interested ones. When researchers have attempted to control for this in various ways, they find that parenting appears to be important independent of socioeconomic status and, crucially, that the impact of inter-

* One compelling example was Doria Pilling's study *Escape from Disadvantage*, described in the Introduction. It showed that children who escaped an extremely difficult start in life often had parents who were interested and ambitious for their future.

ested parents appears to be able to compensate partly for the disadvantages concomitant with a difficult start. The economists too had reached this conclusion. In 2006 Blanden carried out a complex analysis of data from the 1970 cohort to examine what enabled disadvantaged children to succeed in education later in life. Her report, called *Bucking the Trend*, concluded that parental engagement, particularly in the first few years of life, is more crucial than anything else. For example, children whose parents had read to them when they were five and showed an interest in their education at age ten were significantly less likely to be in poverty at age thirty.

Bynner's work pointed to other ways in which people can push life on to a better path – and he became convinced that education, at any time in our lives, can turn things around. He coined a catchphrase – 'Never too early, never too late' – to describe the attitude that should be taken when it comes to improving our life course. With enough motivation and support, people can step up at any time during their lives, and no one need be consigned irrevocably to a trajectory of disadvantage.

Perhaps no one illustrates this idea better than Steve Christmas, the boy in the 1958 cohort who, on paper, was born to fail. Christmas did not have interested parents behind him or an interested school – and with his father's drinking, he had continuous problems at home. He failed his 11-plus and emerged from school with no qualifications and with money so tight that the bailiffs were regular visitors at the family door. After that, he lived at home to protect his 4'6" mum from the verbal abuse that his 6'6" dad delivered when he was drunk. The one thing Christmas could do, however, was work hard, and that's what he did from the moment he left school. The only local jobs were at the village farm, and so he worked there during the day. Then he went straight to a second job as a bouncer at a nightclub in Hastings, the coastal town near his home.

Christmas thinks that things turned around for him when he landed a job as a door-to-door insurance agent. He gave it his all, treated his clients well and was promoted to manager within two years. He learnt book-keeping, computing, letter writing and everything else he needed on the job and, crucially, he earned good money, which he carefully saved so that he wouldn't end up broke like his mum and dad. He eventually left home at thirty-one, married, had a daughter and later passed a string of exams to become an independent financial adviser. Christmas thinks he did OK because he realized that he had control over his life and that he was going to make things work. And he doesn't give up, he says. 'If I can't do something, I'll keep going until I do it right.'

There were hiccups, of course. When Christmas was fifty, he went partially blind with cataracts – his sight dimmed to a point where he couldn't see the tiles on the roof. He has such a phobia of needles, hospitals and anything related to them that it took him five years to agree to have an operation to remove them, but when he did, it was as if he'd been presented with a new life. (Christmas also refused to let the cohort scientists take a blood sample, which means the biobank lacks his DNA.) A second problem arose when the financial industry introduced a new series of exams that Christmas had to pass in order to practise. Christmas does not struggle badly with basic skills, as many in the cohort do, but one of the maths exams proved too much. In 2010, after trying and failing five times to pass it and with his blood pressure sky high, he was forced to leave his profession. But by that point he had saved enough to partly retire and run his own business writing wills.

Christmas's parents stayed together, unable to split despite the drinking and abuse. But after his mother died in 2002, in her mid eighties, Christmas started to make weekly trips to take care of his dad and helped him to cut down on the whisky. Once his dad told him he was sorry for what he'd done and gave him a hug, something that Christmas had never received when he was a child. His father died two weeks later, in January 2003. Christmas now visits his parents' graves in Hastings every two weeks, and makes sure that they are the neatest in the cemetery.

Christmas also takes an interest in the cohort study and has a filing cabinet where he keeps the various bits and pieces that the scientists have sent him over the years. He remembers one report saying that something like one in ten people ends up a failure in life. And he thought, 'Oh my God, am I that one?'

There are other ways to beat the trajectory of disadvantage and Michael Jay, in the 1970 cohort, experienced some dark years before he found a way. His mother had already had five children with other partners before she met Jay's father. Their lives sank quickly under a torrent of abuse – mental, physical and sexual. Jay remembers standing naked in the hallway of the council house where he lived, staring at the terracotta floor with his head facing the door. That was the standard punishment for him and his siblings if they spoke after being sent to bed. Another memory that won't go away is one evening when the children were eating plates of chips, when his dad arrived home. His mum had readied a full meal – but what set him off was that she hadn't made any gravy. He threw the plate at her, hurled their wedding photo through a window – and then he broke her shoulder. But it wasn't until some time later, when he threatened Jay's little brother with a piece of wood, that she picked up the baby and ran. Shortly after that, the police came and took Jay, his brothers and sisters into care.

Jay moved through children's homes and foster parents, was bullied and was a bully himself. And meanwhile, as a young teenager, he was coming to terms with being gay at a time when homosexual acts were a criminal offence for anyone under twenty-one and the subject was still largely ignored. (The cohort scientists didn't ask members of the 1970 cohort about their sexuality until a sweep in 2012.) As Jay freely admits, he was a rebellious 'little sod'. His foster parents couldn't deal with his sexuality or behaviour and threw him out; finally, he walked out of the children's home when a worker there called him a queer. For a while, he was homeless.

Jay stepped off his downward trajectory when he met his partner, Robert, at the age of twenty-one. Robert offered him the stability and love that had until that point been missing, and the two evolved a relationship of mutual support. Now Jay goes out to work – he's been through a string of jobs, including as a trolley dolly, pushing the tea wagon on the trains. Robert, who suffers from a nervous disorder and finds it hard to work, takes care of the home and makes sure the bills are paid. In the time that they've been together, Jay has cut down on his drinking and quit smoking. They are pleased that they got a toehold on Britain's fierce property ladder, managing to buy their council house when the offer came up. In one of those wonderful cohort loops that spool through this story, Jay's participation in the cohort study may have helped him in a way of which he is unaware. He left school without any qualifications and, although he reads a lot, spelling has always been tricky for him and numbers sometimes make him panic. His difficulties ended up in the databanks of the 1970 cohort; as we know, the overall findings helped to convince the government to launch adult education courses; and, a few years ago, Jay reaped the rewards. He took two online courses in literacy and numeracy and easily passed the exams at the end.

Jay is only too conscious that it could all have turned out very differently, and that his trajectory could have continued on its downward curve. A living reminder of this fact comes into his mind every day when his thoughts turn to his brother, who, having committed two murders, may very well end up spending the rest of his life in jail.

PART THREE

Coming Full Circle

7.

The Millennium Children
Cohorts Reborn

By 1999 scientists in Britain had a lot to be happy about. They had four birth cohorts rolling along, started in 1946, 1958, 1970 and 1991. This was reason for incredible pride: no other country was following generations of its people in this way, and using them to understand the roots of mental and physical health. And no other country could claim that high-profile reports based on birth cohort studies were finding their way to the heart of government, where they were starting to drive a sweep of policies concerning social mobility, preschool education, adult literacy and much more. Cohort studies were on the up, and all the discoveries that had been made on past generations were slowly seeping into the present day and making life a little better for the next.

And yet, amidst this celebration, the cohort scientists just couldn't get rid of a nagging regret. They kept on thinking about the missing cohort, the one that should have taken place in 1982 to continue the twelve-year series. That was the one that had died in the Oxford meeting room as a result of Jean Golding's wildly overambitious plans and its poor timing – pitched when funding was drying up and other scientists were becoming enamoured with randomized controlled trials. So, years later, the joy over the cohorts that Britain did have was still soured by the one that it didn't. It was as if the scientists were celebrating a family reunion, but were always dwelling ruefully on the one family member whose death had left an empty place.

That Golding had successfully started a fourth cohort later on – the 1991 one – only provided a little salve for the wound, because in many scientists' minds that study was different and did not properly fill the gap. The fourth cohort only included children in one region, rather than, as the first three cohorts had, spanning Great Britain and representing people across the country. And the 1991 cohort, with its banks of placentas, nails, teeth and DNA, had such a heavy emphasis on modern medical research that it seemed wholly different from its predecessors, which were rooted in previous eras. It was an outsider amongst the cohorts; a study that never really fit.

The growth of science over the last few decades had created a broader split between the four British birth cohorts. Back at the start, James Douglas had been determined that his 1946 cohort should span both social science and medical science, and over the years all the cohorts had vacuumed up reams of information that was relevant to the two disciplines. But, by the millennium, each cohort found itself standing firmly in one discipline or the other – and this was a reflection of the scientists who were running it, using it and paying for it. The 1946 and 1991 cohorts were seen to be biomedical cohorts – focusing on medical research, led by medical researchers and funded by medical research bodies such as the MRC. By contrast, the 1958 and 1970 cohorts were seen to be social science cohorts – led and used by social scientists and mostly funded by the ESRC. The boundaries were certainly not absolute – there was excellent medical research carried out on the social science cohorts and vice versa* – but, in general, the cohorts were moving down two parallel roads. It created a divide, because the scientists working in the disciplines tend to talk slightly different languages and follow different customs.

Mostly this divide was apparent only as an unspoken tension, a slight feeling of 'my cohort is better than yours'. But sometimes the differences erupted into a spat. One of the biggest points of dispute was over data, and how it was stored. The social scientists had long ago made the decision to deposit all their data in the Essex archive and make it freely available to academics, in the belief that this would lead to wider use of the studies and ensure that scientists could repeat and check each other's results. But medical researchers had not done this, because the tradition in that field is for scientists leading a project to keep control over the data: they get the first shot at analysing it, publishing the results and then they only share it with others later, if they are asked. This is partly because medical data is viewed as exquisitely sensitive and confidential – no one wants to risk people's personal health records leaking out – and partly because the field is intensively competitive and scientists are always vying to make discoveries and publish results first. (It is also an increasingly outdated custom because in the last decade or so a movement has sprung up to open up many medical databases for researchers to use, while maintaining the anonymity of people's data.)

These differing approaches to data meant that the social

---

* Although the cohort studies are often viewed from a distance as being either 'biomedical' or 'social science', all of them are involved in both spheres of research. One major example of crossover is the highly successful sweep, starting in 2002, that focused on the biology and health of 1958 cohort members in their forties and that has grown into a major scientific resource.

and medical scientists had a fundamentally different approach to the way in which they ran their cohorts. The social scientists viewed their two cohort studies as a resource that they were running for the benefit of the scientific community: whenever they were planning a sweep, scientists and policy wonks all around the country could suggest hypotheses to be tested by the cohort, help to shape the questionnaires and then use the data. The medical researchers, however, devised their own hypotheses and kept the data close to their chests. This drove a wedge between the studies, because each side tended to think that its approach was best. Some social scientists found it appalling that the medical researchers could run a hugely expensive study, paid for by taxpayers' money, and not freely share the data. They thought the medical scientists were selfish, guarding the data so that they could get first dibs on it, publish all the exciting findings and further their own academic careers. Some medical researchers, for their part, thought that the social science cohorts lacked a clear scientific vision. They thought that the social scientists were acting like servile data collectors and managers – doing whatever policy-makers told them – rather than steering a course for themselves. Because everyone was reserved and British, none of this was ever said openly. Mostly, cohort scientists are unfailingly polite to each other and then snipe behind each other's backs.

So, in 1999, the British birth cohorts were a national triumph, but they were also marred by tension and a mournful sense of what could have been. What made this feeling even worse was that it seemed so typical of Britain as a whole. The nation had found a scientific pursuit – following people's lives en masse – at which it led the world and excelled, but it was now at risk of letting that advantage slip away by not continuing to set up new cohort studies. It was like so many other things that Britain had started – cricket, sandwiches, the computer – that were quickly improved on by others, until we were soundly beaten at our own game. Before too long, some other country would be bound to outdo us at cohort studies too, because we had been too quarrelsome, short-sighted and tight-fisted to start any more.

As it turned out, however, that was not to be the case. And the scientists found this out in the summer of 1999, just a few months before the start of a new millennium. In the wider world, everyone was already making plans for a massive New Year's Eve party: the supermarkets were stocking up on champagne and planning was under way for a spectacular fireworks display over the Thames. In the birth cohort world, the excitement started when a phone rang on the desolate concrete campus of Essex University, and a social scientist called Jonathan Gershuny picked it up. Gershuny didn't have too much to do with the British birth cohorts (he was busy running another large longitudinal study at the time*) but for a short time in 1999 he had nevertheless been placed in charge of birth cohort strategy and was the point person as far as the ESRC was concerned. Gershuny answered the phone. It was someone from the ESRC headquarters in Swindon, with surprising news: 'The Cabinet Office has decided there should be a millennium

---

* The British Household Panel Survey began collecting information on all the members of some 5,500 households across the UK in 1991. Like the birth cohort studies, the household study tracks people over time, but the important difference – and the reason that social and economic scientists like such studies – is that, while birth cohort studies follow *individuals* over time, the household study follows groups of people – all those living in the home – which provides more information on the changing make-up of the household and the relationships between people in it.

cohort study,' he was told. It would be a fifth British birth cohort study – and the first in thirty years to span the country.

Not only that, but the Cabinet Office wanted the cohort to happen right now, and they wanted everyone to know about it. 'Will you please write the press release by lunchtime?' Gershuny was told.

It is very hard to work out where the idea of a millennium cohort was born. By now, John Bynner was directing the 1958 and 1970 cohort studies from offices in London's Institute of Education, which had become known as the Centre for Longitudinal Studies.* Certainly the older cohorts were gaining prominence and momentum, and in the higher echelons of funding agencies and the civil service there was a lot of lobbying in favour of cohorts going on behind the scenes, as well as an awareness that the national cohort series needed to be revived. So there was plenty of enthusiasm and support for a new cohort study. All it needed was a spark.

According to cohort legend, that spark arrived in the form of Peter Mandelson, who was appointed Minister without Portfolio in Tony Blair's new government in 1997. Mandelson was one of the masterminds behind the rebranding of the Labour Party as New Labour, helping it to win its landslide election in 1997, and he later became known for his ruthless approach and for being forced to resign twice from the Cabinet

---

* Neville Butler still maintained a presence: his loyal secretary drove him from Bristol to the office once a week. Butler continued to operate his charity to support the birth cohort studies even though it was making very little money and he himself was nudging eighty. His unwavering devotion to the studies continued until his death, in 2007.

due to political scandals but then staging phoenix-like regen-erations to secure other high-level posts.

But, before that, it was part of Mandelson's job to work out how the government should mark the turn of the millennium. The story goes that as he was sorting through proposals for bridges, domes and a rather implausible-sounding big wheel on the bank of the Thames, it seems that someone – but no one knows who – suggested that it might be impressive to mark this once-in-a-thousand-year opportunity with a major study to learn about the children born at the turn of the millennium. Mandel-son apparently liked the thought – after all, a study of thousands of adorable British babies born at this momentous moment in time has an undeniable dramatic and political appeal. So the word went out that if scientists could come up with a credible plan for a birth cohort to be started in the year 2000, they would receive a substantial sum of money to get it on the road.

When the news of the cohort reached the scientists, they had two reactions. The first was that they loved the idea. The second was that it was impossible. Anyone who had been in the cohort business for a few weeks, let alone a few decades, knew that you needed at least two or three years to start a new birth cohort study. This was easy to understand if you worked backwards from the births themselves. You have to start contacting mothers about six months before the births to enrol them during pregnancy; you need six months before that to start establishing procedures to recruit mothers at antenatal clinics. Add to that at least a year, but realistically two, for researchers to work out how to recruit people across the country and what information to collect. That adds up to two to three years in all. Back in 1979, in fact, when Gold-ing was proposing her ill-fated cohort, one of the stakes to its heart was the timing: it seemed an unworkable rush to get a cohort together in the three short years before 1982. Now, seventeen years later, the government told the scientists in the summer of 1999 that they wanted a birth cohort to launch the following year – even though a substantial number of the babies who would be born in the year 2000 had already been conceived. That is why, when Gershuny first heard of the plan in that phone call from the ESRC, he found himself holding the phone, saying, 'Sorry, we can't do it.'

And the ESRC said, 'Look, if it's not the millennium cohort, it's no cohort at all.'

From the government's point of view, the idea of a millennium cohort had flair, and there was money to blow on millennium events. By contrast, a 2001 or 2002 cohort didn't have the same appeal and the money would be spent elsewhere. So the scientists were stuck: either they raced to launch a study in the year 2000 and risked compromising the science, or there would be no study at all.

The scientists took the first route. They didn't want to let the precious chance of a new cohort slip away so easily; nor did they want to lose the opportunity to restart the cohort series. Peter Elias, an economist and adviser to the ESRC, remembers the situation being discussed at a meeting at the research council. 'We said, "This is crazy, but we can do it. We know we can do it. Let's do it."' So they did. Gershuny wrote the press release in a hurry and the ESRC commissioned him to lead a quick scoping study to show that the cohort was a feasible proposition. (It concluded that it was.) Then the ESRC ran a competition in which it invited any group of scientists to put in a bid to run the new cohort, which would be judged so that the best plan would win. By this time it was already February 2000. The New Year's party was well over, the millennium was already two months old, and no one had even been appointed to take charge. It was going to be very tight.

Bynner and the cohort scientists scrambled to get a plausible-sounding plan together. Starting in February, they had just a few weeks to design the gargantuan study, which would be drastically different from the last national cohort study, some three decades before. This time the births would be collected over a year or more, so that scientists could examine the sometimes substantial effects of being born in different seasons. The data would be entered directly into a computer for the first time, which meant that the researchers needed a crew of expensive, professional interviewers. (There was no way, in the year 2000, that the nation's midwives and health visitors could be convinced to collect information on top of already crippling workloads, nor did they have the time or the expertise.) This study would make it a priority to include the growing populations of ethnic minorities in Britain. And, hard though it is to believe, this would be the first national cohort to survey fathers, as well as mothers, from the start.

There were however a few things to be examined in the survey that were very familiar. In 1999 poverty and inequality were just as hot a topic as they ever had been, and social scientists were keen to learn more about the disadvantaged children. They decided to do this by deliberately over-representing them in the count. Although roughly one quarter of children in the UK lived in poverty at that time, around 30% of those included in the millennium cohort were poor, which increased the power of the study to describe the impact of a difficult start.*

---

* The scientists achieved this by over-sampling in regions of the country where a high proportion of children live in families receiving means-tested benefits. They also over-represented ethnic minorities and children born in Northern Ireland, Scotland and Wales.

All this was written into the plan, and in May 2000 the team received word that they had won the competition to run the study. A social scientist called Heather Joshi would lead it: she was one of the very few scientists to have worked with all three national birth cohorts, which she had used in pioneering work on women's pay and employment. And beside impeccable scientific credentials, she had integrity and determination to her name. But by now, Joshi and her team of scientists were facing a hopeless task. Nearly five months' worth of millennium babies had already been born and the last of the millennium children – the ones who would arrive in December – had been conceived and were making their presence known on pregnancy tests. It was politically unpalatable to rename the study, and therefore it had to include babies born in the millennium year – yet there was no practical way the scientists could start collecting data before the year was up. The team was under immense pressure, the atmosphere was fraught. It was a 'mission impossible' for the cohort scientists: would they be able to save the day?

Joshi rolled up her sleeves and got the job done. She and her team devised a workaround – a massive compromise that would allow them to pull off the cohort and keep the name. They decided to recruit babies who were born from September 2000 onwards – so that they could enrol at least *some* millennium-born babies and justify the cohort's name – but they wouldn't actually *interview* the parents until the year 2001, when the children were around nine months old, giving them time to get the study together. (Joshi identified the eligible children when families registered for child benefit, which most parents in the UK did.) In fact, Joshi realized about halfway through the recruitment phase that she was going to miss the target of 20,000 children because not enough babies were being born. So she stretched out the study to include 'millennium' births in some regions all the way up to January 2002.

This decision to recruit babies so late in their lives marked a major change from the previous cohort studies, which had all recruited families through doctors, midwives and health visitors, and had collected a ream of medical information about pregnancy and birth. Not this time. The impossible deadline for the study meant that the mothers were not monitored during pregnancy, far less information was collected about the medical side of birth, and there was no collection of tissues and DNA. The social scientists didn't worry too much about that – but the medical scientists certainly did.

The earlier cohorts had been ground-breaking in their detailed study of birth; they had established the link between smoking and reduced birth weight, they had been influential in changing obstetric practice, and they had become landmarks in the field of perinatal epidemiology. The birth cohorts had shown that collecting detailed information on pregnancy and birth was scientifically valuable, and it was now well established that foetal and infant development shaped people's health for the rest of their lives. At the same time, genetic research was exploding and it seemed incomprehensible to most biomedical researchers that you would start a huge, expensive, national birth cohort study without collecting a wealth of medical information during pregnancy and birth as well as the mothers' and children's DNA. The chance was missed – jettisoned because of politicians' fixation on having a splashy-sounding millennium cohort. This still causes some medical scientists to press their lips into a disappointed line whenever the millennium cohort comes up in conversation; to them, the start of the study was the squandering of a fantastic opportunity. But it was all very well to criticize from the side lines: Joshi was working her heart out to just get the show on the road before the money and momentum disappeared. 'It was a miracle that we collected as much as we did,' she says now.*

Meanwhile, the progression of time and science was creating other problems for this cohort. In 1946 giving 'consent' simply involved Gertrude Palmer inviting the health visitor into her house. In March 2001, just as the researchers were about to visit the first millennium children, the Medical Research Ethics Committee nearly put a kibosh on the entire study over consent, which had become a hot-button issue in research. They found out that prospective parents were being sent a letter informing them that they could opt out of the study ('please write and let us know if you *don't* want to do it'), rather than opt in ('please let us know if you *do* want to do it'). The committee considered this too coercive. It was an 'absolutely hair-raising experience', says Joshi, who remembers making frantic telephone calls to prevent the cohort from going down. The scientists and ethicists eventually reached a compromise: parents were asked to confirm that they opted in to the study when the interviewers turned up on their doorstep.

So when the interviewers set out, they were armed with consent forms, computers and questionnaires that testify to their moment in time. (Are you married to baby's father / separated /

---

* The social scientists did work with medical researchers when they were designing and launching the cohort – but the tight timetable severely limited what they could do. What's more, the cohort was funded at the start by the ESRC, whose focus is on social science, not medical research.

divorced/closely involved/just friends/not in any relationship?
How many hours of childcare do you pay for each week? Did
you have any medical fertility treatment for this pregnancy?
When it comes to changing baby's nappies, do you do most of
it/does your partner do most of it/do you share it more or less
equally/does someone else do it?)

Despite the impossible deadline, Joshi's army of interviewers managed to recruit 18,818 children — 72% of those eligible.
It was a far cry from the 98% that the 1958 cohort signed up,
but that's because lives and attitudes had changed. When the
first birth cohort was recruiting, all the mothers took part
because they felt an obligation to do their bit for the country.
By the time of the fifth, that sentiment seemed as laughably
out of date as rationing and hand-knitted vests. Today's parents feel no obligation to take part in national science projects:
they are busy, and they tend to wonder what's in it for them.
They also move house more often, which makes them that
much harder to track. And even as the cohort scientists were
working to keep parents involved, they had to maintain the
interest of the government too – if it had started the cohort on
a whim, there was nothing to stop it from turning around just
as suddenly and cancelling the entire thing. The scientists knew
they would have to fight for funds every time they wanted to
do another sweep of the children. But they successfully won
money to survey the children at 3, 5, 7 and 11, and as I write they
are surveying them at 14.

When the millennium cohort started, then, Britain had over
fifty years of experience in birth cohort studies – and yet this
newest one was rushed, a searing disappointment to biologists
and it had an uncertain future. But it was a triumph at the same
time. Scientists had finally got another cohort study on the
road, and had gone a long way towards cementing Britain's

position as a world leader in cohort research. Now there were five cohort studies, and another 18,818 children to put under the microscope. The scientists couldn't wait to plunge into the data to see how the country had changed.

Rebecca Wood remembers when the interviewers turned up on her doorstep asking her, her partner and her son Thomas to take part in a study of children born at the turn of the millennium (or thereabouts). She agreed – in part because she thought she might get a diary of his achievements at the end of it. It was only some years later that she realized this wasn't the case: that all the information was going into some kind of statistical research and that she wasn't going to get anything back. But she wanted to stick with the study. Once she's made a commitment, she says, 'It's not in my nature to pull out.'

When Thomas was born in 2001, Wood was working full time in a bank. The pregnancy went pretty smoothly, but the birth did not. Her baby was facing the wrong way, which meant that the doctors anticipated a difficult birth – and they were right. When she was five days overdue, Wood had her labour induced, endured thirteen hours of pain and was eventually given an epidural anaesthetic to quell her urge to push him out too soon. When he finally emerged at 9.27 a.m., she remembers being utterly exhausted and shocked that there were nine medical staff all crammed into the room to help. The whole experience was unforgettable, she says, although she still keeps all her hospital discharge notes upstairs in a box.

Wood would have liked to take more than six months of maternity leave, but the family needed the money and so she went back to work. There was no way she could afford the extortionate cost of childcare, but she was lucky that her parents lived close enough to be able to help with that. The family has not always been able to afford a holiday, but they do have a mortgage and manage to get the children (Thomas now has a younger brother) what they need. And she knows that many people around her are worse off; the area where she lives is one of the more deprived in the UK.

Wood has always read to Thomas, taught him right from wrong, and made sure he's ready for school and polite. (She didn't need a cohort study to tell her that, she says; 'I think that comes from within.') When Thomas was in infant school she noticed that he was falling behind, but the school told her that it was probably because he was a daydreamer and a summer-born child, so one of the youngest in his school year. It was only last year that he was diagnosed with dyslexia – words appear blurred to him – and he now has assistance at school to read and write. It's something that worries Wood, who wishes the condition had been spotted earlier and wonders if it could affect his future progress and his ability to find a job.

On top of that, Thomas is about to turn fourteen and has entered a stage where he either doesn't talk at all or communicates by grunts. 'I don't know what's worse, giving birth or having a teenager,' she says now.

The millennium children were born into an era of relative prosperity and economic growth, and they were benefiting from a host of changes that the earlier cohorts had helped to introduce. The first cohort had made the case for good maternity benefits and healthcare; by 2000 pregnant women enjoyed free medical care on the NHS as well as a minimum of four months' maternity leave supported by an employer or government stipend. The cohorts had exposed the unacceptably high numbers of children dying at birth; now, thanks in part to the NHS and radical improvements in healthcare, infant mortality had plummeted.

All the earlier cohorts had also shown the lasting impact on children of being born into poverty and disadvantage. Now living standards had risen enormously, and few children suffered the same absolute levels of disadvantage that some children once faced. But in real terms, poverty was still a huge problem. In 1999 New Labour made a prominent pledge to eradicate child poverty in a generation and started pumping money into benefits for families with children. And work on the birth cohorts had shown that educational gaps emerge between upper- and lower-class children even before they reach school, suggesting that intervention to close these gaps had to start very early in life. That was part of the driver for the Labour government when it introduced free nursery school places for three-to-four-year-olds, and the Sure Start programme to support families with young children.

So the country had changed: the Britain that the millennium children were born into was almost unrecognizably different from the one in which the first cohort had arrived, just after the war. These children were taller and healthier; they had refrigerators, computers, TVs, mobile phones and food from all over the world. The new millennium really looked like a wonderful time in which to be born. But, as scientists started combing through the data on the millennium cohort, they found an all too familiar picture: there were signs of inequality everywhere they looked.

By this point, the London economists were infatuated with the cohort data and they leapt at the chance to use the new figures on the millennium children. When they examined the vocabulary of millennium cohort children at the ages of three and five, they found that those from the poorest families were already an entire year behind those in the richest ones – a cognitive chasm just as large as any measured in the generations before. They also plugged the new data from the millennium cohort into their controversial work on social mobility, looking to see whether the decline in social mobility that they had observed between 1958 and 1970 was continuing. They examined the association between children's cognitive test scores and their parents' income and found no sign that social mobility was getting worse – which suggested that the raft of initiatives to support children in the preschool years was helping rich and poor children progress at a more equal rate than they once had. But the economists knew that it was early days and they would have to watch the children pass through the education system, and get jobs, before they could say for sure whether these millennium children were truly less tied to the wealth of their parents than previous generations.

There were other ways in which the data conjured a feeling of déjà vu – particularly when the cohort scientists looked at the disadvantaged children, the ones with the toughest start. One particularly striking study emerged from two social scientists, Ricardo Sabates and Shirley Dex, when they compiled a list of 'risks' that a millennium child might face at the start of life that could put him or her on a difficult trajectory. This included overcrowding, financial difficulties, teenage motherhood, domestic violence, disability, parents' lack of basic reading or numerical skills, alcoholism, unemployment, depression and smoking during pregnancy. Then the scientists added up how many children in the cohort experienced two or more of these risks. The study was, in essence, a rerun of the work in the 1970s bestseller *Born to Fail?*, which had focused on children in the second cohort who had everything stacked against them – the ones in the worst-off families, who lived in houses with no bathrooms or hot water, and received less than £15 net income per week. Since then, living standards had shot up, but many millennium families were still poor, living in overcrowded homes or struggling in other ways. The question that the scientists took on, using their new criteria, was how many millennium children might be born to fail too?

The answer was, quite a lot. The two researchers showed that 31% of babies in the millennium cohort were facing one of the risks in their list, and 8% had three. These figures were comparable to those in *Born to Fail?*, when 36% of children had one risk on the list and 6% had all three. Extrapolated across the country, this meant that at least 83,000 children born into this glorious new millennium – and hundreds of thousands more if you factored in their siblings – were growing up in an environment that, if history were anything to go by, was likely to give them a difficult time ahead. Over sixty years after James Douglas had started to show the difficulties faced by disadvantaged children in the first birth cohort, scientists were discovering that a massive swathe of the most recent generation was facing disadvantages at the very start.

Sabates and Dex then examined the data to see if these children were already showing signs of difficulty as they grew up – and found that they were. Compared with children with one or no risks, those with two or more had a poorer vocabulary at the ages of three and five, and scored worse on measures of behaviour, emotional development, social development and hyperactivity. The scientists only had to glance at the mountain of evidence from the earlier birth cohorts to know that these early-warning signs were pointing them towards trouble. They predicted that these millennium children were more likely than their peers to leave school at the minimum age, win few if any qualifications, end up unemployed or earning a low wage, commit crime, drink dangerously or otherwise rack up measures of adversity as adults. They were headed straight on to the trajectory of disadvantage that Bynner had described based on the earlier cohorts, but this time they would follow that trajectory into the distant future of 2070, 2080 or later.

Things looked worse when, in their analysis, Sabates and Dex also revealed that there were no particular types of risks that tended to cluster together and so could be tackled by policies en masse. The most common combination – smoking, financial stress and teenage motherhood – applied to just 6% of children, but most families had an assortment of risks quite different from those to be found next door. This was a dismal conclusion as far as policy-makers were concerned, because it meant there was no quick fix that could pull these children out of disadvantage. Every troubled family was troubled in its own way – and therefore every family would need a different type of support to escape.

Or, as one cohort scientist summed up the study, 'Crikey, we've got a big problem.'

It was true: Britain did indeed have a problem, and it was hardly new. That there are lots of disadvantaged children, and that they tend to follow a difficult trajectory, hadn't changed since the early days of the birth cohorts when James Douglas exposed the wide inequalities between children in the first cohort. And there was another thing that was being rediscovered – parenting could help.

Back at the start, Douglas had carried out a pioneering analysis on his cohort showing that good parenting was strongly linked to a child's success in school; crucially, the effect of having interested parents appeared to go some way towards overcoming the disadvantages of a working-class start. Over the years, Douglas had collected information from teachers in an effort to assess how interested parents were in their children's education, including how often they visited school to discuss their child's progress. He found that children whose parents were very interested in their children's education secured many more grammar school places than would be expected based on ability alone. In the 1960s, however, when Douglas reported the results, they were widely overlooked – 'unforgivably', as one scientist says now.

But things were different in millennial Britain. A wealth of evidence by this point – from the British cohorts and elsewhere – suggested that having interested and aspirational parents helped children to overcome the setbacks presented by poverty, low class or other measures of disadvantage; it was associated with better outcomes in school and a generally smoother path through life. But, on the ground, out there in the arduous world of parenting, what everyone wanted to know is what being an engaged and interested parent actually *meant*. If parents – and society – wanted to do the best for their kids, what were they supposed to *do*?

Scientists had made some progress on this front, often using cohort studies, since Douglas's day. They had taken the association between 'interested' parents and good outcomes, and broken it down into more specific behaviours that interested parents tend to display. It is now widely accepted, for example, that reading to a child every day, from a very young age, is strongly correlated with good performance at school. And so is a host of other things. One cohort study in the UK has followed 3,000 children since the age of three and focused intensively on best practices in bringing up children during the early years. It concluded that whatever parents did to create a good 'learning environment' at home was more important for children's intellectual and social development than their parents' job, education or income. Reading with a child, teaching them songs and nursery rhymes, painting and drawing, showing them the alphabet and numbers, visiting the library, taking children on trips and visits – all of these were associated with higher intellectual, social and behavioural scores as the children grew up. Other studies have padded this out, and highlighted the importance of parental involvement as children get older too. Talking to children about what they are learning at school, supporting homework, expressing ambitions for their future and talking up the idea of further education are all associated with improved academic achievement. Pretty much any attention paid to a child's education seems to be highly predictive of success.

The millennium cohort has looked at a broader spectrum of 'good' parenting behaviours than those associated with learning. It found that talking and listening to a child, responding to them warmly, instituting regular mealtimes and bedtimes, and authoritative discipline are all strongly correlated with a brighter future. (Harsh discipline, such as smacking, was associated with poor outcomes.) To some extent, the motivation to parent children well seems to be as important as the exact methods by which it is carried out. Inspiring them, reading to them, taking them out and spending time with them may ultimately be more productive than sinking energy into moving to the catchment area for a particular school.

The difficulty in all of these studies lies in filtering out the confounders. Parents who read to their children, take them to the library, put them to bed on time and do all the other 'good' parenting behaviours are also more likely to be of higher socio-economic status – with more money, more education and better jobs. So does 'good' parenting really lead to better outcomes in children, or are they actually a result of having more money and better-educated parents at home? This is something that social scientists are still working to understand, and work from the millennium cohort has helped.

One recent study on 10,000 of the millennium cohort children found an association between regular bedtimes and good behaviour – one of the biggest studies to examine the impact of sleep schedules on young children. What made this study stand out was the evidence that the bedtimes were a *cause* of the behavioural problems, rather than just being associated with them. The scientists showed that children who experienced irregular bedtimes throughout their early years – when they were 3, 5 and 7 – were more likely to have problem behaviours than those who had irregular bedtimes at only one of those ages, even when they stripped away the possible confounders. And they showed that children who had once had irregular bedtimes, but who later in life switched to a regular sleep schedule, showed a significant improvement in behaviour – all supporting the idea that instituting consistent bedtimes could actually bring about an improvement in children's lives. Scientists even had a good idea why: disrupted sleep is thought to upset the brain's innate 24-hour clock, leaving children in a state much like perpetual jet lag, which interferes with the working of their brains and messes with their behaviour.

This is hardly rocket science. The sleep study made headlines not because it was surprising but because it threw the weight of science behind what is already parenting common sense. The same is true of many of the cohort findings, which offer evidence to support what people already know they should be doing – reading to their children, talking to them and so on – rather than rewriting the rules. Still, knowing this can strengthen parents' resolve. One cohort scientist has found the birth cohorts to be invaluable when she is battling to get her headstrong teenager to eat breakfast or get to bed. In these types of arguments, it really helps to have the scientific literature on your side.

That said, all these findings about parenting come with the usual caveat from cohort studies, which is that there are no guarantees of success. Reading regularly to a child is associated with good educational outcomes when examined across a group; but this says little about what will happen if you read regularly to an individual child. It might do them some good, and it's unlikely to do them any harm. What it does not do is guarantee them success in life.

From the parents' point of view, all this risks fanning the everyday, smouldering worries about the quality of their parenting into a guilty blaze. As so often in science, there are no simple take-home messages and no guarantees. But the likelihood is that if you're reading this, or thinking about how to do the best for your child, you're already a long way towards being the engaged, interested parent that you want to be.

Right from the start, birth cohorts had shown that both poverty and parenting mattered. In the new millennium, inequality was still a huge topic of discussion, and politicians were still making efforts to reduce it, although the conversation had a lot less energy than it once had: there was no appetite for tackling inequality with the ambition present after the war, when the welfare state had been introduced. The actual policies to reduce inequality – such as offering free hours at nursery school – looked a little lacklustre by comparison. But, while poverty was still important, the attention being paid to the parenting part of the equation had ramped up.

All the work on the subject, from the cohorts and elsewhere, was thrust firmly into the limelight. There was some sense that the pendulum had swung too far in one direction, and that now parenting should be the priority. After all, it can be convenient to put the emphasis on parenting; that way, you can say disadvantaged children could do just as well as those of the well-to-do if their parents simply did a better job at home. According to this line of thinking, a lot of educational inequality would go away if only poor parents started to show more of an interest in their children, reading to them every day and getting them to bed on time. This idea received an airing in a speech by David Cameron in 2010, when he pointed to some of the recent research. The differences in outcome between a child born in poverty and a child born in wealth were no longer statistically significant when both had been raised by confident and able parents, he said. The discovery that parenting could compensate for poverty was the new law of social mobility. Parenting, Cameron asserted, mattered *more* than poverty.

When they heard this, some cohort scientists were aghast. As usual, the scientific picture was far more nuanced than it might seem. In fact, some scientists had come to question a number of old studies suggesting that having interested parents mattered quite so much. When they sat down and thought a bit more carefully about the way in which 'parental interest' had been measured in the past cohort studies – when teachers were asked to rate how interested parents were in their child's education – they saw a problem: teachers weren't always in a good position to judge. In many cases, parents weren't encouraged to go past the school gate and they typically met the teachers during the single annual parents' evening at school.

This meant that the teachers barely knew the parents, and they were very likely to be judging their interest based on what they thought of the child, including his or her behaviour, appearance, social class and performance at school. So some of these early measurements of parental interest were far more subjective and unreliable than most scientists had realized. This didn't negate the idea that parents were important in their children's performance at school, but it did say that the early studies should be viewed with caution, and that interested parents might not be as important as some studies had made out.

And anyway it could hardly be said that today's parents were *not* interested in, and ambitious for, their children's future. When researchers surveyed parents of the millennium cohort when their children were seven, they found that almost all of them had high aspirations – 97% wanted their child to attend university, for example. This meant that parental ambition on its own was a useless indicator of future success, because clearly not all of those children would do well enough at school to go on to attend university. This statistic alone defied the idea that difficulties faced by disadvantaged children could be overcome if only their parents were more engaged and ambitious for them; according to this data, their parents already were.

One study on the millennium cohort children has shown quite clearly that both poverty and parenting matter a lot. It examined the effect of poverty and the quality of parenting on the children's achievement in their first year of school, when they were aged between four and five. Children living in persistent poverty were falling behind those who were better off from an early age, but good parenting appeared to offset the disadvantage to some extent. (The scientists rated parenting based on a series of measures that included how often parents read to a child, did home learning activities, took them to the library, attended parents' evenings, as well as whether they interacted warmly with them, breastfed them, instituted regular bed times and meal times, and fed them a healthy diet.) But good parenting reduced the gap by only about 50%; it didn't close it. The scientists argued that focusing on good parenting without efforts to tackle poverty would therefore never close the gap between rich and poor.

Parents on their own cannot provide all the support that children require: they need the right landscape around them to help. Many experts in education want to see major investment in initiatives to support children in their early years, including access to affordable, full-time childcare for disadvantaged children; good-quality, widely available preschool education; parenting courses; and a concurrent effort to establish better evidence on what type of interventions to support children really work. The one thing that is clear is that you can't just tell parents to be better parents, because most of them are already trying as hard as they can.

Poverty and how to escape it is a very old problem indeed for Britain. Before too long, however, the millennium cohort was pointing up a very new problem besetting the country: children were growing obese.

In the early 2000s, when the scientists were holding a pow-wow to plan what to ask of the millennium children at age three, one of those around the table was a paediatric doctor and researcher called Carol Dezateux, who was about to be sucked into the cohort world as if by quicksand. At that meeting she put up her hand and said, 'My goodness, you've got to measure these children's height and weight.'

The issue at the forefront of Dezateux's mind was, of course, obesity. The earlier cohorts had shown how quickly British adults were gaining weight and by now it was clear that children were too. An epidemic of childhood obesity was well under way, and the millennium cohort offered an ideal opportunity to investigate the causes by tracking which children gained weight. Doing so turned out to be Dezateux's first lesson in the challenges of collecting human data by the thousand. Even something as simple as measuring height and weight is very difficult when it has to be done very precisely for several thousand children scattered around Britain. It involved buying and calibrating hundreds of sets of scales and height gauges, briefing the field workers who would take the measurements and then working out whether the workers would break any health and safety regulations – which are famously overzealous in the UK – if they had to lug the heavy kit up the stairs to a council flat.

The effort was worth it, however, for it produced alarming results: 23% of children were either overweight or obese by the age of just three, and a similar percentage by the age of five. The work opened many people's eyes to a looming medical crisis, because overweight children are more likely to grow up into overweight adults, with all the associated high risks of chronic diseases such as heart disease and diabetes. So this generation, aside from being just as divided by inequality as the ones before, was also a whole lot fatter. Researchers are still desperately trying to unpick the tangle of factors associated with a higher risk of being overweight as a child, which include lower levels of parental education, introducing solid food to babies very early in life, and children watching more than three hours of television a day.

The cohort scientists also found an association between childhood obesity and having a mother who works. They are still trying to figure out why this should be the case. It could be that children of families with working mothers rely more on unhealthy, pre-prepared foods, or have less time to get out and be active, or it may be that the association is spurious and can be explained by some unknown confounder. What is clear is that the study hit a raw nerve, because it implied that working mothers were neglecting their children and failing to feed them properly. The results of the study were so deeply unpopular that when the BBC website ran a news story on it, the page received around 1,000 comments within three days – and many of those were vitriolic rants.

A few years later Dezateux and her collaborators filled out the picture on childhood obesity when they posted accelerometers – little gadgets that measure how much a person walks and runs – to seven-year-olds in the millennium cohort and asked them to wear the devices around their waists for a week so they could record how active they are. The children seemed to love it, and nearly 10,000 of them wore the accelerometers and posted them back. The scientists then spent about eighteen months trying to make sense of the data, which was far more taxing than it might seem. For one thing, they had to work out whether some children had really been sitting very still or whether they had taken the device off. One child seemed to have a very peculiar pattern of activity, and when a researcher went out to visit the family the child confessed that he had strapped the accelerometer to the family dog. The results were published in August 2013, and the study made headlines by showing that only 51% of children overall – 38% of girls and 63% of boys – took part in an hour of physical activity each day, as the current guidelines recommend. For once, the social-class gradient favours those at the bottom of the socioeconomic scale, because children of mothers who were not employed were slightly more active than those of mothers who worked. This may be because better-off parents are more likely to drive their kids around and put computers in their rooms, which means they are sitting around for more of the day.

As the years have passed, the rushed start to the millennium cohort has been forgotten and forgiven in the torrent of invaluable research that the study has produced. It may be the youngest of the cohort studies, but it is already prized by scientists around the world. And some of those hasty decisions about its design have paid off handsomely – such as the one to collect the births over the course of a year, rather than over one week. Several studies have examined how the month in which children are born has an impact on their progression through school. This is a big problem: a body of work has shown that English children born in the summer months are most likely to fare poorly on academic tests and to suffer other problems at school, in comparison with those born at other times of year. This is because schools in England use the end of August as the cut-off date for dividing one school year from another, so children born in June, July and August become the youngest in the school year while those born in September, October and November become the oldest. (A similar 'month of birth effect' can be seen for the youngest children in a school year in other countries, even when the cut-off dates are different.) The advantages of being September-born are so well known that sometimes, when a child is born in the dying hours of 31 August, midwives will do parents a favour and record a baby's birth as being in the early hours of 1 September.

The millennium cohort study came up with explanations as to why summer-born children developed such disadvantages.

It showed that because children born in the summer months often perform worse at school, they are more likely to be placed in low-ability groups by the age of just seven, which may then entrench the differences between summer- and autumn-borns. The older children gain confidence and ability in the high-ability group, while the younger children may lose confidence and have less opportunity in the lower one, which deepens and perpetuates the differences between them. Studies on the millennium cohort have also shown that summer-born children show social and emotional differences, as well as educational ones, to autumn-borns. They are more likely to doubt their own ability, to dislike school and to be bullied. Education experts are still debating what to do about the month-of-birth effect: shifting the cut-off date would simply shift the problem on to another group of children. The recommendation from cohort researchers is to adjust test scores based on the child's age, something that policy-makers have shown no sign of doing as of yet. In general, many educational differences narrow a lot by the time children have reached their late teens, although they don't seem to disappear altogether.

Collecting data on births over the course of a year also proved very useful in demonstrating the benefits of breastfeeding. The roots of this study can be traced all the way back to the first maternity survey in 1946, when James Douglas found that women were more likely to start and continue breastfeeding when they had good antenatal support from doctors, midwives and health visitors. This is widely accepted today: the entire NHS is committed to encouraging women to breastfeed, and many hospitals employ a midwife to patrol the postnatal wards in order to help women establish breastfeeding in the first day or two after the birth – the critical window for the practice. But when an economist called Emla Fitzsimons spent a Saturday night having her baby at a London hospital, she noticed that the service was patchy: there was very little support for breastfeeding at the weekend, whereas on Monday there was plenty. The NHS, under permanent pressure from the government to cut costs, pares down to only the most essential staff at the weekends and Fitzsimons wondered if breastfeeding support was one of those things that are cut.

Breastfeeding is associated with many measures of improved health, development and cognition in children – but mothers who breastfeed are also more likely to be of higher socio-economic class, so the challenge lies in working out whether breastfeeding really causes better outcomes when class is discounted. Fitzsimons and her husband, an economist called Marco Vera-Hernandez, realized that the staffing patterns of British hospitals provided a natural experiment that would allow them to study the causative associations with breastfeeding. Women who had their babies during the week were more likely to have good postnatal support and would be more likely to continue breastfeeding than those who happened to have their babies at the weekend, regardless of class. All they had to do was to compare the two groups. The previous national cohorts were no good for this, because they spanned one week and so some chance event in that week could have muddied the waters. They needed to examine births over many weeks in the year, which is exactly what the millennium cohort had done.

The two economists divided up the millennium cohort children into those who had been born on a weekday (good support, more likely to have been breastfed) and those who had been born on a weekend (less support, less likely to have been breastfed) and then looked at various measures of health and development as the children grew up. They found that breastfeeding was causally associated with better cognition – but the associations with other measures of good health did not hold up. (This mirrors the findings of George Davey Smith, in Chapter 5, who identified causal associations with breastfeeding by comparing cohorts from different countries, with different class structures.) Fitzsimons and Vera-Hernandez's clever study also exposed the massive, unexpected repercussions of money-saving efforts in healthcare: the simple decision to cut back support staff at the weekends leads to less breastfeeding of weekend-born babies, which potentially affects brain development for the rest of these children's lives.

While the fifth cohort was growing up, something quiet but dramatic had been happening at the helm of the British birth cohort studies, something that is best illustrated if we think back to the very start of the story, when the Population Investigation Committee came together to launch the 1946 maternity survey. At that time almost all the doctors and academics around the table were men, and the two key scientists who got the cohort going – the doctor James Douglas and the social scientist David Glass – were men. Since then, the cohorts had passed through the hands of a string of men: Neville Butler, John Bynner and Mike Wadsworth. There had been two notable exceptions in Mia Kellmer Pringle – who complained that being a woman held her back – and Jean Golding, who hardly let anything hold her back. But, nevertheless, the cohorts and academia had largely been a man's game. Through the 2000s, however, there was a sea-change: the cohorts had moved almost exclusively into the hands of women.*

* The exception was the 1991 cohort, which moved from the hands of a woman – Jean Golding – into the hands of a man, George Davey Smith.

The cohort studies had produced a ream of influential research showing the steady rise of women in the workplace since the 1970s, and now this came to be mirrored in the leadership of the studies themselves. In 2004 Jane Elliott took charge of the 1958 and 1970 cohorts. Elliott was an unwitting beneficiary of John Bynner's decision in the 1980s to draw new scientists into the cohorts by creating sample data sets for them to play with. Bynner had no idea that this decision would actually hook his own successor, but it did. In 1986 Elliott was a student at Cambridge, where she had switched from studying mathematics to social sciences, and she was given one of those data sets as part of her course. At that time, the only way to use computers was to walk to the university's central computer room, which was filled with men and the odour of old socks. Elliott didn't mind. She was captivated by this generation of people who had been born only eight years before her and yet seemed so grown up. The data left such an impression on her that, nearly thirty years later, she can still recite some of the codes by heart.

As she entered academia, Elliott went on to investigate divorce; she was one of the researchers who produced the surprise finding that the impacts of divorce could be seen on children's cognition and behaviour before their parents actually divorced (as mentioned in Chapter 2). After Elliott took the reins of the 1958 and 1970 cohorts, she soon sensibly realized that two cohorts were too much for one person to handle. She kept the 1958 cohort, and brought in Alice Sullivan, a researcher in sociology and education, to lead the 1970 one. Sullivan also mirrors some features of the cohort that she directs: she is roughly the same age – born four years after them – and she has no desire to have children, just like many women in her generation.

The newest additions to the team are Alissa Goodman, an economist who in 2012 assumed leadership of the 1958 cohort, and Emla Fitzsimons, who took over the millennium cohort the following year. Goodman was involved in cohort work that demonstrated how a higher education could pay off richly in terms of securing more lucrative employment: women who had a university degree earned nearly 40% more per hour than women who had A-levels alone by the time they were thirty-three.* As for Fitzsimons, her studies on breastfeeding convinced her that the millennium study was strong. The women work in a maze of ageing offices on London's Gordon Square, where the 1958, 1970 and millennium cohorts are based. The birth cohorts – these unique studies built up over decades of work – are run out of humdrum offices with worn carpets that look and smell like so much of British academia, chronically deprived of recognition and cash.

Sullivan, Elliott, Goodman and Fitzsimons are all extraordinarily clever, articulate, talented, efficient scientists who love their work – and yet they couldn't be more different from Douglas and Butler, the men who dominated the early life of the cohorts and kept them going with wartime resolve, charm, self-assurance and a big dose of luck. But those characteristics won't keep a cohort study going these days. What the studies need now, if they are to stay alive, is people who can fight for them in the modern world: people who can not only lead the science, but also write convincing reports for the government that list all the ways in which they have influenced policy; and who can send in dense grant applications, on time, to make a

---

* Cohort work showed so convincingly that people with a university degree earn more over their lifetime that it helped to convince the government to introduce tuition fees for university in 1998.

financial case to funders that they should support the next sweep. That is one of the many things that these women do exceptionally well, and that is why they are absolutely essential for the cohorts – without them, the entire scientific legacy would be lost. Just as vital is the team that works behind the scenes: the data experts, survey managers, communications staff and huge fieldwork agencies that ensure the studies run with the tight professionalism necessary in the research business today.

There are other ways in which the cohort leaders now are different from those of the past. They don't necessarily see the job of running a cohort as a job for life. This has produced some turnover at the top. When Joshi relinquished leadership of the millennium cohort in 2011,* her successor Lucinda Platt stayed in the job for less than three years before leaving to become a professor elsewhere. In 2014 Jane Elliott quit the cohorts to become head of the ESRC, so that she is now directing the organization that funds most of the country's social science research, including the cohorts. This turnover is good and bad: good, because it means that scientists steeped in the cohort studies are rising upwards, so the cohorts have support at the highest levels of British science; bad, because some cohort leaders have a shorter, more distant relationship to their studies than the early leaders did, and because some of the rich history of the studies is inevitably forgotten and lost when new scientists come in.

But the struggle to secure the next round of funding for the cohort studies goes on and on. No sooner have the scientists

---

* Like many other cohort scientists passionate about their subject, Joshi didn't actually stop work when she retired: she continued her research and went on spreading the word about cohort studies around the world.

secured one short-term tranche of money than they have to start pleading for the next. This is time-consuming, exhausting and emotionally draining for them, and it means that they can never make plans with the surety that the studies have a future. It has to be said that running a birth cohort today sounds like a lot less fun than it did back at the start, when the scientists were tallying every baby born in a single week, watching the girls play netball and desperately trying to raise money by spilling coffee on to Mrs Thatcher. Today a cadre of scientists sit in offices with computers, devising smart hypotheses and striving to get grant applications in on time.

On the other hand, the cohort scientists no longer have to work quite so hard to sell the idea of birth cohorts. The entire world seems to have noticed that they are a splendid thing to do.

The appeal of tracking human lives has led scientists to start other cohorts of different shapes and sizes in all corners of the world. The British scientists helped to set up some of them. In the 1970s Butler helped to start a study of births and perinatal deaths in Cuba that went on to become a cohort study. (This led to one memorable linguistic misunderstanding when Butler drove into a village to find a big banner strung across the road reading WELCOME, AND LONG LIVE PERINATAL MORTALITY.) In the 1980s Golding started a perinatal survey in Jamaica encompassing over 10,000 births, which eventually helped bring down the number of deaths from pre-eclampsia. South Africa has been running a study since 1990 called Mandela's Children, because the 3,273 babies enrolled in it arrived in the year that Nelson Mandela was released. There are many more like these.

What happened as the millennium approached, however, was that everyone's cohort ambitions seemed to grow. Suddenly massive birth cohort studies were *the* thing to have. It was as if everyone wanted one.

There were two major reasons for this. The first was that scientists had developed a wider appreciation that tracking people's lives from cradle to grave was a genuinely valuable pursuit, rather than just an odd thing that the British did. A lot of the impetus came from medical research and epidemiology – and particularly from the rapid spread of David Barker's ideas showing that chronic diseases have their origins in pregnancy and the first few years of life. If pregnancy and childhood are crucial to our lifelong health, this meant that it was important to study people from their conception and on through their lives.

Second, technology had made it possible to carry out cohort studies more easily than ever before. James Douglas had only followed 5,362 children in his 1946 study, because that was all that one man and a tabulating machine could handle. Those constraints are now laughable. A laptop computer can crunch statistics on tens of thousands of children within minutes; a robot can process thousands of biological samples; and advanced statistical programmes have made it possible to eliminate confounding factors from an analysis while the scientists pop out for a bite to eat. Dealing with data from cohort studies is no longer the laborious, cumbersome task it once was. What's more, scientists had developed a taste for big, splashy projects in science. The Human Genome Project paved the way by showing that, with enough money and chutzpah, it was possible to pull off an ambitious, mega-biology project. This heralded a wave of projects – sometimes called Big Science – involving lots of people, money and big ideas. Birth cohort studies were certainly big, bold and expensive, and now they seemed like a great thing to have. So, as Britain was gearing up to launch the millennium study, scientists around the world began to establish birth cohorts that were far bigger than any that had gone before.

In 1999 scientists in Norway started recruiting women into what has become the largest birth cohort study so far, with over 110,000 children. Denmark started to track about 100,000 of its children a few years before that. Giant cohorts like this are easier to pull off in countries with pre-existing, national databases of personal, health and educational data, because researchers can simply tap into the databases and sweep up swathes of information from them on the cheap, as long as they get their permission from the participants first. The Norwegian cohort, for example, used national identification numbers to link up its study members with the country's extensive databases including birth and death registries, a cancer registry, a prescription database and vaccination registry.

The cohort craze spread wider than this. France recruited over 18,000 children from maternity hospitals in 2011, and scientists in the Netherlands have enrolled what is now nearly 10,000 children in a birth cohort called Generation R in the city of Rotterdam. When scientists in China recorded the births of over 13,000 children in Anhui province, starting in 2008, they emerged with the staggering statistics that 67% of children were born by caesarean section and that 115 males were born for every 100 females. This lopsided ratio is a product of China's one-child policy and its preference for sons; once ultrasound scans could be used to identify the sex of children before birth, abortion of female foetuses became widespread. Closer to home, in 2007 researchers started a project to follow a few hundred children born in the city of Bradford, and some years later had recruited 13,500 of them instead.* There are other birth cohorts under way in Canada, Japan, Australia, New Zealand, Germany, Finland, India, Guatemala, the Philippines and Brazil.** One inventory of birth cohorts listed eighty-seven at the last count; if you wrap in cohort studies that recruited children after birth, the number shoots up.

Scientists found themselves in the middle of a birth cohort boom. They began gathering at an international meeting on longitudinal studies – and having a dedicated conference is a sure sign that a scientific field has come of age. There, they swapped lessons and results. They also sighed over shared enemies: the drop-out of participants, which can kill a cohort if it's not kept in check; the dread that a breach of confidentiality could expose the identities of the cohort members and jeopardize their trust; and the eternal struggle to keep politicians interested enough to continue stumping up the cash.

This was all excellent news for the British birth cohorts, which, after years of being side-lined or ignored, had become the subject of great interest abroad. The 1946 cohort was, by this stage, the longest continuously running birth cohort in the world – and the whole British series was considered a pioneer by scientists in the field. It wasn't unusual to hear scientists elsewhere refer to them in awestruck terms. 'They're kind of

---

* This effort, called Born in Bradford, has been run so cheaply that its director calls it the 'Poundland of birth cohorts'. It is designed to understand the high rates of childhood death and disability in a multi-ethnic population that includes some of the most deprived regions in the UK.

** The city of Pelotas, in Brazil, has a series of birth cohorts separated by eleven years, starting in 1982, 1993 and 2004. (A fourth one was getting underway in 2015.) This is by far the most impressive series of birth cohorts outside Britain. George Davey Smith used one of these cohorts to find the causal associations with breastfeeding.

one of the wonders of the world, you know?' said one. 'I don't
think you can beat the British cohorts.'

This flurry of birth cohorts might create the impression that
starting one has become a completely trivial exercise, when
nothing could be further from the truth. If you want an example of how difficult it is to start a major birth cohort, the United
States is one place to look. There, researchers and policy-
makers spent over a decade and more than $1 billion mired
in arguments about how to track 100,000 children from birth to
twenty-one, and eventually gave up. This effort, called the
National Children's Study, had the potential to be one of the
biggest and best. But it all went horribly wrong.

The concept of a US birth cohort emerged around the same
time as the British millennium cohort, and when many other
major studies were taking shape. In 2000 Congress asked the
National Institutes of Health to launch a national longitudinal
study that would examine the health and development of children. On paper this seemed do-able. The Americans could draw
on the fifty-plus years of experience that Britain and other countries had amassed in starting birth cohort studies, and they could
see the enormous difficulties that come if you try to start a
cohort with sprawling, unfocused hypotheses and overly ambitious plans for recruiting mothers. But few people in the US
were taking much notice of what a bunch of quirky British scientists had been doing with its studies of children since the end
of the war. And anyway, cohort studies, just like babies, tend to
encounter their own unique troubles at the time of birth. So,
whatever mistakes the British cohort scientists had made over
the decades, the US scientists proceeded to make in a more spectacular fashion and with a few extra twists of their own.

The Americans wanted a cohort that was as big and bold as

the best of them, and so they embarked on a colossal planning and consultation exercise spanning several years and involving, by one estimate, some 2,500 experts. They wanted a sample of 100,000 children chosen at random from across the country so that any conclusions could be generalized to all American children. This made sense – but the process they came up with for finding potential mothers was extraordinarily labour intensive. In the UK, the NHS provides care for almost all pregnant women, and so offers a centralized means for recruiting them, following them and collecting their medical information. But there is no such system in the United States, where healthcare is provided by a patchwork of privately financed providers. So the scientists had to devise a different plan. They decided to select 105 counties scattered across the US, choose random blocks of houses there, and then send out interviewers to walk along and knock on doors until they found women who were pregnant or planning to get pregnant. This was complicated, and was made more so by the scientists' aim to recruit some women before they even conceived – which meant they would have to follow around subjects for many months, as they had no idea who would conceive or when. And it seems highly unlikely that a federal government official standing on the doorstep and asking if a woman was thinking about getting pregnant would be warmly invited inside.

The cohort study also became completely bogged down by the huge number of scientists involved, who all had their own interests and wanted to see their questions crammed into the questionnaires. It became overloaded with hypotheses and plans to collect an immense amount of data. The aim was to carry out detailed interviews with all 100,000 sets of prospective parents and to collect environmental samples – such as drinking water, air, dust and soil – as well as a full set of biological samples from the very start of pregnancy. Many of the scientists involved were openly voicing doubts that it could work.

Still, the study kicked off, and started recruiting pregnant women into pilot studies in 2009, by which point the estimated costs had doubled to some $6.9 billion – and the effort was already consuming over $190 million each year. (These types of sums make the British cohort scientists weep; for comparison, the sum assigned for the last sweep of the millennium cohort was £3.5 million, or about $5.5 million.) But soon the plans started to unravel, and then they came undone. The pilot studies confirmed that the doorstep strategy wouldn't work, the study had yet to find a clear scientific direction, and politicians were baulking at the spiralling costs.

In December 2014, with several thousand children already enrolled and over $1.3 billion spent, word came that the study was to be scrapped. Mothers and their children who had been drafted into the pilot study were left in limbo, and felt betrayed by the scientists who had talked them into taking part. The scientists involved, some of whom had been working on the study for nearly fifteen years, were left angry and shocked. Many researchers feel that the effort has been a costly train wreck and a national embarrassment. Over the time it took for the US to plan, pilot and then cancel its birth cohort, the Norwegians and Danes both reached their target of recruiting 100,000 children into their studies, and the British scientists visited their smaller millennium cohort five times. Back in Britain, no one in the birth cohort community took any pleasure from the fiasco across the water, it just made them realize how fortunate and thrifty they had been. Britain is more used to playing David to the United States' Goliath when it comes to scientific research – but in this case it was leading the way, running a string of birth cohorts for just a fraction of the price of the projected

American one. Epidemiologist Michael Marmot compares the British economical style of doing things to a sharp shooter with a pistol, and the US approach to a fleet of B52 carpet bombers. Theirs was supposed to be 'the biggest, bestest thing ever', he says. 'Well, the British did it differently and carried it off.'

The failure of the National Children's Study gave some scientists pause for thought. They started to wonder where the birth cohort boom would end. Not every country needs a giant 100,000-child cohort. Even the most ardent cohort fans questioned how much of the cohort boom was now being driven by science, and how much by a sense of national pride. There was a sense that some countries wanted a birth cohort just because that was the done thing.

And even if the US scientists did get a cohort going,* they would still be seventy years behind. Because in the birth cohort business, you can't play catch-up, no matter how much money you have to throw around. It's true that the British birth cohorts have had a troubled history, routinely starved of cash and frequently on the verge of collapse. But what the British scientists have done is to push on, get the job done and keep collecting data whenever they could.

The reason that the British cohorts are still here is because the scientists did what the British have always done: kept calm and carried on.

At the start of the twenty-first century, birth cohorts turned full circle. As new ones were springing up around the world,

* This could yet happen, because although the National Children's Study was cancelled, the idea of a major longitudinal study of children's health is still alive. The most recent plan is to do this by knitting together existing cohort studies rather than start a brand new one.

the children in the first and original study – the ones born in March 1946 – were reaching old age. In 2011 they would turn sixty-five, the age at which many people in the UK retire and, as such, a milestone in British life. This raised a question: should the scientists throw a birthday party to celebrate the study and its members having got this far? As the birthday approached, this was being turned over in the mind of Diana Kuh, the economist who had developed the idea of life course epidemiology while working with the cohort. In 2007, when Mike Wadsworth retired, Kuh took charge of the 1946 study. It was a heavy mantle of responsibility. This cohort was the grandfather of them all, and scientists around the world were in awe that it had survived this long.

However, none of this stopped the MRC, which was still paying for the study, from threatening to close it down when Wadsworth retired. The research council is under permanent pressure to control its costs, and so it took the opportunity of a change of leadership at the cohort to consider whether the study should go on at all. But, once again, chance, politics and grim determination helped to keep it on the road. At just the time when the MRC was considering the cohort's future, a House of Lords report called attention to the country's ageing population, and asked the research councils why on earth they weren't doing more to investigate the situation. Suddenly, a cohort study of Brits in their sixties sounded like a terribly worthy pursuit.

To Kuh, it was inconceivable that the cohort would not go on. One of Kuh's colleagues describes her as a mother tiger for her protective yet aggressive care of the cohort, and if you can superimpose sensible bobbed hair and spectacles on that idea, you have a rather good description of her. Kuh cares deeply for the cohort, and she'll claw out the eyes of anyone who threatens it.

Kuh set about taking the cohort on to its next stage, the one that would study the cohort members as they grew old. Until that time, nurses had still been travelling regularly to the homes of the cohort members to carry out medical examinations, but by this time they were staggering under the weight of all the equipment. If the study was to keep up with the rapid developments in medical research, Kuh argued, she needed to get people to a clinic where scientists could carry out more thorough examinations. By 2008 she had convinced the MRC to pay for every willing cohort member to spend half a day in one of a number of clinics around the country and complete their most intensive interrogation to date, including ultrasound scans to examine their hearts and body scans to look for weakening bones and thickening fat. (They were also put through a battery of low-tech tests to measure how well their bodies and brains were holding up. Please can you balance on one leg with your eyes closed? How many words can you remember from this list?) The study members loved the attention and like to call it their MOT. The MRC also reinstated the cohort as a dedicated research unit, just as in Douglas's time, and it is now housed in a Georgian terrace on Bedford Place, sandwiched in between upmarket London hotels. Here, Kuh goes up and down carpeted steps all day to and from her office on the second floor.

As the sixty-fifth birthday approached, however, the prospect of a party was causing Kuh great concern. None of the national birth cohorts had held a birthday party since 1989 – when Neville Butler threw his wild bash for the third cohort at Alton Towers – because scientists now tend to think that they should be passive observers of their cohort. If they were to bring them together at a party, they risked influencing the participants' life course in some way, which is a bit like tampering

with your own experiment. (The main concern was that someone might get drunk and get off with someone else in the
study, so that the party inadvertently led to a marriage breaking up.) And even if Kuh did throw a party, how could she
accommodate all the thousands of cohort members across the
country if everybody wanted to come? Or, worse, what if
nobody came?

In the end, Kuh decided that the benefits outweighed the
risks, because the party would recognize and reward the cohort
members for sticking with the study for so many years. She
solved the inclusivity problem by planning four parties across
the UK. (She also wrote a letter to Buckingham Palace to
request an invitation for the study members to one of the
annual royal garden parties. A few months later the palace
wrote back: would fifteen cohort members like to come? The
chosen ones were over the moon.) Meanwhile, the other parties were getting oversubscribed. The cohort members were
curious to meet others like them, even if they had a few reser-
vations about signing up. They worried that a guest list made
up of scientists and pensioners would make for a really dull
evening, and that the MRC would be stingy when it came to
paying for the drinks. 'I thought one glass and that would be it,'
Philip Cheetham said. The first party was set for 3 March 2011,
in a function room of London's British Library, sixty-five years
to the day after the first Douglas Babies were born. All the
cohort members would turn sixty-five that week.

In the end, all the worries were for nothing: the evening was
a triumph and the cohort members were abuzz. They wished
each other a happy birthday and talked about rationing and the
terrible diets of their grandchildren. Kuh, who was too busy to
be nervous, made a heartfelt speech. There was plenty of wine,
and it didn't look like any cohort members were getting off

with each other either, although you never really know. There were glowing articles in the newspapers about this extraordinary treasure of British science, and the remarkable scientists who had kept it alive. It was a high point in the life of the study. And, because it was a party full of 65-year-olds and scientists, everyone arrived on time – and then left early, to make sure they caught the last train.

About a year later, the buzz of the party had faded and Kuh was close to getting ill trying to keep the cohort going for another few years. The MRC subjects all its research units to a rigorous performance assessment, called the quinquennial review, every five years. It is a deadly serious business: if scientists are not up to par, they can be kicked out and their funding can be slashed. Douglas and Wadsworth, her predecessors, had sweated blood every time they had to get through one. But the 2012 review would be the first for which Kuh was solely responsible, and she did not want to go down in history as the one cohort director who hadn't managed to get the study funded. The pressure was enormous; she had the 65-year legacy of the study resting on her shoulders.

In order to pass the review, Kuh had to write a telephone directory of a document summarizing the cohort's achievements – which by that point added up to eight books and 700 publications – as well as her future plans. She rented a flat near the research unit in London partly so that she could focus on the review. She would get up at 5 or 6 a.m. thinking about the cohort, walk the short distance to the office, work all day on the review, and be the one locking up the building at night. She would go back to the flat, collapse in bed and get up to start all over again. She sent in the document in June, responded to forty-five pages of comments on it, and then waited for a crucial two days in November, when a panel of reviewers would visit the unit and decide its future. They were scheduled to meet in the boardroom, downstairs at the unit in Bedford Place.

On the morning, Kuh was exhausted and yet wired on adrenalin at the same time. In the boardroom, the scientists each gave a short talk and then the review panellists talked privately among themselves, before calling her back in and giving her the verdict – a short report with scores for the unit out of 10. She got a string of 9s, which is as close to perfection as anyone in science is going to get. The reviewers recommended that the unit should receive nearly £9 million to take it through until 2018, when the cohort would be turning seventy-two. The study had won the latest reprieve in its long life. The scientists celebrated – they popped champagne and went to the pub. Then, the next day, they were in early to work again. They have so much to do in such a short time. Because, now that she has money, Kuh has the sad scientific task of carefully watching the cohort members grow old, fall ill and die.

The truth is that if funders don't kill this cohort, time, inevitably, will. Some 13% of the subjects had died by that point – and the study has plenty to say about the fate of the rest. Now that the scientists have traced the cohort for so long, it is possible to draw associations between some of the earliest events in people's lives and their state of health today, as if they were sketching lines through decades of time. In one of their recent papers, Kuh's team looked for correlations between the cohort members' social class as children and how well they performed on those medical MOTs in their sixties. It seems amazing to think that the social class of your parents at birth could, over six decades later, have any bearing on how long you can balance on one foot with your eyes closed, or how well you can remember a list of words. But it does. The cohort members who had been born into lower socioeconomic positions tended to perform the worst on every one of the tests.

This fulfilled a prediction made by James Douglas, when the cohort members were still in their twenties. He had said that the differences between those in the upper and lower classes would become more prominent with the passage of time. The idea was that those who were already scarred by disadvantage as children would more rapidly succumb to disease and the deterioration that arrived with old age, while those who'd had a more comfortable life would enjoy a healthy trajectory for more years. No one would argue with that now, when study after study from the cohort has shown that those born into the lower classes have been more likely to develop almost every problem in the medical book.

Still, the beauty of scientific inquiry is that it often kicks up a curious stone, and when it comes to death, the correlations haven't emerged as neatly as you might expect. A few years ago Kuh put together graphs showing the proportion of the cohort members surviving up to age sixty, categorized according to their social class at birth. Disadvantage never stops showing its hand: those study members from the poorest backgrounds were 60% more likely to have died than those from the better-off ones. But the picture was not so simple when the survival rates were divided not just by class but by sex. When the figures were diced this way, it became clear that middle- and upper-class men were dying at roughly the same rate as lower-class men and women – whereas women from better-off backgrounds had a death rate about half that of everyone else. The scientists have not yet explained why this is – it doesn't seem to be because of anything obvious such as these women smoking less than the other groups. Kuh suspects that these middle- and upper-class women were better able to take advantage of the opportunities afforded by post-war Britain to improve themselves: attending grammar school and securing good healthcare on the NHS. The opportunities given to them by Beveridge's reforms allowed them to get educated, get a job and stay healthy, which have all helped them stay alive longer than others in the study. Kuh has a personal interest in the graph, because she is only six years younger than the cohort and she knows that she is a middle-class woman who benefited from grammar school and the welfare state – so the graph tells her something about her own chances of survival too.

A few years after the death graphs, the scientists published another simple but powerful analysis of the cohort's decline. They took all the detailed MOTs that Kuh had collected and counted up how many medical disorders each person had out of a list of fifteen, including cardiovascular disease, hypertension, raised cholesterol, diabetes, obesity, osteoporosis, psychiatric problems, cancers and respiratory disease. They found that a whopping 85% of the cohort had at least one of these conditions and that, on average, they had two disorders apiece – even though most of those people, when asked, said that they were in good health and a large number of the conditions had never been previously diagnosed. It was a sobering picture of ageing, *tout ensemble*, and one with important implications for Britain and for the rest of the world. The 1946 birth cohort contains the very first members of the baby boom, the surge in births that started after the end of the Second World War. Now the boomers are starting to enter retirement and so the population as a whole contains more and more elderly people. (Some 17% of people in the UK were aged sixty-five and over in 2010, a figure that is expected to rise to 23% by 2035.) A similar phenomenon is happening elsewhere, where growing life expectancy and falling fertility rates mean that the over-sixties are the fastest-growing proportion of the population in countries around the world. The cohort study shows that many of them will have some type of chronic disease. It is acting as a bellwether, an early indicator of the tsunami of illness that this rapidly ageing population is going to bring in its wake.

It could also be a best-case scenario, because the people in the cohort study were cushioned by the brand-new welfare state and brought up on healthy, if meagre, rations. Those coming along later, when obesity was arriving on the scene, could find themselves suffering more disease. Kuh also sees a way for the cohort study to help, and at the same time for it to return to its roots. At the start of its life, the study shaped maternity services in the fledgling NHS; now its observations of pensioners could guide the NHS as it prepares for the onslaught of age-associated disorders that is heading our way. Quite how the NHS is going to cope with the enormous expense of a sick and ageing population is the topic of regular talks and hand-wringing at very high levels of the health service, but no one seems to have come up with any clear solutions to the problem.

At present the cohort scientists are also busy working out how to continue tracking the cohort members as they age. They are particularly interested in carrying out a further MOT that focuses on their brains, because a big slice of the cohort is expected to develop dementia over time. The team has just started to bring about 500 of the cohort members into London to carry out state-of-the-art scans of their brains, looking for early signs of Alzheimer's disease and other deterioration of the mind.

All that is more than enough to fill the next five years, but Kuh won't take the cohort through its next big review, because she'll be close to retirement age herself – and, much as she loves the cohort, she doesn't think she has the energy to see it through another round. Like her cohort, Kuh has her two clinical conditions and she doesn't want any more. She is thinking a lot about who will take over from her. Her goal is to hand on the baton, passing the cohort study safely into another scientist's hands.

It's hard to resist the morbid temptation to look far into the cohort's future when, one day, someone will have a very hard decision to make. When, finally, should the cohort study be allowed to die? There are currently about 3,000 study members left – because of those who have died or dropped out – and with a little extrapolation of her survival curves, Kuh predicts that there will be about 1,400 left by the time they are eighty-four and just 300 around to celebrate their hundredth birthday in 2046. When the scientists strip away whatever emotional attachment they have to the cohort, they know that at some point it won't make scientific sense to keep collecting the data any more. There will be too few surviving members for the study to have any statistical power and therefore to produce meaningful results.

Most cohort members don't know the detailed plans that the scientists are making in order to watch them die. Even if they do think about it, they are completely unruffled about science accompanying them all the way to the grave. Most like the attention and feel that if their mothers signed them up for the study, it's their duty to see it through to the last. 'It's something you said you would do, and you do it,' says one cohort member stoically. And very occasionally, someone who had dropped out of the cohort gets back in touch. One long-lost member e-mailed the scientists in 2015. He'd been in Canada for the previous forty years, but now he was back in Britain and had seen the study in the news. Could he please join up again? Kuh, who treasures all her remaining cohort members, couldn't have been more pleased.

Dropping out hasn't even occurred to Patricia Palmer, who was born into the first birth cohort, in March 1946. Palmer is one of those who should, statistically speaking, have had a difficult life because of her tough start: born into a poor, working-class household, with a father who drank and left home when she was five. She failed her 11-plus and, although she wanted to train to be a teacher, knew her mother wouldn't be able to afford it and left school at sixteen. It's something that she still bitterly regrets.

Sixty-five years later, Palmer lives in a well-to-do suburb on the fringes of Cheltenham, just a mile or two from where she was born. Somewhere in her house is a collection of birthday cards that the cohort scientists have sent her almost every year since she was born, but she can't quite remember which drawer it's in. In the decades that her cohort has been going, four more British birth cohorts have been started and she has become just one of the more than 70,000 people that the scientists have now enrolled. But Palmer has been busy living her own life, which is the stuff from which the study is built.

In her case, it's hard to find a neat explanation for the way life turned out apart from chance and a strong work ethic – something that she inherited from her own tireless mother. She flourished in secondary school and, after leaving at sixteen, learnt secretarial skills at GCHQ and went on to sell cosmetics in department stores. But she gave up work at twenty-one when she married a divorced man and found herself stepmother to his two young children.* (Her mother was absolutely horrified, she recalls.) Within a few years, Palmer bore a daughter of her own. Her husband earned a good wage and eventually Palmer went back to work, and ended up managing the finances of a large school. She moved to Luxembourg with him, and it was there that – like many of her cohort – she started to gain weight. She thinks it was the pâté, baguettes and all the hormonal changes that accompany the menopause that pushed her slowly up from 11.5 stone to 15.

Now that she's back in the UK, the weight has come off. (She knows that she has to keep going to Slimming World and make morning visits to use the cross-trainer at the gym.) It helps that she spends her afternoons picking up three of her grandchildren from school, which she does to support her daughter and son-in-law, who both have busy jobs. It's exhausting, she says, but she loves seeing so much of the children too.

Although Palmer was born in difficult circumstances, she thinks that she could have chosen almost whatever she wanted to do because of the time in which she was born. Everyone found it tough to some extent after the war, but people were mostly happy with their lot. 'I feel very lucky, actually, the way

---

* Palmer changed her surname to Malvern when she married.

that my life has gone,' she says. She thinks that it's harder for children who are born into disadvantage today, because they are surrounded by toys and computers and they expect so much more. She also worries that the opportunities for her grandchildren aren't as great. The cost of living is spiralling upwards, and the price of a university education could put it almost out of reach for them. It's sad, she reflects, to see anyone denied an education because of money, just as she was over fifty years ago.

For most of Palmer's life, the cohort study was just like a shadow that followed her around – always present, but something that was attached to her rather than the other way around. But that changed when she received the invitation to attend one of the cohort's sixty-fifth birthday parties. She decided to go to the one in Birmingham, where she met Diana Kuh and the other scientists, and she even agreed to make a short speech. She told a little joke about the scientists following her until the end. 'I wonder,' she said, 'when we reach the pearly gates, whether there'll be somebody from the study standing there, you know, with their clipboard, waiting for our last comments.'

8.

Bridging the Divides

Cohorts Face the Future

Starting birth cohorts is like the process of birth itself. At the time, it is so extraordinarily painful that no one ever wants to go through it again. But soon enough amnesia sets in. The physical scars heal up, the sleepless nights pass, and the difficult memories are erased by the love and fascination felt as the child blossoms and grows. In time, the entire process begins again. It really wasn't so bad, mothers think, and it *would* be fun to have another one.

This may explain why, just a few years after the rushed, stressful beginning of the millennium cohort, some scientists were starting to think about doing it all over again. In this case, it wasn't just that the pain had faded – there was also a sense that a sixth cohort was an obligation the scientists had to fulfil. After all, they had wanted so much to restart the cohort series, and the millennium cohort had realized that goal. Now they had an unrivalled series of studies that was tracing generation after generation and was envied by the rest of the world. It should not, must not stop.

As it happened, the opportunity to start a sixth cohort arose from a confluence of events involving a big pot of money in London and some deep thinking in a holiday cottage in Wales. It also grew out of the intellectual inheritance from all the previous ones, because scientists who had cut their teeth studying the earlier birth cohorts were now rising to positions of power.

In 2003 a social statistician called Ian Diamond took over as the chief executive of the ESRC – the organization that had already funded three of the cohorts – and went on to chair the Research Councils UK Executive Group, the umbrella organization that oversees all seven research councils (including the ESRC and MRC). Diamond was already a huge cohort fan. Early in his career, he had studied the age at which women in the 1946 cohort had children (he found that those with involved parents, ambition and higher levels of education, had children later). Now Diamond had a powerful position overseeing the way that the UK funds its research, and he saw an opportunity to give social science a huge boost.

Diamond knew that the government put aside a large sum of money – about £100 million a year – into something called the Large Facilities Capital Fund, which was designed to support major research facilities or infrastructure projects that would strengthen the country's science base but that are so expensive they are beyond the standard budgets of each research council. Basically, it was a bank account stuffed with gold to which scientists could apply when they needed a particularly expensive piece of kit. And it had been used to support some very impressive science projects indeed. These include a research station in frozen Antarctica, a 90-metre-long Royal Research Ship that roams the oceans in the name of science, and a world-leading laboratory that monitors for deadly infectious diseases. The bank account also supports a vast doughnut-shaped particle-accelerator in Oxfordshire, where scientists generate beams of light ten billion times brighter than the sun and then use them to probe the insides of viruses, minerals and much more.

That was all very well, but Diamond knew that something was amiss: while lots of other research councils had been tapping into this bank account, the ESRC had not. This was because of an old-fashioned view that economists and social scientists didn't need pricey bits of equipment to do their research. Diamond and the heads of the other research councils thought this was out of date. Like other disciplines, social science was now embracing ambitious, Big Science projects, and this meant that it needed major cash infusions to build up its data banks. That's why, in July 2004, an economist called Peter Elias got a call from the ESRC. Elias had just accepted a job advising the research council on data strategy. Now he was asked to work out how the ESRC could make a bid for money in the stuffed-with-gold account. What everyone wanted was a great, big, bold scientific scheme for social science that would sound as eye-catching as a particle collider or ocean explorer. At the same time, the plan needed to be just four pages long, so it could be easily digested by civil servants. 'We need it to be done now. You've got a week,' he was told. Elias was on holiday in a cottage in remote Wales, so he started the project right there.

Like Diamond, Elias was also steeped in the birth cohorts. Early on in his career, he had made his name as an economist by analysing the work histories of people in the 1958 cohort and found that those from lower-class backgrounds struggled to get the good jobs. In more recent times, he had worked behind the scenes, helping to set up the millennium cohort and throw open more of the cohort data so that scientists would use it. He, Diamond and others at the ESRC knew that Britain's series of cohorts were rare treasures that were finally coming into their own. And so, in 2004, when Elias was in Wales, trying to think up an expensive, exciting-sounding project for the ESRC, the birth cohorts were the obvious place to start. On one rare sunny day, he was sitting inside, thinking about the rich history of the cohorts, and about what could lie ahead for them. He started to type – and the four pages that he wrote outlined an ambitious new future for the cohorts.

Elias proposed that the country should build what he called a Research Laboratory for the birth cohort studies. It would be a laboratory in the figurative sense, in that it would form a home to all the cohort studies and be a place where scientists could come together and analyse them. Elias knew that all the cohorts had evolved separately, and that each still tended to carve out its own path. That was partly because of their different historical roots, and the cultural divide between medical and social scientists – and even more so because the leaders were so busy keeping their own cohort going that it was difficult to find time or money to build collaborations between them. He thought that this needed to end, and that the studies would only reach their full potential when scientists could easily compare and contrast the generations – to find out, for example, how the arrival of the obesity epidemic had affected each of them in turn. Elias knew he was writing a pitch for civil servants, and he really went for the hard sell. This laboratory would have no parallel in the world, he wrote. It would ensure that the UK had the most advanced social science data infrastructure in the world, it would cement the UK as a leader in global science, and it would attract researchers from everywhere. It was a pitch worthy of Madison Avenue.

And there was, of course, another thing that the laboratory could do, something that would make the proposal more forward-thinking and give it some oomph. It would launch a new birth cohort, one that would start in 2010 or 2011. In effect, what Elias was arguing was that the birth cohorts are to social scientists what a research ship is to oceanographers or a particle collider is to physicists: an essential data-generating machine, churning out the information from which scientific discoveries are built. This meant that they deserved the same huge level of investment. He estimated that the laboratory and the new cohort would come in at about £46 million.

The idea of this laboratory was not, in fact, new: more than twenty years earlier, when the leaders of the first three cohorts got together to shoot their video in Bristol, Mia Kellmer Pringle had wished for just such a place – 'an institution whose job it would be to mount these studies and build in comparisons'. But at that time, in 1982, when social science was out of favour and the cohort leaders hardly spoke to each other, she had dismissed it as a dream. Now, in the mid 2000s, the political climate for cohort science was considerably warmer. Should Elias and Diamond be able to convince the government to give them some of the Large Facilities Capital Fund, the idea had a chance of becoming a reality.* And having Ian Diamond behind it was going to help. He was determined that social science should no longer be viewed as a cottage industry. He took every opportunity to talk about big social science, and to sell the idea that the cohort studies were a jewel in Britain's crown.

Despite all this, however, the idea of a birth cohorts laboratory didn't exactly take off – it floated about, while the cohort scientists tried to build support behind the scenes. And a few years later, when the project came up again in a meeting, everyone realized what a very good idea it actually was. One of the things going for the project was that it was interdisciplinary: it spanned the social and medical sciences. This had been problematic in the early cohort days, when James Douglas had

---

* Given the history, it would be wrong to say that the ideas in Elias's pitch were his alone. Although he wrote the original draft, many of the concepts in it were already in the air and the proposal was refined and polished as it passed through others' hands.

found himself an outsider by attempting to bridge disciplines; but today, interdisciplinary science is considered very desirable, because scientists (and funding organizations) have recognized that solutions to many important problems can come only from research that bridges traditional boundaries between disciplines. In that spirit, the project gained the support of the MRC, which, together with the ESRC, submitted the bid to those who control the Large Facilities Capital Fund.

The delay had offered the scientists another fortuitous way to embellish their pitch, because, by then, the new birth cohort had been shunted to 2012. This would, fittingly, resume the twelve-year interval between this cohort and the one before. But the new date also meant it would coincide with the 2012 Olympics in London, about which there was mounting excitement. The UK was throwing a colossal amount of money at a new stadium and facilities to host the games, and it was conscious that the country would be thrust into the international spotlight for a few short weeks of sporting glory in August 2012. That same summer was also special because it would coincide with the Queen's Diamond Jubilee – it was sixty years since she had assumed the throne – and there were plans for a great big flag-waving national party, which Britain doesn't often do. So the hope was that a 2012 birth cohort might be attractive to politicians because it would capitalize on this sudden appetite for expensive, patriotic projects on the world stage. And it seemed to work. When the bid for the new cohort was submitted to the government fund in 2009, all the signs were that it would go ahead.

The research councils put out a call for scientists who would be interested in running the new cohort. They quickly whittled the responses down to two serious bids. One of those was from Carol Dezateux, the professor of paediatric epidemiology who had measured the weights and activity levels of the millennium cohort children. When Dezateux heard about the idea of a 2012 cohort, she was ready for a new challenge and dropped everything to pull a team together and write a bid. She had learnt to handle sleepless nights as a doctor on call, and now that skill was again put to use. As the deadline approached, she was so frantic in preparing the application that she went three days straight without sleep.

Across London, the social scientists who were already running three of the existing cohorts were working just as frantically to prepare their own application. This made for an interesting contest. Dezateux was a qualified doctor and medical researcher, so her application put questions about biology and medicine at its heart. She had energy and audacious plans, but she had never run a cohort before. Her competition were social scientists with somewhat different passions, and with years of experience with cohort studies under their belts. Although it may not have been articulated, the tension between the two academic cultures about how best to run a cohort was coming to a head in a battle for the biggest and most expensive one of the lot.

In the end, Dezateux's team won. The panel of scientists tasked with choosing a winner wanted this new study to have a strong focus on health, just as most of the earlier cohort studies had intensively studied the medical side of birth. But they told Dezateux that she had to beef up the social science side of the study so that scientists in both disciplines would come on board. Even then, she and her new cohort were not yet home and dry. She launched into a frenzy of work to force the proposal through the excruciating governmental bureaucracy necessary before the money was finally signed off. Everything went smoothly, and by May 2010 the proposal had been moved into the science minister's in-tray. All it needed was his signature, and the new cohort would move ahead. But before that could happen, politics once again intervened in the life of the cohorts. The Labour government was ousted in the general election and the Conservative/Liberal Democrat coalition came to power.

The cohort scientists had seen this film before – and they knew it didn't end well. It was exactly the same script as in 1979, when Thatcher, with her dislike of social science, had come to power just as the proposal for the 1982 cohort was hanging in the balance. At that time, the change to a Conservative government had led to a difficult era for the birth cohorts: all of them had been starved of money, and the idea of the 1982 cohort had been knocked on the head. So now, when David Cameron took over as the first Conservative prime minister in fifteen years, every expectation was that this would be a painful rerun. Within weeks, Cameron had made clear his plans for sweeping cuts across the government – and the easiest thing to trim is money that you haven't actually spent. It's even easier when the money is tens of millions of pounds for a study of babies that is guaranteed to show that lots of children are being born into disadvantage in modern Britain and that wouldn't produce any results until the government had left power. What politician was going to pay for that? The newest cohort was surely doomed. Dezateux and the cohort scientists felt as if they had won the trophy, only to have it plucked out of their hands.

But in fact, this film had a different twist. A few months later, hope arrived in the form of David Willetts, who had been appointed as the Minister for Universities and Science. Willetts was widely known to be a friend of the social sciences; he had written a book called *The Pinch*, in which he drew on social science research, including cohort data, to make a case that the baby boom generation had amassed wealth and power at the expense of their children. He had even earned the nickname 'Two Brains' for his academic approach – as well as his high, boffin-like hairline.

On 1 March 2011 Willetts announced that both the birth cohorts laboratory and the new birth cohort would go ahead with a £33.5 million grant. (The scientists' scheme to sell the cohort on the back of the Olympics seemed to have worked: he referred to those in the new cohort as the children of Olympics 2012.) Willetts showed himself to be a true cohort enthusiast: he even admonished the previous Conservative government for not funding a cohort in the 1980s, and promised that the new government would support the social sciences as a whole. He said that the entire effort would be central to the government's commitment to tackle the social mobility problem that the earlier cohorts had brought to light. 'A crucial ambition of the coalition is for children born next year to have greater opportunities to make their ways in life than the children born at the start of the millennium. This database will enable our performance to be judged over years to come.'

As word of the new cohort whipped around the world, everyone in longitudinal research was thrilled and relieved. Elias was in Paris when he received a text message letting him know the news. He'd been working on this project for years – from the four-page proposal back in 2004 to seeing the government back it with serious money. He and a colleague bought a couple of huge cocktails and toasted the fact that they'd got it through.

At the moment of Willett's announcement, the birth cohorts were on a high. There was Willetts, the government minister responsible for science, describing the cohorts in glowing terms. That very same week, the first and original cohort celebrated its sixty-fifth birthday. The speech was just about the most high-level, ringing endorsement that the birth cohorts had ever received. Britain was finally recognizing the ruby in the very centre of its imperial crown. And *this* time around, scientists surely wouldn't make the same mistakes they had before. This cohort would have a smooth arrival into the world – or, at least, it was Dezateux's responsibility to make sure that it did.

Carol Dezateux has a book on her shelf that reminds her how dramatically the lives of women have changed. Called *Maternity Letters from Working Women*, it is filled with the poignant words of working-class mothers from 1914, who described their difficult experiences of birth and infant death. 'It is my last three babies that I have buried,' wrote one woman matter-of-factly. 'The doctor says I must not have any more; it will be fatal to me if I do.'

Nearly one hundred years later, Dezateux's thoughts turned back to that book as she was thinking about how to record the experiences of women having children today. In some ways, she was simply repeating history: like her predecessors, James Douglas and Neville Butler, she was a clever, curious doctor who was launching a nationwide survey of British births. But she and her study were also worlds apart, because organizing a cohort study had become orders of magnitude more difficult than it was just after the war. She wanted to recruit 80,000 children, four times more than any of the British cohorts before.

Dezateux found herself in an excruciatingly difficult spot. She had to design and deliver a study that reflected the long history of the British birth cohorts, while anticipating the way that science would unfold many decades in the future. She had to overcome any past divisions between the social sciences and medical sciences, and collect detailed information that would keep those in both disciplines happy. She had to answer to the government bodies funding the work – assuring them that the study was relevant to policy – while simultaneously promising a demanding scientific community that she had academic control. She had to negotiate the tangled thicket of bureaucracy and administration that came with a government grant of tens of millions of pounds, all the time aware that at any moment the government could decide to pull the plug. The committees, advisers, stakeholders, boards and administrators were stacked up on her like smothering layers of bedclothes, and every stakeholder wanted to have a say. It didn't help to learn that the one cohort study trying to be as ambitious as this one – the one of 100,000 children in the United States – had failed.

After the 2012 cohort got the go-ahead, Dezateux came under intense pressure to get it going as fast as possible. But she took on board a lesson from the past. She was determined not to rush the study, as the millennium cohort had, just to keep the cohort anchored to its provisional name. She quickly abandoned the idea of a 2012 cohort and instead branding consultants were brought in. Soon, the enterprise emerged under the timeless moniker Life Study. Then she set about planning a study that would, if it worked, eclipse every birth cohort that had come before.

Back when Douglas was collecting data on the first British birth cohort, technology continually held him back. He could only follow 5,362 children, because it was all that his administrative staff and tabulating machines could handle. And when he carried out his study on the health impacts of air pollution in the 1960s, he had to use records provided by the Local Fuel Overseers as a crude way of estimating the amount of pollution in the region in which each child lived. At that time, there was no way of working out the exact amount of pollution that someone was exposed to as they walked from home to school.

Nearly fifty years later, as Dezateux sat down with her team to discuss what information to collect on the massive new birth cohort, air pollution was near the top of the list. The killer smogs of 1950s London have dissipated, but cities are still awash with the emissions of modern cars and industries, including carbon dioxide, carbon monoxide, sulphur dioxide and the tiny particles emitted by diesel engines that bury themselves deep in our lungs. In the last few years, the scientific literature has exploded with papers associating air pollution with poor health. In one study, US scientists tracked a cohort of Californian children from the age of ten and found that those who had grown up within 500 metres of a busy freeway – and who were therefore continually exposed to traffic exhaust – had lungs that were significantly smaller and weaker by the time they were eighteen than those who lived 1,500 metres away. Because of this, many of these children will suffer respiratory problems for the rest of their lives. Now scale this up: consider how ubiquitous major roads have become in many parts of the world, and how population expansion forces more and more people to live and work next to them. That is one reason why the World Health Organization in 2014 declared air pollution to be the single biggest environmental threat to public health, accounting for about one in eight of all deaths in the world.

The pollution study that scientists devised for the new cohort was a wonderful example of how old ideas plus new technology can create potentially powerful ways for scientists to investigate the causes of disease. In the new cohort, the scientists would have an opportunity to monitor exposure to pollution using all the tools that modern technology could provide, and from the start of life. They planned to calculate something of a personal pollution chart: a gauge of the pollutants that each pregnant woman and her growing baby would be exposed to as she moved around the city. (The scientists would start with London, where their pollution data was best.) They would hardly rely for data on coal-rationing records. Now, they could really knock themselves out. They could draw on a computer-generated map of air quality so detailed that it could distinguish the different pollution levels from one block to the next. The team would marry up this map with the home address and workplace of each pregnant woman enrolled in the new cohort, and then use it to estimate her daily dose of pollutants. As the years went by, they would be able to look for associations between the levels and types of pollutants that their mothers breathed and the health of their children.

This type of study would throw open a fascinating window on inequality. Scientists know that cheaper housing is often in the less desirable areas – such as closer to busy roads, where the pollution concentrations are highest. One reason that poor or disadvantaged children suffer increased risks of disease could be that they are more likely to live in these areas, and they therefore suffer the unavoidable penalty of breathing more polluted air. So high-tech pollution studies like these could start to unpick the associations between disadvantage and poor health by identifying the active ingredients involved – the things that disadvantaged mothers and children are actually exposed to that put them at higher risk of sickness.

The pollution data was just a fraction of the information that the cohort scientists planned to collect on the new birth cohort. The objectives in epidemiology, finding the causes of ill-health by tracking people over time, were still the same. What had changed was the size of the operation, which involved so many more children and so much more data that it was almost industrial in scale. Old wine in a new jar.

The scientists wanted to build as complete a picture as they could of the environmental influences in the modern world, and how they might affect a child as it develops in the womb and, later, in the world. They would ask water companies to supply them with a breakdown of chemicals in tap water, and use that to work out what each pregnant woman consumed; they would try to ascertain the cocktail of chemicals that she encountered elsewhere by asking her about her use of cleaning products, hair dye, nail varnish, skin creams and more. They would ask permission to access her mobile phone records, to find out how often she used her phone, and they would use this to build up a picture of her and her baby's exposure to electromagnetic radiation. (Some parents now station a mobile phone next to the cot as a baby monitor.) The scientists hoped to ask about all this without worrying parents, because there is little concrete evidence so far that any particular factors do cause harm. If they could carry it off, it would be a landmark in epidemiology because no one had attempted to monitor the environments of so many people in such detail from birth. Once the data came in, it was possible that just one of those things – a certain pollutant or chemical, say – would be associated with slower growth, or greater risk of a disease, just as smoking was once linked to lung cancer. But the thinking now in epidemiology is that the answers are more complicated than that, and that some as-yet-unknown mixture of environmental exposures can increase the risk of disease somewhere down the line. Quite what those mixtures are, and whether they affect health during childhood, or middle age, or old age, no one knows.

Scientists weren't thinking about the environment on its own; they wanted to understand how all those environmental factors interact with the children's cells and DNA. The plan was to collect more biological samples than any birth cohort study had ever done anywhere before. They would freeze down mothers' blood, urine and saliva and gather bits of placenta, umbilical cord and cord blood at birth.

One of the foulest samples that the scientists planned to collect was the baby's first stools and a smear of the mother's too. That's because it is currently all the rage in biology to comb through samples of human faeces in order to study microbes – mostly bacteria and viruses – which live in and on the human body, something which scientists call the microbiome. That all of us are harbouring billions of bacteria on our skins and in our guts, mouths and every orifice was largely ignored until the 2000s, but it has now become a red-hot area of research. Advances in DNA technology have made it possible to sequence and identify the microbes, and this has led to the recognition that they have a huge impact on our health: they are now thought to play a crucial role in our susceptibility to obesity, diabetes and many other diseases. It also means that routine medical practices, such as the use of antibiotics and caesarean sections, are being viewed in a new light.

One controversial hypothesis says that the rise in childhood asthma, eczema and allergic diseases could partly be explained by the increasing number of births by caesarean section – over 25% of children are born this way today, compared with 13% in the early 1990s. (These rates are modest compared to those of some other countries: one third of children are born by C-section in the United States and a remarkable 45% in Brazil.) Children who are born by caesarean section pick up different microbes as they emerge to those who come out via the vaginal route, where they are bathed in microbes from the mother's vagina and faeces. The theory is that the C-section children, who don't encounter all the standard microbes, end up with immune systems that later react to things that they shouldn't – producing allergic diseases. If the cohort scientists could collect faeces from tens of thousands of babies, they could one day analyse the microbes in them and look for associations with such diseases when they were diagnosed. And if researchers found evidence of long-term health risks associated with caesarean sections, they could start to look less like the benign operations they are widely assumed to be.

Once the scientists had collected all the environmental measures – pollution, chemicals, phone records and so on – and the biological ones such as DNA, tissues and faeces, it seemed likely that a mesh of even more complicated associations would emerge. It might be that exposure to a particular cocktail of chemicals places children at more risk of asthma – but that they only develop the disease if they also inherit a genetic predisposition to it from their parents, something that DNA analysis would reveal. Or it may be that children with particular types of bacteria in their guts, as revealed from their stool sample, are more susceptible to food allergies, but only if they encounter that food at a particular time as a child. Given the enormous number of variables that the scientists were attempting to collect, the answers were not going to be simple, nor were they guaranteed. Epidemiology is akin to a mathematical fractal curve, in which zooming into one part of the curve reveals an elaborate pattern that replicates the intricacy and complexity of the whole. The roots of disease appear just as complex with every step towards the answer that we take.

The scientists had other wild ambitions that the explosive growth of technology had thrust onto the scientific stage. One scheme was to capture movies of the mothers interacting with their infants, in order to look for certain indicators of a child's brain development. There is evidence, for example, that children who go on to develop autism-spectrum disorders find it harder to pay attention to a book or toy along with a parent, something which could be seen in a video. On paper, it sounded reasonable to collect snippets of digital video that could be stashed away and examined in five, ten or twenty years' time. In practice, it would be like trying to capture that perfect, precious movie of a baby's first birthday party, under time pressure, and 80,000 times over. On the other hand, there were huge repositories of data that the scientists could use for free, as long as they received permission from the cohort families first. They wanted to be able to link participants to information in health records, school and university databases, and government records of taxes, benefits and savings. That way, data on the children and their families could be hoovered up from databases cheaply and for the rest of their lives.

Taken together, the scale of data collection in this cohort would be vast: 80,000 babies, warehouses of stool samples and placentas, gigabytes of video clips, several hundred thousand questionnaires and much more. The landscape of science is so broad and data storage so cheap and plentiful that there is almost no limit to the amount of information that scientists can collect. But as cohort history shows, super-ambitious studies of pregnancy and birth can run into problems without the right constellation of planning and support. The trouble with Big Science is that it also comes with big risks.

As Dezateux and her team mapped out their new cohort, they kept stumbling over two overarching problems, both of which were familiar yet freshly acute. The first was the almost paralysing difficulty of planning a study that would only come to full fruition in fifty or even a hundred years' time, when the instigators would be old or dead. The chronic diseases that would kill the children of 2015 would probably peak when they were over seventy – and lengthening life expectancy meant that a remarkable one third of all babies born in this cohort were predicted to live beyond a hundred. The scientists could hardly begin to imagine what types of data their successors would wish they had collected by that time.

The second question was much simpler and more immediate: would women even sign up? There was no shortage of potential pregnant women: the birth rate in Britain was on the rise. But Dezateux could hardly get them to take part with just a secretary, a series of polite letters to local health authorities and an army of health visitors, as Douglas once did.

The spiralling birth rate meant that antenatal clinics were already bursting at the seams, and there was a chronic shortage of midwives and health visitors. They couldn't collect all the information as part of their normal duties – so Dezateux came up with a different plan. She would try to convince pregnant women to travel to special recruitment centres set up for the study and then spend two hours there, answering questions and giving their samples of urine and blood. The aim was to enrol most of the mothers during pregnancy, and then see them again when their child was six months and twelve months.* This was a far more sensible way of running things than the approach of all the previous cohorts, which had little long-term planning. But it was a terrible challenge for Dezateux, who had to organize several sweeps of the cohort from the start and persuade women to commit to them too. What's more, she was asking them for all kinds of personal information at a time when many people are becoming anxious about the security of their data in the digital world.

It was a lot to ask, and there was no guarantee that busy, working women would want to give up their precious time. And even if eligible women did come, would 50% of them come or would only 5% of them come? Because if it was only 5%, the scientists would have to give up. It wouldn't be enough.

The agonizing answer to this question became clear in the summer of 2015, as I wrote the end of this book. The women didn't come – and the study was cancelled, although the reasons for its closure are still a matter of bitter dispute.

The new cohort was years in the planning, but it took only a few months to go down. In January 2015, Dezateux and her team opened the first of their dedicated recruitment centres for pregnant women, in King George Hospital, Ilford, on the outskirts of London. The location was chosen partly because the local area is ethnically diverse. One big aim of the study was to enrol women from ethnic minorities as well as those in socially disadvantaged groups. But this added to the challenge,

---

* The 80,000 child study was actually divided into two parts. 60,000 expectant families would be recruited at special centres in a few locations, and another 20,000 children would be recruited from across the UK and visited at home at around six months of age. This would allow the collection of detailed medical information during pregnancy, while still ensuring that the study included children from the population as a whole.

because scientists knew that it could be more difficult to encourage people from these groups to take part.

According to the most optimistic scenario, Dezateux and her team would recruit some 16,000 women in the first eighteen months of the study. But between January and June, a mere 249 women signed up. The numbers looked catastrophically low.

Dezateux knew this, but she also knew that this was a test phase and that there were ways to put it right. Because it was a risky project, she and her team had long ago built in plans to adjust the recruitment strategy as things went along. They had just started offering women a £20 shopping voucher to reward them for taking part, and they were going to reduce the time demanded of pregnant women by collecting all the information for the study at a routine ultrasound appointment, rather than requiring a second trip. And anyway, the signs were that recruitment was starting to pick up. In late September, when the team opened a second centre in Leicester, they contacted some 800 women and got an enthusiastic response.

Unfortunately, it was too late. Behind the scenes, everything was falling apart. The ESRC, which was leading the management of the study on the funders' side, was becoming deeply concerned by the low recruitment numbers and in July 2015 it requested a special review. The new cohort study had passed all its previous reviews with glowing marks – but this one came back with major concerns. On 10 July the ESRC discussed the situation at a high-level meeting in order to work out what to do.

At 6 p.m. that evening, Dezateux received a terse email informing her of the outcome. The funders had decided to close the study, a decision that was finalized and made public in October. Dezateux wrote to the mothers who had signed up to tell them that recruitment had ended. The hugely ambitious cohort study had been scrapped, years of energy and investment had been for nothing, and the remarkable series of British birth cohorts had, once again, hit a wall.

The cancellation of the new cohort left a sour taste in many people's mouths. Dezateux and many of her colleagues were angry and upset – they felt that they were not given a fair chance to get the study going, and they didn't understand why. 'It's a catastrophic decision that doesn't make any sense,' says Dezateux. She thought that one option was to scale back and run a smaller cohort study, rather than stop it dead.

To the ESRC, the recruitment numbers were a red flag that couldn't be ignored. By the time the study closed, it had consumed around £9 million* and the research council didn't want to risk putting more money into a project that appeared to be failing. The ESRC decided that whatever could be done to rescue the study wouldn't be enough. Privately, there was speculation amongst scientists that the research council was under particular pressure to cut costs because of an imminent government spending review and organizational shake-up that could lead to cuts in research. But at this stage, no one knows the full story.

For the scientists running other birth cohort studies at home and abroad, the news was a dagger to the heart – especially coming just a year after the massive American children's study had been cancelled. Now the two most high-profile, ambitious efforts to launch new birth cohorts had both crashed. It was incredibly sad, and scientists suspected that it would be difficult to propose another study like it for many years.

---

* While this is undoubtedly a large sum, it is still a sliver of the more than \$1.3 billion consumed over fifteen years by the National Children's Study, when it was shuttered.

There is now some hard thinking to be done about how future birth cohorts are designed. One valuable lesson is that scientists running cohort studies have to be cognizant of the growing demands on people's time and try not to ask too much of study members or they might say no. 'You can't see a film without being handed a questionnaire,' as Davey Smith puts it – the risk being that a questionnaire from a cohort study will end up in the trash with all the other stuff we don't have time to read. A second, familiar lesson is that a cohort study can try to do too much. Both the recent failed studies were extraordinarily ambitious in their design by trying to collect information from a large representative sample of a population, including all ethnic minority and socioeconomic groups, as well as extensive biological samples such as blood and tissues. Perhaps, in future, scientists will need to scale back.

Meanwhile, there is deep mourning for the science that has been lost. The chance to collect swathes of exciting and valuable information on this generation has evaporated. The DNA will not be collected, the videos will not be shot, the hypotheses will go untested and the lives of 80,000 children as they blossom and grow will go unrecorded by scientists.

For Dezateux and others in the cohort world, one loss hurts the most, and that's the opportunity to understand how disadvantage is affecting the children of today. If anything, the debate about inequality is raging just as fiercely now as at any time in the history of the cohort studies. Things have got dramatically better in real terms: living standards have risen enormously, and poor families don't receive meagre £2 maternity grants as they did in 1946. But in relative terms, poverty and disadvantage still affect a large proportion of the population. Around 25% of children are in families that live below the poverty line after paying for housing costs, a statistic that makes it imperative to understand the impact of deprivation on children's lives. Much of the academic and political discussion now centres on growing income inequality: the share of overall income going to the richest members of society is increasing, producing a widening gap between the rich and poor in many countries around the world. That's why, in 2013, President Barack Obama said that rising inequality was the 'defining challenge of our time'.

In 1946 the British government addressed inequality by working hard to equalize life chances through rationing and the creation of the welfare state, with its National Health Service and overhauled schools. In more recent years, the government has still been talking about equalizing life chances and improving social mobility, while at the same time introducing sweeping changes that will abrogate many of those equalizers, such as legislation that cuts welfare benefits, reforms schools and restructures the NHS, allowing private companies to attempt to make profits where profits should, in theory, not come into the equation. Critics say that all of these changes will be felt worst by the poorest and most disadvantaged, widening inequalities even further. Whether it worsens or not, it's clear that inequality is not going away.

If the new study had gone ahead, it would therefore have shown that there are plenty of children being born into disadvantage and that, on average, these children are likely to follow more difficult life paths. The earlier cohort studies had revealed this too. But the newest one would have gone further, by allowing scientists to use the tools of modern science to unpick why, and what can be done to help. By doing so, it would have continued a seam of work on disadvantage that started with the very first cohort, in 1946. When David Willetts launched the new cohort, he had said that the data would allow the government's efforts to improve the life chances of children to be judged in years to come.* But now it won't. No results will emerge from this study in a few years' time to remind everyone that poverty and disadvantage leave a scar on children's lives, and to help us understand why. That valuable information has slipped out of scientists' grasp.

The loss of the new cohort was extraordinarily painful, but it also emphasized the value of the studies that Britain already had. And the other part of that four-page proposal – the birth cohorts laboratory – was successfully taking shape. The laboratory is more mundane than its name suggests, because the infusion of money did not produce a brand-new building for the birth cohorts or anything swanky like that. What actually happened was that the extra cash was wired to the ageing offices in London that already house the 1958, 1970 and millennium cohorts, where Jane Elliott – one of the super-efficient cohort scientists – took charge of spending it. (The laboratory also got a relatively small sum of the money from the pot-of-gold account, because Dezateux's mega-cohort took the lion's share.)

What is still strong is the sentiment behind the new laboratory, which is to promote research across all the British cohorts. This sounds simple but is not; and data, once again, is getting in the way. One of the biggest problems for researchers wanting to compare the cohorts is that the data doesn't always allow it – it has been collected in slightly different ways in each study, which makes matching the figures up difficult. Take, for example, body height and weight.

---

* Willets left government at the election in 2015, which removed a key political champion of the studies.

These seem like straightforward measures, but once you start digging into the data, things look a lot more complex. In older sweeps, height and weight were recorded in imperial units and in more recent ones they were metric. Sometimes cohort members were asked to get on a set of scales, but sometimes they were asked their own weight – and people often don't know or they don't tell the truth. Sometimes the height measures were rounded up to the nearest quarter of an inch, and sometimes they weren't. And sometimes the idiosyncrasies of the data only become apparent after a little investigative work. This was superbly illustrated when scientists who wanted to look at obesity across all the cohorts began trying to harmonize the data, and saw something odd about the weights of the seven-year-old children in the second cohort: none was more than 45 kilograms (or 99 lbs). This couldn't be right. In the sixties, when these weights were being collected, it was certainly rare for children to weigh more than 45 kilos but at least some children were that big.

The researchers realized that the data had been constrained by the body weight expectations of the time; obesity was so rare that whoever was responsible for cleaning up the data and plugging it into the computer had simply cut off any weights that seemed too high. There *were* children who weighed more than 45 kilos, but their data had been dismissed as wrong. So the researchers had to use computer models to fill in the missing weights.*

---

* They found other, similar mistakes in the data – for example, they discovered that the heights of the 1970 cohort at age twenty-six had been cut off at close to 1.98 metres (about 6'6") tall.

Yet the effort to marry up the heights and weights produced the first big result to emerge from the birth cohorts laboratory, and it is one that the scientists are excited about: a comparison of the way that people in all five have gained weight during their lives. The study was gargantuan, wrapping in 273,843 measurements of body mass index on 56,632 cohort members. No one has previously been able to watch obesity as it crept up on consecutive generations, and it doesn't make a pretty sight.

The scientists had already found that obesity hit hard when our lifestyles changed in the 1980s, because they observed a rise in the weight of subjects in both the 1946 and the 1958 cohorts at that time. Now it was clear that the 1970 cohort fit neatly into the pattern, because many of them also became overweight in the 1980s, when they were just teenagers. As for the later generations, the wave of obesity had already swept in by the time they were born, and so the data showed that they were more likely to be overweight or obese as children. The graphs produced by the laboratory show neatly the remarkable and rapid changes that are sweeping across the developed world, causing each generation to get fat at ever younger ages and bringing with it the increased risks of heart disease, diabetes and more.

However, the data did give some reason for hope. Many people were getting heavier, but not *everyone* was. A good proportion of each cohort has been able to maintain a healthy weight. So now cohort scientists want to understand what is so special about this subgroup. What special combination of genes and lifestyles makes these people seemingly immune to all the pressures around us to pile on the pounds? This is the glass-half-full approach to epidemiology – rather than study why the overweight people got heavy and sick, it looks at how others manage to stay healthy and trim.

Marrying up body measurements may have been difficult at the laboratory, but matching up socioeconomic measures across the cohorts has proved to be much worse. Over the years, income has been measured in myriad ways. Sometimes gross income, sometimes net; sometimes people gave a precise figure, sometimes they were placed in approximate income bands. Sometimes just the father's earnings were recorded, but at other times the income for the entire household, including benefits, was noted instead. Sometimes cohort members were asked to tot everything up in their heads; sometimes an interviewer walked them through it to reach a more accurate estimate. Getting all this data into a form in which it can be compared is a crucial but tedious task, which involves downloading all the data from the Essex archive and painstakingly converting it into new categories – such as a bog-standard, comparable figure of the income of parents when all the children were ten. It's a bit like collecting all your payslips, bank statements and receipts for the last seventy years and trying to enter them into a tidy spreadsheet. But once it's done, the reordered data should help fill in some gaps from the past. The controversial work from the economists showing that social mobility had decreased mainly took in figures from men's jobs, but, using the new standardized measures, scientists now hope to flesh out the picture by looking at a household's entire income – including women's earnings, benefits and other sources too.

This work to iron out kinks in the data is really a continuation of the process that John Bynner started in the 1980s, when he tried to encourage more scientists to use the information in the Essex data archive. Now the idea is to lower the bar for entry – make the data more inviting so that more scientists will want to dive in. The laboratory team is building an impressive new search platform that will allow anyone to interrogate the cohorts for terms that are related to, say, smoking – something that has never been possible before. And they are trying to ensure that university students studying social science will get a chance to use cohort data in their projects; the team are keen to lure in the next generation of cohort scientists while they're young. If the cohort laboratory survives long term, there are ambitious plans for its growth. It might even be possible to incorporate international cohort studies and to start making comparisons with those abroad. But meanwhile the scientists are excited about a development relating to the missing cohort, the one from 1982 that was always mourned. It turns out that there was a spare cohort study lying around in Britain, looking for a home, and it might enable scientists to fill that empty hole.

This study was started by the Department for Education, which identified about 16,000 children who were born in 1989 and 1990 and started to follow them when they were aged 13–14. They tracked them for seven years, as they moved from school to work or higher education. But the department lost interest in the group as they got older and moved outside their remit, so staff there started to ask around if anyone wanted to take on a study of thousands of young people. The cohort scientists most certainly did. They put in a bid for it, and formally adopted the group in early 2013. This cohort comes with no data on birth and early life, and it would be too much to expect that it would perfectly plug the gap of a 1982 birth cohort. Nevertheless, scientists expect a great deal from the study, because it already has a lot of educational data in the bank, the participants are spread across the entire country, and they are similar in number to the other national cohorts. The scientists are now fleshing out their records by surveying them at the age of twenty-five. This group is particularly interesting to them because the subjects were entering the job market just as the global recession hit in 2008, and the team want to examine the impact this may have had on their lives. Getting a foot on the housing ladder is a major headache for this generation, and the scientists will want to look at this as well. Those in the first two cohorts were able to afford their own homes and contentedly watched the value of their houses climb. But incomes failed to keep up with the rise in property prices, and later generations have suffered the consequences. Far fewer people in the 1970 cohort own their own homes than do those in the two preceding cohorts. Among those born in the 1990s, only the wealthiest young people can afford their own home – often with the aid of inherited wealth – and everyone else is consigned to paying rent or to living at their parents' home.

While the new laboratory is working hard to spur research across all the British birth cohorts, it also has the remit of promoting the studies in general and raising their profile. More than anything, the cohort scientists wish that the wider world knew more about them. It would be wonderful if they were appreciated in the same way that the country values the BBC or the NHS – as a British institution, cherished both for its history and for all its flaws. The scientists have realized that affection for these incredible studies, which have stretched their tentacles into almost all aspects of British life, could be the cohorts' salvation, because if the nation learns to love them, the funders and politicians are more likely to support them too.

But, until that happens, it is only the love of the scientists that keeps the studies alive. And there is no time to stop and get sentimental in the cohort world. The scientists are running to stand still – frantically planning and carrying out sweep after sweep on the cohorts just to gather up all the information that they can on their study members, and stuff it into the data-banks, before time washes it away.

In 2012, when interviewers started fanning out for the latest sweep of the 1970 cohort, the scientists were confronted with a brand-new challenge in birth cohort science: Facebook.

A few years back, one of the cohort members had started a group on Facebook when he realized that he knew no one else in the study and he was curious to find out more. Since then the group has amassed over 200 cohort members – only a sliver of the 10,000 or so who still take part. The scientists were taken aback when they found out about the group, because it was a development that was out of their control. They worried that someone might post something incorrect or negative about the study that could discourage cohort members – and they were a little nonplussed that they were bending over backwards to keep the identity of the cohort members confidential, only to find a bunch of them casually revealing their names, birth dates and identities on a website for anyone to see. It was one of those occurrences in birth cohort science that no one could have envisioned at the start.

But so far the Facebook page has had no negative repercussions. The busiest it gets is in the April week when everyone celebrates their birthdays and they post pictures of the birthday card that the cohort scientists have sent. (They have developed their own cohort vernacular, such that those with a birthday on the 5th call each other 5-ers, and so on through the week until the 11-ers). In 2012, however, the year that the cohort turned forty-two, there was a flurry of posts when the interviewers started arriving with the latest questionnaire.

'Had my interview today, not too bad,' wrote one member. 'So when do we go back to Alton Towers, lol.'

'Interview set for this afternoon – quickly doing the pre-interview questionnaire just now!' wrote another. 'So . . . am I a racist, TV-watching, apolitical, non-religious, lazy, depressed, miserable alcoholic . . . ??? Hmm, off to have a think about it.'

Needless to say, this wasn't exactly the way the cohort scientists approached the questionnaire when they were putting it together a year or two before. It was the first sweep directed by Alice Sullivan, who has run the study since 2010. Sullivan wanted to probe some of the issues facing this generation as it rolls into middle age: why fewer women are having children (Have you not had children because of an infertility problem/you have not wanted to/you have not got round to it/you have been focused on your career/you never met the right person/other?); and why obesity is on the rise (How often do you eat ready meals; convenience foods; take-aways; a home-cooked meal made from basic ingredients?). Sullivan also resurrected a vocabulary test that the cohort had completed at age sixteen that asked the children to identify the meanings of twenty words, starting with QUICK and increasing with difficulty to PUSILLANIMOUS, which you will be either relieved or shocked to hear that hardly anyone knew.* 'All those who have done the survey, was it just me or was the vocabulary test really hard!! Not sure I had even heard of some of the words,' read another Facebook post. (Sullivan

---

* The word means timid, lacking in courage or determination.

was relieved that no one posted the actual words on Facebook, which would of course have allowed people to cheat on the test and skewed the results.)

With the data still so fresh, Sullivan and her team are still deep in the analyses. They found that a big proportion of the cohort members are, in fact, not that far off the description in the Facebook post. Many of them are TV-watching, apolitical and non-religious, and by some measures they are also lazy, miserable and, if not alcoholic, drinking more than they should. She found that 68% of men and 49% of women are overweight and obese – more than the 1958 cohort at the same age – and that around three quarters of both sexes fail to follow the government guidelines of exercising for thirty minutes, five days a week. Well over half of them say they are often worried and 40% are tired most of the time. In many categories, there was a strong link between lower social class and either ill-health or the behaviours that lead to it. Sullivan has now deposited the data in the Essex archive and is encouraging researchers around the globe to dive in.

Even as she wades through the new data, Sullivan is wringing discoveries from the old. In 2013 she pulled out of the archives information showing how often the 1970 cohort members had read for pleasure during their childhood – and then linked that up to their test results at school. She compared children from the same social background who were equally clever, based on tests at five and ten, and found that childhood readers tended to advance further in vocabulary, spelling and maths between the ages of ten and sixteen. It even seemed that reading for pleasure had a stronger influence on children's test results than having a parent with a university degree. That study led to a record-breaking 75,000 hits on the scientists' website and a flurry of media interviews; eventually it found its way into all sorts of campaigns to support reading and libraries.

A few doors down from Sullivan at the cohort office, Emla Fitzsimons, the new leader of the millennium cohort, is planning the next survey of the children, which will take place when they are fourteen. It will be the most ambitious sweep to date. The scientists are finally going to collect DNA from the children, which will go a long way to compensating for the rushed start of the study when the collection of detailed medical and biological information was forced to one side. And the scientists will draw on other strands of cohort history. They will ask the children to wear accelerometers, just as many of them did when they were seven years old. (Accelerometer technology has advanced apace, and this time they will wear gadgets on their wrists rather than strapped around their waists.) They are also making plans to collect diaries from the teenagers – just as Neville Butler did from thousands of teenagers in 1986. This time, however, the adolescents will be able to fill in what they are doing in every ten-minute slot of the day using an online form or an app on their phones. The plan is to compare the diaries of 2015 with those of 1986 to find out if today's teenagers are happier, more sociable or more sedentary than those decades before. The scientists were so ambitious for this sweep that their plans got a little out of control. Their £4 million budget would allow them to pay interviewers to spend three hours with each child and their parents. But there was so much to cram into the time* that when the team did pilot

---

* The questions covered school, religion, friends, family, relationships, smoking, risky behaviours, illegal and anti-social behaviour, cyber-bullying, food, dieting, moods and feelings, and more. It also included a gambling task to examine decision-making and risky behaviour.

tests they found that the interviews were taking more like four and a half hours – one took six – and they had to scale back what they wanted to ask.

Elsewhere, scientists working with the other cohorts are all gathering up information as fast as they can. In London, Diana Kuh, the mother tiger looking after the 1946 cohort, is still up at 5 a.m., sending e-mails and worrying about who will look after the study when she retires. She knows it is ironic that the study is being fêted for being the longest-running birth cohort in the world – the members are nearly seventy – and yet it still has to fight for a life extension every few years. The dramatic closure of the youngest cohort study only amplifies her concerns.

But history allows the scientists to find a little comfort and hope. Back in the 1970s, Jean Golding's plans for an ambitious cohort were shot down – but she found a way to launch a smaller study a few years later instead. And in 2000, when her country called her to get a millennium cohort going against unbelievable odds, Heather Joshi stepped up and delivered the goods. When the scientists encounter setbacks, they don't give up.

And that's why, once the pain of the most recent failure has faded and the political winds are again blowing in the right direction, someone is bound to bring up the idea of doing it all over again. Perhaps they'll propose a 2020 cohort, or one in 2025. Maybe your children or grandchildren will be enrolled in it – or perhaps they will even run it. Governments and funding come and go, but what lasts is our fascination with watching human life unfold, as well as the desire to record it and understand the different paths we set out on.

So the scientists keep soldiering on. They will keep driving on the studies that they already have, and if they get the opportunity, they will track tomorrow's children too. Perhaps those children will help resolve some of the mysteries about science and society that 70,000 lives, so far, have not.

Epilogue: Where are They Now?

Writing about birth cohorts shares the same difficulties as directing them: you are always running to keep up. Time slips past, the people in the cohorts get older, the scientists embark on the next sweep of data collection, and discoveries about the cohorts flood out. By the time I had written about what is happening in the cohort world today, tomorrow had come.

But even if the cohort studies do not end, this story must. My solution is to draw a finishing line in the autumn of 2015, as I write the end of this book, by giving a snapshot of each of the studies at this moment.

1946 cohort

Diana Kuh is planning another birthday party for her cohort, whose members will turn seventy in March 2016. It is a milestone she feels it's important to mark. This party will be less elaborate than the 65th-birthday celebration was – just one-day events in London and Manchester to which scientists and all the cohort members will be invited. There will be science talks, tea and birthday cake. It's likely that the parties will be packed, because the cohort members are so loyal. When Kuh's team posted out the last set of questionnaires, 83% of cohort members sent them back – a far higher response rate than most cohort studies obtain. (Kuh, who had promised to make all her colleagues a home-cooked lunch if they got an 80% response, then had to make a large batch of home-made soup and quiche.)

When she is not celebrating the survival of the cohort, Kuh is still busy watching their numbers dwindle. One recent paper in the *British Medical Journal* revealed a little more about who might be likely to die first. The study, led by epidemiologist Rachel Cooper, looked at just three simple tasks that the cohort members had been asked to do when they were aged fifty-three: how hard they could grip with their hands, how quickly they could stand up from a chair, and how long they could balance on one leg with their eyes closed. All these tasks seemed like a bit of fun to the cohort members, but they were actually carefully validated measures of muscle strength and coordination. The scientists looked for links between people's performance on these tests and death.

Kuh and her team found that 177 people had died over the following thirteen years, and that those who had performed poorly on the tests in their fifties had a higher mortality rate than those who had done well – even when they eliminated confounding factors such as having an unhealthy lifestyle. (Perhaps unsurprisingly, the ones who fared worst of all were those who had been physically incapable of performing any of the tests at age fifty-three: they had a mortality rate twelve times higher than the group that could manage all three.) The study is important because it shows that quick and simple tests, carried out in middle age, could identify those people in the population who are most at risk of life-threatening health conditions within the next few years and so those who might benefit the most from more intensive medical care or help to improve their fitness and health. No one would deny that the NHS, which is stretched to breaking point, could benefit from quick, cheap ways to work out how to target its limited resources.

The scientists are now carrying out the next sweep on the cohort members, at age sixty-nine, by dispatching nurses to their homes. As the cohort edges towards seventy, the risks of dementia and cognitive decline are very real, so the scientists are also well into their study to monitor this in a smaller sample of the group. The aim is to examine the brains of 500 cohort members in great detail, using memory tests, neurological examinations and advanced brain scanning. Then they will monitor who develops dementia over time and tap the lifetime of data in their computers to work out what predisposes people to the condition and what protects others. The hope is to find better ways to predict who will develop dementia, and when.

The 1946 cohort is the longest continuously running major birth cohort study in the world, and one of the longest-running studies of human development.

1958 cohort

The 1958 cohort is heading rapidly towards its 60th birthday. This prospect may not be relished by the cohort members, but it is by the scientists behind the study. The team, now led by Alissa Goodman, has ambitious plans to turn the cohort into a study of ageing. They are planning a sweep of the cohort at age 60 to collect many measures of health that, they hope, will cement the study's position as an interdisciplinary cohort, straddling biomedical and social science. Goodman is particularly interested in picking through the lifetimes of data to explore what factors in middle and old age – exercise, wealth, social networks or more – can reverse the effects of disadvantage early in life. The Centre for Longitudinal Studies, which runs the 1958, 1970 and millennium cohorts, won a major ESRC grant in April to support its cohort studies for the next five years.

The scientists have also found the money and the means to revive the 13,000 or so essays that were written by the cohort members when they were eleven years old. Advances in computing mean that there are now automated tools that can make sense of text like this en masse. The plan is to analyse the children's language, and then see if there are patterns and associations with people's health and well-being as their lives played out. It could be that the innocent words of these children actually contained important indicators of their present and future psychological traits and mental health.

In the 1958 cohort, scientists are still trying to understand why some children have followed relatively successful life trajectories, while others have floundered and failed. One idea that has recently taken hold centres on the importance of self-control in childhood as a predictor of success later in life. The most famous example of this is known as the 'marshmallow test' – experiments started in the late 1960s by psychologist Walter Mischel at Stanford University. Pre-school children were presented with one marshmallow (or a cookie or other treat) and told they could either eat that one now, or wait up to twenty minutes and get two treats instead. Some children gobbled up the single marshmallow the moment that the scientists' backs were turned, while others were able to resist temptation, even if they had to cover their eyes, make up songs or kick at the table to distract themselves. Years later, the psychologists followed up the children and found that the ones who had better self-control had gone on to perform better on college-entry tests, were better able to cope with frustration and stress and – less surprisingly – maintained a lower body mass index. The idea that childhood self-control pre-dicts our future health and wealth has since taken off. Cohort studies provide a brilliant way to test it, while disentangling confounders such as intelligence and social class. In a swathe of recent work, sci-entists have been plumbing the 1958 and 1970 cohort data to see if it holds true. It is a lovely example of new ideas blossoming from old data.

In one study, scientists identified children in the 1958 cohort who appeared to have poor self-control based on some of the seven- and eleven-year-old tests. (Does the child constantly need petty correction; misbehave when teacher is out of the room; not know what to do with himself; never stick at anything long? Is he or she sometimes eager, but sometimes doesn't bother?) In general, children are considered to have self-control if they can delay gratification, control their emotions and behaviours, maintain attention and persevere at a task. The scientists linked up the answers to a range of health measures taken at middle age such as blood pressure, cholesterol and body mass index, which they combined into one measure of physiological health.

Children who scored poorly on these measures were more likely to have poor health as adults – even when confounding factors were stripped away. Similar studies are showing that cohort children who had strong self-control have been more likely to secure a higher socioeconomic status and move into a managerial position at work, and have been less likely to spend time unemployed. Some scientists now think that skills such as patience and perseverance are such a crucial predictor of success in life that they should be taught from a young age.

It all adds up to the growing realization that when it comes to finding happiness, health and wealth in life, it really helps to build social and emotional skills, as well as intellectual ones. Success at many jobs and life challenges requires people to be diligent, reliable and to get the job done, rather than having bountiful raw intelligence.

1970 cohort

The scientists have just received funding of nearly £4 million from the MRC and ESRC to do a major biomedical sweep of the cohort, starting in 2016. Nurses will visit the cohort members at home and take measurements, including blood pressure, heart rate, tests of cognition, grip strength, height, weight, body fat, mental health and more. People in this cohort will also be asked to fill in a diet diary, provide a blood sample for extracting DNA and wear fitness trackers – to get more accurate measures of how active they are through the day.

The focus on health is a new one for this social sciences cohort, which has not had a major collection of medical information since Neville Butler's survey at the age of sixteen. The reason for collecting more medical information now is that the cohort members are getting on into middle age, which means they are showing more early signs of chronic disease such as obesity, diabetes and heart disease. So the scientists want to store away detailed baseline measures, which will serve as a starting point from which they can follow people's health into the future.

Alice Sullivan, who directs the 1970 cohort, has recently taken a fresh look at the issue of social mobility. She wanted to know how people get to the top – the highest social class, and the best jobs and incomes. Specifically, she wanted to test the idea that attending private schools and elite universities helped people to get ahead, in terms of earnings or social class. She compared people who went to private schools and state schools, and compared those who went to one of the Russell group universities – a group of twenty-four prestigious institutions including Oxford, Cambridge, Edinburgh and Bristol – with those who did not, while controlling for their social backgrounds, intelligence, school-exam results and other confounders. The aim was to look solely at the impact of the educational institution itself.

When she crunched the numbers, she saw an interesting but complex picture emerge, with differences determined by sex. For men, attending a private school was associated with getting ahead – so that even if you compared boys with identical family backgrounds and exam results, the ones who had attended private school were more likely to do well. It's possible that boys who attend these schools emerge with strong old boys' networks that help them to advance. For women, the type of school didn't matter so much, but attending an elite university did.

The other exciting news from this cohort is that the remarkable leisure diaries collected back in 1986 – during Butler's mega-sweep – have found a use. It always seemed a stretch to think that the mundane details of four days in the lives of 7,000 teenagers would be of much value. But the curiosity of scientists is boundless, and, as it happens, there is now a research centre in Oxford whose speciality lies in analysing diaries from across decades and around the world, in order to understand how people spend their time. Over the last two years, researchers there have dug into the 1970 cohort's diaries, and they think that they are now unique in the world, because they can be linked to more than forty years' worth of information on the diary-keepers' lives. In one of their first studies, they found that sixteen-year-olds who took part in physical activity every day were likely to have better mental health as adults – perhaps a predictable link, but one that is stronger when it is based on hard data. Now the scientists are looking at when and how often the teenagers were socializing with others, and how that might have links with physical and mental health too.

The 1991 cohort

The scientists in Bristol are preparing to survey members of the 1991 cohort at the ages of twenty-four and twenty-five. This presents new problems, because the cohort members are leaving home, moving not only around the country but around the world – and the scientists have to convince them to journey back to the Bristol clinic to be examined. They are offering to pay their travel and accommodation costs, and are making sure the clinic has free Wi-Fi, tablet computers and other amenities that appeal to the twenty-something crowd.

The 1991 cohort is also in the midst of a modernization exercise – under pressure from its funders – to make sure that its data is available and easy to use. Right now, scientists are employing five 'Data Buddies', who help researchers get hold of the information they need for their work. In future, the hope is to automate more of that process and perhaps eventually create an online data library, in which scientists with the necessary permissions can simply click on the data they would like to view.

The logistical challenges of running the 1991 cohort and handling the data have proved so enormous that, in 2014, the cohort brought in a second director, Paul Burton. Now George Davey Smith directs the science, and Burton is lumbered with the dry but essential work of keeping the cohort on the road. (Burton doesn't mind that he got the short straw: he loves maths, methodologies and data infrastructure, and, anyway, he says it makes him seem a bit of a martyr.) So, whereas all of the other cohorts are now directed by individual women, the 1991 cohort is led by two men.

This cohort, which has led the way in genetics and epigenetics, is also pushing into other frontiers in biological research. Cell biologists around the world are currently in thrall to a cell type that they make in the laboratory: induced pluripotent stem cells, or iPS cells. These are much like the cells in a very young human embryo, with the incredible ability to sprout into almost any cell type in the body. iPS cells can be studied in a laboratory dish in order to understand how cells normally develop, and what goes wrong when diseases arise. Scientists on the 1991 cohort have ambitions to make a whole bank of these cells, each grown from a cohort member. The aim is to identify someone in the cohort with specific behavioural problem, disease or an interesting mutation in their DNA that put them at risk for a disease – and then turn to their cells to grasp how it affects the ability of tissues to grow and develop. Banking the cells allows them to carry out experiments that they wouldn't be able to conduct on the people themselves.

The 1991 study started with 14,062 children, but now just over 40% respond to any one questionnaire and just 50% visit the clinic when asked. It is not unusual to see this level of attrition in a birth cohort study. The study is, however, growing in another way: the scientists have now recruited over 330 children of the cohort members and approximately four to five more are being born and entered into the study every month.

The millennium cohort

Emla Fitzsimons, who directs the millennium cohort, is in the middle of surveying the children at age fourteen. This sweep is considered important because it is the first time that the participants will have put their childhood firmly behind them (see Chapter 8).

Fitzsimons recently had an idea to start a 'policy bank' for this and other cohorts, which is a collection of news headlines and other records of major events, changes in policy, shocks or natural disasters. It's a little like a diary for the country, and it could prove valuable to scientists in the future wanting to answer questions employing cohort data long after the events themselves have faded from memory. Scientists might, for example, use it to explore the impacts of the general election in 2015, or perhaps the future arrival of an infectious disease, or extreme weather driven by climate change. The aftershocks of such events might leave traces in the lives of cohort members that researchers can one day detect.

Life Study

Dezateux and her team are still coming to terms with the closure of their study, and are working out how to move on with their science and their lives. A few elements of the study may continue in some form. One of those is a collection of stool samples from a few thousand mothers and newborn babies, for which the team secured separate funding. The aim is to understand how vaginal and caesarean births, as well as the common use of antibiotics at birth, affect the microbes in the guts of babies, and how that in turn might shape children's health and development. The scientists are planning a small meeting in January 2016 to recognize their four and a half years of hard work, and discuss what can be learnt from it.

In March this year, scientists in London held a conference to showcase some of the important work from the British birth cohorts. It lasted for two days and attracted hundreds of scientists spanning many disciplines; yet it could still only include a tiny sample of the work pouring from the cohort studies today. One of the most shocking presentations used 1958 cohort data to estimate that children who experience psychological problems will lose an average of more than £300,000 over their lifetimes, thanks to the lasting impacts of these problems on their education, employment and other aspects of their lives. Added up across the population, poor childhood mental health could be costing the UK some £550 billion in lost earnings.

Economist Alissa Goodman had just taken over the Centre for Longitudinal Studies, which houses the 1958, 1970 and millennium cohorts, and so it fell to Goodman to thank the organizers, the funding bodies and the scientists for their work. And then she finished by making the most important thank you of all. 'Nothing is possible without the generosity of our cohort members,' she said. 'Many feel that they don't have much of a voice in society   and all the research that you do, that uses the studies to change society for the good – it gives them a voice.'

Several times a week, when I travel into St Pancras Station in London, I walk past a hidden reminder of the British birth cohorts. It is a spot where, in 2011, a brass time capsule was buried beneath the Francis Crick Institute, a massive new medical research centre that is being built. Amongst the items the capsule contains – letters from renowned scientists, architects' sketches, and photographs – is memorabilia from the 1946 cohort. The capsule is a symbol of the aspirations of scientists for future generations, and it will not be unearthed for many decades. By then, the members of that original cohort will be long gone – but, with luck, the remarkable life project that originated with that study will still be going, tracking the generation already born and hopefully the generations yet to come.

Bibliographical Notes and Sources

Much of this book is based on extensive interviews conducted over five years with scientists, cohort members and others connected with the cohorts.

The studies have generated a vast range of publications across many disciplines and I have also drawn from this body of work. The sources I consulted are too numerous to list comprehensively. The following notes therefore feature a selection that were particularly valuable, important or enlightening, as well as providing references for some of the key studies mentioned. They are intended both as an acknowledgement and as a pointer to further reading.

General

A Companion to Life Course Studies, edited by Michael Wadsworth and John Bynner (2011), provides a detailed picture of the social, scientific and historical context in which the five British birth cohort studies have taken place. Michael Wadsworth has meticulously documented the history of the 1946 cohort, which he relayed to me in extensive interviews, and which he has also written up in two papers: 'The origins and innovatory nature of the 1946 British national birth cohort study', *Longitudinal and Life Course Studies* 1 (2), 121–36 (2010), and 'Focussing and funding a longitudinal study of health over 20 years: the MRC National Survey of Health and Development from 16 to 36 years', *Longitudinal and Life Course Studies* 5 (1), 79–92 (2014). I also drew on documents from the archives of the Medical Research Council held in the National Archives in Kew, Richmond, provided to me by Michael Wadsworth along with the handwritten notes he had made.

The history of social sciences and the Economic and Social Research Council (ESRC) is summarized in two invaluable documents: *SSRC and ESRC: The First Forty Years* (2005) and *The Social Sciences Arrive* (2000) by Alexandra Nicol. On the history of epidemiology, Kenneth Rothman's second edition of *Epidemiology: An Introduction* (2012) and Rodolfo Saracci's *Epidemiology: A Very Short Introduction* (2010) both provide for the reader what their titles promise.

A fascinating overview of the history and major findings of the 1958 cohort study is given in a report published to mark the cohort's fiftieth birthday, *Now we are 50* (2008), edited by Jane Elliott and Romesh Vaitilingam. This is also a good jumping-off point to further literature on the subject.

New research from around the world using cohort and other longitudinal studies is regularly published in *Longitudinal and Life Course Studies* and presented at the annual conference of the Society for Longitudinal and Life Course Studies.

The website for each cohort study provides an overview of the studies, a more comprehensive bibliography and, in some cases, details of questionnaires and other data collected:

1946 cohort: http://www.nshd.mrc.ac.uk/nshd/

1958, 1970 and millennium cohorts: http://www.cls.ioe.ac.uk

1991 cohort (ALSPAC): http://www.bristol.ac.uk/alspac/

Introduction

Escape from Disadvantage (1990) describes Doria Pilling's journey to trace the 1958-born children who were born in difficult circumstances but went on to find relative success. The feature story that I wrote about the 1946 cohort is 'Study of a lifetime', *Nature* 471, 20–24 (2011); a few excerpts of which appear in this book.

PART ONE: *Coming into the World*

1. *The Douglas Babies*

The health visitor's call on Gertrude Palmer was reconstructed based on interviews with her daughter Patricia and a visit to her childhood Cheltenham house as well as the questionnaire used in the 1946 maternity survey. The early history and results of the 1946 maternity survey are told in *Maternity in Great Britain* (1948), largely written by James Douglas but credited to the Joint Committee of the Royal College of Obstetricians and Gynaecologists and the Population Investigation Committee. The follow-up book, *Children Under Five* (1958), by James Douglas and J. M. Blomfield, fills out the early childhood years of the cohort.

Michael Wadsworth's book *The Imprint of Time* (1991) was also essential in understanding the story of the 1946 cohort from birth to adulthood. *The Population Investigation Committee: A Concise History to Mark its Fiftieth Anniversary*, by C. M. Langford (1988), explains the concerns about Britain's population decline, the formation of the Population Investigation Committee and the rationale for the 1946 maternity survey.

For James Douglas's history with Solly Zuckerman, I drew on papers in the Zuckerman Archive at the University of East Anglia, which offer an astonishing and grisly insight into the classified work of scientists in the Casualty Survey as they documented the impacts of bomb blasts during the war. The Penguin paperback *Science in War* was published anonymously in 1940, but was authored by the

Tots and Quots, a London dining club of young scientists formed by Zuckerman. The origins of social medicine are covered in John Pemberton's paper 'Origins and early history of the Society for Social Medicine in the UK and Ireland', *Journal of Epidemiology and Community Health* 56, 342–6 (2002).

For the biographical details of James Douglas, I drew on interviews with Douglas's family members and colleagues, and was fortunate to be able to consult a collection of letters, newspaper articles and other private papers provided to me by his widow, Rachel Douglas, who compiled it at his death in 1991.

The history of the cohort study methodology is drawn from sources including R. Doll, 'Cohort studies: history of the method. I. Prospective cohort studies', *Sozial- und Präventivmedizin* 46, 75–86 (2001). William Farr's 'Report upon the Mortality of Lunatics' was published in the *Journal of the Statistical Society of London* 4 (1), 17–33 (1841). For additional reading, *The Emperor of all Maladies* (2011), by Siddhartha Mukherjee, and *Tom's River* (2013), by Dan Fagin, are both Pulitzer prize-winning books which open a window on the history of epidemiology.

For the origins and history of the 1958 and 1970 cohorts, I drew on the archives of the National Birthday Trust Fund, housed in the Wellcome Library in London. The transcripts of the press conference at which the results of the 1958 cohort survey were first presented are a few sheaves of paper within an overwhelming stack of folders in these archives that document the sometimes farcical-sounding organization of the studies. The history of the National Birthday Trust Fund itself, the maternity surveys of 1946, 1958 and 1970, as well as the changing attitudes towards pregnancy and birth in Britain, are all meticulously documented in *Women and Childbirth in the Twentieth Century* (1997), by A. Susan Williams, a book which proved a precious resource.

For the biographical details of Neville Butler, I drew on interviews with Butler's colleagues and friends. The Centre for Longitudinal Studies also gave me a copy of a DVD featuring Butler and his work on the cohorts: *Generations: The Life and Works of Neville Butler* (2006).

Many details of the history and results of the 1958 Perinatal Mortality Survey are covered in the two major publications from its early years: *Perinatal Mortality: The First Report of the 1958 British Perinatal Mortality Survey* (1963), by Neville Butler and Dennis Bonham, and *Perinatal Problems: The Second Report of the 1958 British Perinatal Mortality Survey* (1969), by Neville Butler and Eva Alberman.

2. Born to Fail?

The Home and the School (1964) reports James Douglas's work on the educational trajectories of the 1946 cohort. Douglas continued to document the children's differing educational trajectories during secondary school in *All Our Future* (1968), which he authored with Jean Ross and Howard Simpson.

The revival of the 1958 cohort and the wealth of findings on the sweep at age seven are documented in the appendix to the Plowden Report: *Children and Their Primary Schools: A Report of the Central Advisory Council for Education (England)* (1967). The results were later written up in the books *11,000 Seven Year Olds* (1966), by Mia Kellmer Pringle, Neville Butler and Ronald Davie, and *From Birth to Seven* (1972), by Ronald Davie, Neville Butler and Harvey Goldstein. The *Sunday Times* magazine article 'An Unequal Start' (4 June 1972), by Ronald Davie, summarized the results in the latter book and caused the major embargo break by the British press.

The origins of the National Children's Bureau and the years during which it housed the 1958 cohort are covered succinctly in *30 Years of Change for Children* (1993), edited by Gillian Pugh. I was also fortunate to be able to consult two dusty books at the National Children's Bureau in London which are stuffed with press clippings about work from the 1958 cohort study during the 1960s, 70s and 80s. These also hold the minutes from the Bureau's annual general meetings.

The slim book *Born to Fail?*, by Peter Wedge and Hilary Prosser, is just as powerful now as it was when it was selling out from station bookshops in 1973. It reveals the difficult life trajectories of children born into disadvantage in the second of the British birth cohorts – a story continued in the follow-up book, *Children in Adversity* (1982), by Peter Wedge and Juliet Essen. A thorough overview of the country's education system is provided by *Education in England: A Brief History* (2011), by Derek Gillard (www.educationengland.org.uk/history). For more information on the research programme inspired by Sir Keith Joseph's speech, see *Cycles of Disadvantage* (1976), by Michael Rutter and Nicola Madge.

Elsa Ferri's illuminating report on children of one-parent families in the 1958 cohort is *Growing Up in a One-Parent Family* (1976). The key studies on the impacts of divorce from the 1958 cohort are summarized in the aforementioned report *Now we are 50* (2008), edited by Jane Elliott and Romesh Vaitilingam. For the study showing that differences in children of divorced parents are in evidence before parents separate, see B. J. Elliott and M. P. M. Richards (1991), 'Children and divorce: educational performance and behaviour before and after parental separation', *International Journal of Law, Policy and the Family* 5, 258–76 (1991). A comparison of the impacts of divorce on children in the 1946, 1958 and 1970 cohorts was published as M. Ely, M. P. M. Richards, M. E. J. Wadsworth and B. J. Elliott, 'Secular changes in the association of parental divorce and children's educational attainment: evidence from three British birth cohorts', *Journal of Social Policy* 28 (3), 437–55 (1999).

The details and results of the 1970 British birth survey are described in *British Births 1970* (1975), by Roma Chamberlain, Geoffrey Chamberlain, Brian Howlett and Albert Claireaux.

3. In Sickness and in Health

Accounts of the 1952 London fog can be found in reports from the Meteorological Office (http://www.metoffice.gov.uk/education/teens/case-studies/great-smog) as well as newspaper articles of the time. James Douglas's work on the lasting effects of air pollution is described in J. W. B. Douglas and R. E. Waller, 'Air pollution and respiratory infection in children', *British Journal of Preventive and Social Medicine* 20, 1–8 (1966), and later publications.

The way that epidemiology came to focus on chronic disease, and the role of adult cohorts in driving that change, is described in *A Life Course Approach to Chronic Disease Epidemiology* (1997, and its second edition of 2004), edited by Diana Kuh and Yoav Ben-Shlomo – and Chapter 2 in particular (D. Kuh and G. Davey Smith, 'The life course and adult chronic disease: an historical perspective with particular reference to coronary heart disease').

The way in which epidemiological studies revealed the link between lung cancer and smoking is covered in R. Doll, 'Cohort studies: history of the method. I. Prospective cohort studies', *Sozial- und Präventivmedizin* 46, 75–86 (2001), a reference already noted above. Other sources include C. White, 'Research on smoking and lung cancer: a landmark in the history of chronic disease epidemiology', *Yale Journal of Biology and Medicine* 63 (1), 29–46 (1990); G. Davey Smith and M. Egger, 'The first reports on smoking and lung cancer – why are they consistently ignored?', *Bulletin of the World Health Organization* 83 (10) (2005); and J. Cornfield et al., 'Smoking and lung cancer: recent evidence and a discussion of some questions', *Journal of the National Cancer Institute* 22, 173–203

(1959), a paper reprinted in *International Journal of Epidemiology* 38, 1175–91 (2009).

Doll and Hill's case control study was published as R. Doll and A. B. Hill, 'Smoking and carcinoma of the lung', *British Medical Journal* 2, 739–48 (1950). For the results from the British Doctors' Study, see R. Doll and A. B. Hill, 'The mortality of doctors in relation to their smoking habits: a preliminary report', *British Medical Journal* 1 (4877), 1451–55 (1954).

The history and impact of the famous Framingham cohort are well told in a review published in the *Lancet* on the study's sixty-fifth birthday: S. S. Mahmood et al., 'The Framingham Heart Study and the epidemiology of cardiovascular disease: a historical perspective', *Lancet* 383, 999–1008 (2014).

The story of how the 1958 cohort data helped lead to a consensus that smoking could cause low birth weight is summarized in H. Goldstein, 'Smoking in pregnancy: some notes on the statistical controversy', *British Journal of Preventive and Social Medicine* 31, 13–17 (1977). The key paper from the study was N. R. Butler, H. Goldstein and E. M. Ross, 'Cigarette smoking in pregnancy: its influence on birth weight and perinatal mortality', *British Medical Journal* 2 (5806), 127–30 (1972). For the painfully condescending editorial about pregnant women and smoking, see 'Smoking, pregnancy and publicity', *Nature* 245, 61 (1973). The advertisements featuring a pregnant, smoking woman are in V. Berridge and K. Loughlin, 'Smoking and the new health education in Britain 1950s–1970s', *American Journal of Public Health* 95 (6), 956–64 (2005).

The history of the 1946 cohort told in this chapter, including the MRC's great debate about what to do with the study when Douglas retired, is explained in M. Wadsworth, 'Focussing and funding a longitudinal study of health over 20 years: the MRC National Survey of Health and Development from 16 to 36 years', mentioned above.

Two of the studies from the 1946 cohort that linked respiratory illness in childhood with chronic cough in adults are: J. R. T. Colley, J. W. B. Douglas and D. D. Reid, 'Respiratory disease in young adults: influence of early childhood lower respiratory tract illness, social class, air pollution and smoking', *British Medical Journal* 3 (5873), 195–8 (1973), and K. E. Kiernan, J. R. Colley, J. W. Douglas and D. D. Reid, 'Chronic cough in young adults in relation to smoking habits, childhood environment and chest illness', *Respiration* 33 (3), 236–44 (1976).

The Bedford survey of 1962 and its 25,000 bottles of urine are reported in W. J. H. Butterfield, 'Diabetes survey in Bedford 1962', *Proceedings of the Royal Society of Medicine* 57 (3), 196–200 (1964).

PART TWO: *Coming of Age*

4. Staying Alive

The difficult years faced by the social sciences and the SSRC described here drew on the previously mentioned source *SSRC and ESRC: The First Forty Years* (2005).

The account of the years that Neville Butler ran the 1970 cohort in Bristol was based largely on interviews. The publications and funding sources during that period are summarized in J. Elliott and P. Shepherd, 'Cohort profile: 1970 British Birth Cohort (BCS70)', *International Journal of Epidemiology* 35 (4), 836–43 (2006).

The history of the fourth perinatal mortality survey – the one that would have ideally started in 1982 – is based on interviews. Other sources include a plan for the survey provided to me by Jean Golding and a report on the proposal submitted to the DHSS in May 1979, *Desirability and Feasibility of a Fourth National Perinatal Survey*, a copy of which was given to me by its author, Iain Chalmers. I also consulted the annual reports of the National Perinatal Mortality Unit from its early years, kindly lent to me by Alison MacFarlane.

Iain Chalmers's studies on the risks and benefits of the increased medicalization of birth are published in I. Chalmers, J. E. Zlosnik, K. A. Johns and H. Campbell, 'Obstetric practice and outcome of pregnancy in Cardiff residents 1965–73', *British Medical Journal* 1 (6012), 735–8 (1976), and I. Chalmers, J. G. Lawson and A. C. Turnbull, 'Evaluation of different approaches to obstetric care: Part 1', *British Journal of Obstetrics and Gynaecology* 83 (12), 92–9 (1976).

The backlash over the increased medicalization of birth is covered in J. Russell, 'Perinatal mortality: the current debate', *Sociology of Health and Illness* 4, 302–19 (1982), and A. Susan Williams's *Women and Childbirth in the Twentieth Century* (1997).

Austin Bradford Hill's randomized controlled trial of streptomycin is reported in 'Streptomycin treatment of pulmonary tuberculosis', *British Medical Journal* 2 (4582), 769–82 (1948). Archie Cochrane's seminal book *Effectiveness and Efficiency: Random Reflections on Health Services* (1972) helped change the way that medical treatments are evaluated. An oral history of evidence-based medicine, including an interview with Iain Chalmers and other key figures, is available at http://ebm.jamanetwork.com/.

The questions in the 1982 sweep of the 1946 cohort were made available to me by cohort member David Ward, who kindly allowed me to browse through his files and talked me through his and his parents' answers.

Information on the International Centre for Child Studies was gathered largely from interviews, as well as a 1982 brochure for the centre and other documents shown to me by Diana Pomeroy and Colleen Daley, who worked closely with Neville Butler. I also went to Ashley Down House, the imposing ex-orphanage building that Butler used as the centre's headquarters in Bristol.

All the survey instruments from the 1986 sweep of the 1970

cohort, including the leisure diary, are available on the website of the Centre for Longitudinal Studies, http://www.cls.ioe.ac.uk/. Information on the sweep is also available in the UK Data Service as http://dx.doi.org/10.5255/UKDA-SN-3535-2.

A copy of the video recording of the three cohort leaders, *Three Generations of Children*, made in March 1982, was given to me by Harvey Goldstein. A transcript of the video was published in *Paediatric and Perinatal Epidemiology* 12, Suppl. 1, 15–30 (1998) – a special issue of the journal dedicated to the memory of Neville Butler.

5. Older and Wiser

A few excerpts from this chapter were previously printed in a feature that I wrote about the 1991 cohort, 'Coming of age', *Nature* 484, 155–8 (2012).

An excellent oral history of the early years of the ALSPAC cohort, recounted by Jean Golding and many others involved, is available as a 'Witness Seminar' (May 2011), 'History of the Avon Longitudinal Study of Parents and Children (ALSPAC), c.1980–2000' at http://www.histmodbiomed.org/witsem/vol44. An overview of the cohort and its publications is provided by A. Fraser et al., 'Cohort profile: the Avon Longitudinal Study of Parents and Children: ALSPAC mothers cohort', *International Journal of Epidemiology* 42 (1), 97–110 (2013), and A. Boyd et al., 'Cohort profile: the "Children of the 90s" – the index offspring of the Avon Longitudinal Study of Parents and Children', *International Journal of Epidemiology* 42 (1), 111–27 (2013). The cohort team also published a book about the study to mark its twenty-first birthday: *Twenty One Years: Our Journey* (2012), available to download at http://www.bristol.ac.uk/alspac/go/21st-book/.

A potted history of the Human Genome Project can be found on the websites of two of the major institutions involved, the Wellcome Trust Sanger Institute (http://www.sanger.ac.uk/about/history/hgp/#tabs-1) and the National Human Genome Research Institute (http://www.genome.gov/10001772). In 1990 Marcus Pembrey articulated the case that a birth cohort study would help decipher the human genome in a short letter to *Nature*: see M. E. Pembrey, 'Cohort of Genes', *Nature* 348, 280 (1990).

The paper from the 1946 cohort which found a correlation between weight at birth and blood pressure at age thirty-six is M. E. J. Wadsworth, H. A. Cripps, R. E. Midwinter and J. R. T. Colley, 'Blood pressure in a national birth cohort at the age of 36 related to social and familial factors, smoking, and body mass', *British Medical Journal* 291 (6508), 1534–8 (1985).

The history of the idea that foetal and child development can influence risk of chronic disease is summarized in the aforementioned chapter D. Kuh and G. Davey Smith, 'The life course and adult chronic disease: an historical perspective with particular reference to coronary heart disease', in *A Life Course Approach to Chronic Disease Epidemiology* (1997), edited by Diana Kuh and Yoav Ben-Shlomo. Other sources include G. Davey Smith and D. Kuh, 'Commentary: William Ogilvy Kermack and the childhood origins of adult health and disease', *International Journal of Epidemiology* 30 (4), 696–703 (2001), and D. Kuh et al., 'Life course epidemiology and analysis', in *Oxford Textbook of Global Public Health*, 6th edition (2015), edited by Roger Detels, Martin Gulliford, Quarraisha Abdool Karim and Chorh Chuan Tan; as well as a slide presentation shared with me by Diana Kuh.

The story of David Barker's work is based in part on an interview with him in 2013. This history and Barker's ideas are also well explained in a November 2007 profile of Barker by Stephen S. Hall in the *New Yorker* magazine at http://www.newyorker.com/magazine/2007/11/19/small-and-thin), and *Size Matters: How Height Affects the Health, Happiness, and Success of Boys – and the Men They Become* (2006), also by Stephen S. Hall.

For the death atlas, with the green and red maps showing the distribution of heart disease deaths, see Martin J. Gardner et al., *Atlas of Mortality from Selected Diseases in England and Wales, 1968–1978* (1984). Barker's ideas are also explained in D. Almond and J. Currie, 'Killing me softly: the foetal origins hypothesis', *Journal of Economic Perspectives* 25 (3), 153–72 (2011). An overview of the Hertfordshire cohort is in H. E. Syddall et al., 'Cohort profile: the Hertfordshire Cohort Study', *International Journal of Epidemiology* 34 (6), 1234–42 (2005).

Two of Barker's key publications are D. J. Barker and C. Osmond, 'Infant mortality, childhood nutrition, and ischaemic heart disease in England and Wales', *Lancet* 1 (8489), 1077–81 (1986), and D. J. Barker et al., 'Weight in infancy and death from ischaemic heart disease', *Lancet* 2 (8663), 577–80 (1989).

The history of the Whitehall Study and Whitehall II can be found at http://www.ucl.ac.uk/whitehallII/history. Whitehall II is also the subject of M. Marmot and E. Brunner, 'Cohort profile: the Whitehall II study', *International Journal of Epidemiology* 34 (2), 251–6 (2005).

The links between childhood developmental milestones and later risk of schizophrenia were described in P. Jones, B. Rodgers, R. Murray and M. Marmot, 'Child development risk factors for adult schizophrenia in the British 1946 birth cohort', *Lancet* 344 (8934), 1398–402 (1994).

The study linking menopause to early development is D. Kuh et al., 'Childhood cognitive ability and age at menopause: evidence from two cohort studies', *Menopause* 12, 475–82 (2005).

The book on life course epidemiology is the previously mentioned *A Life Course Approach to Chronic Disease Epidemiology* (1997), edited by Diana Kuh and Yoav Ben-Shlomo. The ideas are also introduced in Y. Ben-Shlomo and D. Kuh, 'A life course approach to chronic disease epidemiology: conceptual models, empirical challenges and interdisciplinary perspectives', *International Journal of Epidemiology* 31 (2), 285–93 (2002).

The 1991 cohort findings on babies' sleeping position were published as L. Hunt, P. Fleming and J. Golding, 'Does the supine sleeping position have any adverse effects on the child?: I. Health in the first six months', *Pediatrics* 100 (1), E11 (1997), and C. Dewey, P. Fleming and J. Golding, 'Does the supine sleeping position have any adverse effects on the child? II. Development in the first 18 months', *Pediatrics* 101 (1), E5 (1998).

For the findings of studies showing that eating fish during pregnancy is associated with better eye and cognitive development in children, see C. Williams et al., 'Stereoacuity at age 3.5 y in children born full-term is associated with prenatal and postnatal dietary factors', *American Journal of Clinical Nutrition* 73 (2), 316–22 (2001); J. L. Daniels et al., 'Fish intake during pregnancy and early cognitive development of offspring', *Epidemiology* 15 (4), 394–402 (2004); and J. R. Hibbeln et al., 'Maternal seafood consumption in pregnancy and neurodevelopmental outcomes in childhood (ALSPAC study): an observational cohort study', *Lancet* 369 (9561), 578–85 (2007).

The FTO gene association study was published as T. M. Frayling et al., 'A common variant in the *FTO* gene is associated with body mass index and predisposes to childhood and adult obesity', *Science* 316, 889–94 (2007).

The study charting and comparing the BMI of the 1946 and 1958 cohorts is L. Li, R. Hardy, D. Kuh, R. Lo Conte and C. Power, 'Child-to-adult body mass index and height trajectories: a comparison of 2 British birth cohorts', *American Journal of Epidemiology* 168 (9), 1008–15 (2008); for the study showing the strength of association between BMI and variants of the genes FTO and MC4R, see R. Hardy et al., 'Life course variations in the associations between FTO and MC4R gene variants and body size', *Human Molecular Genetics* 19 (3), 545–52 (2010).

For an overview of the Boyd Orr cohort, see R. M. Martin et al., 'Cohort profile: the Boyd Orr cohort – an historical cohort study based on the 65 year follow-up of the Carnegie Survey of Diet and Health (1937–39)', *International Journal of Epidemiology* 34 (4), 742–9 (2005). For a more colourful history and pictures of the original handwritten ledgers, see David Blane's presentation at https://www.ucl.ac.uk/icls/publications/op/index/edit/boydorr.pdf.

George Davey Smith's career is affectionately documented in a file put together by his colleagues in 2013 called 'The First One Thousand: Reflections on the Publications of George Davey Smith', a copy of which was given to me by Davey Smith.

For the study comparing the causal effects of breastfeeding in the 1991 cohort with the Pelotas birth cohorts in Brazil, see M.-J. A. Brion et al., 'What are the causal effects of breastfeeding on IQ, obesity and blood pressure? Evidence from comparing high-income with middle-income cohorts', *International Journal of Epidemiology* 40 (3), 670–80 (2011).

Work using Mendelian randomization to unpick the effects of drinking alcohol during pregnancy is described in L. Zuccolo et al., 'Prenatal alcohol exposure and offspring cognition and school performance: A "Mendelian randomization" natural experiment', *International Journal of Epidemiology* 42 (5), 1358–70 (2013).

The epigenetic study on cord blood samples of children in the 1991 cohort is published as C. L. Relton et al., 'DNA methylation patterns in cord blood DNA and body size in childhood', *PLoS ONE* 7 (3), e31821 (2012). Barker's study on the placentas of the 1991 cohort is D. Barker et al., 'Maternal cotyledons at birth predict blood pressure in childhood', *Placenta* 34 (8), 672–5 (2013).

The study establishing a link between iodine deficiency in mothers and mental development in children was led by Margaret Rayman at the University of Surrey, UK, and published as S. C. Bath et al., 'Effect of inadequate iodine status in UK pregnant women on cognitive outcomes in their children: results from the Avon Longitudinal Study of Parents and Children (ALSPAC)', *Lancet* 382 (9889), 331–7 (2013).

6. *Opening Up*

The history of the UK Data Archive at Essex University is described in a publication celebrating its fortieth anniversary: *Across the Decades – 40 Years of Data Archiving* (2007). Other details on the archive were provided to me by Mike Knight and Jack Kneeshaw, who kindly showed me around the data centre.

John Bynner contributed to *The Sexual Behaviour of Young People* (1965), under the main authorship of Michael Schofield, and his work on smoking behaviour was published as *The Young Smoker: A Study of Smoking among Schoolboys Carried Out for the Ministry of Health* (1969).

Bynner's report on the 1958 cohort data and why it wasn't being used is *Secondary Use of the National Child Development Study: A Report Prepared for the Economic and Social Research Council* (1984), a copy of which he kindly gave to me. The data dictionary for the cohort studies is available on the website of the Centre for Longitudinal Studies at http://www.cls.ioe.ac.uk/datadictionary/default.asp.

A mountain of research and publications has emerged from the cohort studies since the early 1990s, most of which could not be covered in this book. However, for an insight into the wealth of findings from the adult sweeps of the 1958 and 1970 cohort studies, see *Life at 33* (1993), edited by Elsa Ferri, *Twenty-something in the 1990s: Getting on, Getting by, Getting Nowhere* (1997), edited by John Bynner, Elsa Ferri and Peter Shepherd, and *Changing Britain, Changing Lives* (2003), edited by Elsa Ferri, John Bynner and Michael Wadsworth and the publications on the website of the Centre for Longitudinal Studies.

The account of the economists' work with cohort data is based largely on interviews. The tests taken by the 1970 cohort children at age 22 months and 42 months are available on the Centre for Longitudinal Studies website.

For an accessible explanation of Leon Feinstein's work, see L. Feinstein, 'Very early evidence', *CentrePiece* 8 (2), 24–30 (2003). His study was published as L. Feinstein, 'Inequality in the early cognitive development of British children in the 1970 cohort', *Economica* 70 (277), 73–97 (2003). The Feinstein graph in this book is based on the one published in that paper. For the paper challenging part of Feinstein's analysis, see J. Jerrim and A. Vignoles, 'The use (and misuse) of statistics in understanding social mobility: regression to the mean and the cognitive development of high ability children from disadvantaged homes', DoQSS Working Paper No. 11–01 (April 2011).

The economists' research on social mobility is published in a series of papers, of which just a few are mentioned here. For a digestible summary of the work and the ensuing academic debate, see Jo Blanden, 'Big ideas: intergenerational mobility', *CentrePiece* 13 (3), 6–9 (Winter 2008/9).

For the study assessing intergenerational mobility in the 1958 cohort, see L. Dearden, S. Machin and H. Reed, 'Intergenerational Mobility in Britain', *Economic Journal* 107 (440), 47–66 (1997).

For the comparison of social mobility in the 1958 and 1970 cohorts, see J. Blanden, A. Goodman, P. Gregg and S. Machin, 'Changes in Intergenerational Mobility in Britain', in Miles Corak (ed.), *Generational Income Mobility in North America and Europe* (2004), and J. Blanden and S. Machin, 'Up and down the generational income ladder in Britain: past changes and future prospects', *National Institute Economic Review* 205, 101–17 (2008).

For the work showing a strengthening relationship between parental income and children's progression in education, see J. Blanden, P. Gregg and L. Macmillan, 'Accounting for intergenerational income persistence: non-cognitive skills, ability and education', *Economic Journal* 117, C43–60 (2007).

For John Goldthorpe's position on the debate, see J. Goldthorpe, 'Understanding – and misunderstanding – social mobility in Britain: the entry of the economists, the confusion of politicians and the limits of educational policy', *Journal of Social Policy* 42 (3), 431–50 (2013); and the analysis of social mobility across four birth cohorts is E. Bukodi, J. H. Goldthorpe, L. Waller and J. Kuha, 'The mobility problem in Britain: new findings from the analysis of cohort data', *British Journal of Sociology* 66 (1), (2015). The economists' six-years-in-the-making response is J. Blanden, P. Gregg and L. Macmillan, 'Intergenerational persistence in income and social class: the effect of within-group inequality', *Journal of the Royal Statistical Society* 176 (2), 541–63 (2013).

The report examining the family income and cognitive ability in childhood of those who later enter top professions was L. Macmillan, *Social Mobility and the Professions* (2009) at http://www.bristol.ac.uk/media-library/sites/cmpo/migrated/documents/socialmobility.pdf.

The cohort work on literacy and numeracy is summarized by John Bynner in 'Skills and Lifelong Learning', Chapter 9 of *Now we are 50* (2008), and in a report by David Budge, *The Impact of Adult Literacy and Numeracy Research Based on the 1970 British Cohort Study* (2014), available on the website of the Centre for Longitudinal Studies. Much more detail is provided in a series of reports on the website of the National Research and Development Centre for Adult Literacy and Numeracy (http://www.nrdc.org.uk/). For example, see J. Bynner, and S. Parsons, *New Light on Literacy and Numeracy* (2006).

The Moser report is *A Fresh Start: Improving Literacy and Numeracy. The Report of the Working Group Chaired by Sir Claus Moser* (1999).

John Bynner's work tracing the trajectories of adults with poor basic skills is summarized in S. Parsons and J. Bynner, *Illuminating Disadvantage: Profiling the Experiences of Adults with Entry Level Literacy or Numeracy over the Lifecourse* (2007). It is also discussed in J. Bynner, 'Never too early, never too late', in *Adults Learning* (2008).

Glen Elder's book, influential in the development of life course theory, is *Children of the Great Depression* (1974), which was extended and updated in a twenty-fifth anniversary edition published in 1999.

Jo Blanden's report showing the importance of parental interest and engagement in children's trajectories is *'Bucking the Trend': What Enables Those who are Disadvantaged in Childhood to Succeed Later in Life?* (2006) at dera.ioe.ac.uk/7729/.

PART THREE: *Coming Full Circle*

7. *The Millennium Children*

The beginnings of the millennium cohort were pieced together mostly from interviews, as well as two reports on the history and origins of the study: *The Millennium Cohort Study Annual Report to ESRC & ONS* (2001), provided to me by Heather Joshi, and *Millennium Cohort Study: First, Second, Third and Fourth Surveys: A Guide to the Datasets* (2012), edited by Kirstine Hansen and available on the website of the Centre for Longitudinal Studies.

For the results from the early years of the millennium cohort children, see S. Dex and H. Joshi (eds), *Children of the 21st Century: From Birth to Nine Months* (2005), and K. Hansen, H. Joshi and S. Dex (eds), *Children of the 21st Century: The First Five Years* (2010). For an overview of the millennium cohort study, see R. Connelly and L. Platt, 'Cohort profile: UK Millennium Cohort Study (MCS)', *International Journal of Epidemiology* 43 (6), 1719–25 (2014).

The economists' analysis of the cognitive scores of the millennium cohort children at the ages of three and five is published in J. Blanden and S. Machin, 'Intergenerational inequality in Early Years assessments', a chapter in *Children of the 21st Century: The First Five Years*. Ricardo Sabates and Shirley Dex's study of risks in millenium cohort children is in the Institute of Education publication *Multiple Risk Factors in Young Children's Development* (2012).

James Douglas's analysis of the links between interested parents and better progress through school is in Chapter 7 of *The Home and the School* (1964). The cohort study following 3,000 children is the Effective Pre-School, Primary and Secondary Education (EPPSE) research project and its results are published in a series of reports available at http://www.ioe.ac.uk/research/153.html. For the study of bedtimes and behaviour in millennium cohort children, see Y. Kelly, J. Kelly and A. Sacker, 'Changes in bedtime schedules and behavioral difficulties in 7 year old children', *Pediatrics* 132 (5), e1184–93 (2013).

For the millennium cohort study arguing that both poverty and parenting matter, see K. E. Kiernan and F. K. Mensah, 'Poverty, family resources and children's early educational attainment: the mediating role of parenting', *British Educational Research Journal* 37 (2), 317–36 (2011). For a useful review on parenting and education, see the report by Charles Desforges and Alberto Abouchaar, *The Impact of Parental Involvement, Parental Support and Family Education on Pupil Achievements and Adjustment: A Literature Review* (Research Report 433) (2003).

The findings on childhood obesity in the millennium cohort are summarized in L. J. Griffiths, S. S. Hawkins, T. Cole, C. Law and C. Dezateux, 'Childhood overweight and obesity', in *Children of the 21st Century: The First Five Years*. For the study on working mothers and childhood obesity, see S. S. Hawkins et al., 'Maternal employment and early childhood overweight: findings from the UK Millennium Cohort Study', *International Journal of Obesity* 32, 30–38 (2008). For the study in which the children wore accelerometers, see L. J. Griffiths et al., 'How active are our children? Findings from the Millennium Cohort Study', *BMJ Open* 3, e002893 (2013).

The cohort work on summer-born children is largely summarized in a report published by the Institute for Fiscal Studies: C. Crawford, L. Dearden and E. Greaves, *Does When You are Born Matter? The Impact of Month of Birth on Children's Cognitive and Non-cognitive Skills in England* (2011).

For the study examining the causal effects of breastfeeding using the millennium cohort, see E. Fitzsimons and M. Vera-Hernandez, 'Food for thought? Breastfeeding and child development', Institute for Fiscal Studies Working Paper W13/31 (2013).

The changing role of women in the workplace has been studied extensively using the British birth cohorts and is beyond the scope of this book. It is covered in *Now we are 50* (2008) and *Unequal Pay for Women and Men: Evidence from the British Birth Cohort Studies* (1998), by H. Joshi and P. Paci. Some of the work on the financial returns to education is also summarized in *Now we are 50.*

For an overview of major birth and child cohort studies, see C. Pirus and H. Leridon, 'Large child cohort studies across the world', *Population* 65 (4), 575–629 (2010). The annual international meeting on longitudinal studies is the aforementioned conference of the Society for Longitudinal and Life Course Studies (http://www.slls.org.uk/).

The challenges of starting new birth cohorts are well described in D. A. Lawlor, A.-M. Nybo Andersen and G. D. Batty, 'Birth cohort studies: past, present and future', *International Journal of Epidemiology* 38 (4), 897–902 (2009). An inventory of birth cohorts is available at http://www.birthcohorts.net/bch2.

Information on the US National Children's Study is online at https://www.nichd.nih.gov/research/NCS/Pages/default.aspx. The plans for the study were outlined in A. E. Guttmacher, S. Hirschfeld and F. S. Collins, 'The National Children's Study – a proposed plan', *New England Journal of Medicine* 369 (20), 1873–5 (2013). The story of the study's origins and challenges is well told in Jocelyn Kaiser, 'The Children's Study: unmet promises', *Science* 339 (6116), 133–6 (2013).

A lovely brochure celebrating the sixty-fifth birthday of the 1946 cohort is available at http://www.nshd.mrc.ac.uk/nshd/65th-birthday-brochure/ and a gallery of all the birthday cards sent to the cohort members since the practice started in 1962 can be viewed at http://www.nshd.mrc.ac.uk/nshd/birthday-card-gallery/. Some interviews from the London birthday party are part of an NPR radio piece on the cohort available at http://www.npr.org/blogs/health/2011/12/23/144192370/poked-and-prodded-for-65-years-in-the-name-of-science.

For the paper showing correlations between the 1946 cohort's childhood socioeconomic position and performance in the medical MOTs in their sixties, see L. Hurst et al., 'Lifetime socioeconomic inequalities in physical and cognitive aging', *American Journal of Public Health* 103 (9), 1641–8 (2013).

For the study examining mortality in the cohort, see D. Kuh et al., 'Do childhood cognitive ability or smoking behaviour explain the influence of lifetime socio-economic conditions on premature adult mortality in a British post war birth cohort?', *Social Science and Medicine* 68 (9), 1565–73 (2009). And for the tally of medical conditions suffered by each 1946 cohort member, see M. B. Pierce et al., 'Clinical disorders in a post war British cohort reaching retirement: evidence from the first national birth cohort study', *PLoS One* 7 (9), e44857 (2012).

8. Bridging the Divides

The impressive scientific facilities supported by the Large Facilities Capital Fund can be found in a roadmap document from 2010 at http://www.rcuk.ac.uk/Publications/policy/lfr/.

A copy of the four-page pitch to the fund for a research laboratory for the birth cohort studies was given to me by Peter Elias. The case for a new British birth cohort and for the scientific importance of cohort studies as a whole was also articulated in influential reports by the think tank Longview, available at http://www.slls.org.uk/#!longview-reports/c8a5. For an earlier effort to coordinate research across cohort studies, as part of a project called Healthy Ageing across the Life Course (HALCYON), see http://www.halcyon.ac.uk/.

The Pinch: How the Baby Boomers Took Their Children's Future – and Why They Should Give it Back (2011), by David Willetts, earned the author a review as a 'one man think tank'. A copy of his March 2011 speech announcing the funding of the 2012 birth cohort is available at https://www.gov.uk/government/speeches/the-arts-humanities-and-social-sciences-in-the-modern-university.

The 1915 book *Maternity Letters from Working Women,* by Margaret Llewelyn Davies, is as powerful now as it was one hundred years ago and offers a compelling insight into the past conditions in which women bore and frequently lost children. The website for Life Study is http://www.lifestudy.ac.uk/homepage.

For the cohort study documenting the impact of air pollution on children living near a freeway, see W. J. Gaudernman et al., 'Effect of exposure to traffic on lung development from 10 to 18 years of age: a cohort study', *Lancet* 369 (9561), 571–7 (2007).

The birth cohorts laboratory was launched under the name CLOSER (Cohort and Longitudinal Studies Enhancement Resources) in 2013 and details can be found at http://www.closer.ac.uk/. The adopted cohort of around 16,000 children born in 1989–90 was known as the Longitudinal Study of Young People in England, or LSYPE, but was rebranded by the cohort scientists as Next Steps. Information can be found at http://www.cls.ioe.ac.uk/page.aspx?&sitesectionid=124 68&sitesectiontitle=Welcome+to+Next+Steps+(LSYPE).

For the study comparing body weights across several cohorts, see W. Johnson, L. Li, D. Kuh and R. Hardy, 'How has the age-related process of overweight or obesity development changed over time? Co-ordinated analyses of individual participant data from five United Kingdom birth cohorts', *PLoS Medicine* 12 (5), e1001828 (2015).

The preliminary results on bodyweight in the 1970 birth cohort were published by the Centre for Longitudinal Studies in a report by Alice Sullivan and Matt Brown, *Overweight and Obesity in Mid-life: Evidence from the 1970 Birth Cohort Study at Age 42* (2013).

The first findings from the sweep of the 1970 cohort at age 42 were reported in a series of papers in *Longitudinal and Life Course Studies* 6 (2) (2015).

The correlation between childhood reading for pleasure and later educational performance is reported in A. Sullivan and M. Brown, 'Social inequalities in cognitive scores at age 16: the role of reading' (2013), available on the website of the Centre for Longitudinal Studies.

All other reports, studies and plans for future sweeps on the 1958, 1970 and millennium cohorts can be found on the website of the Centre for Longitudinal studies at http://www.cls.ioe.ac.uk.

Epilogue: Where are They Now?

For the study connecting physical tasks in middle age with mortality, see R. Cooper et al., 'Physical capability in mid-life and survival over 13 years of follow-up: British birth cohort study', *British Medical Journal* 348, g2219 (2014).

The famous marshmallow experiments are described in *The Marshmallow Test: Mastering Self-Control* (2014) by Walter Mischel. Evidence for the importance of social and emotional skills across the life course is provided in 'Social and emotional skills in childhood and their long-term effects on adult life', by A. Goodman, H. Joshi, B. Nasim and C. Tyler (2015), available at http://www.eif.org.uk/wp-content/uploads/2015/03/EIF-Strand-1-Report-FINAL1.pdf. One study showing the lasting impacts of early psychological health is A. Goodman, R. Joyce and J. P. Smith ,'The long shadow cast by childhood physical and mental health problems on adult life', *PNAS* 108 (15), 6032–7 (2011).

Acknowledgements

I have many people to thank. My agent Sarah Chalfant, for believing that my idea could be a book; my editor Helen Conford at Penguin for her vision and always-right advice; and Donna Poppy, who with her skilful editing transformed my flawed draft into a story. My early readers: Tim Appenzeller, David Adam and Geoff Brumfiel. Rowena Purrett, who faithfully transcribed my interviews. The many friends, writers and editors who provided encouragement and support, in particular Sara Abdulla and Meredith Wadman, and my colleagues at *Nature* who patiently tolerated my infatuation with cohort studies.

I owe enormous thanks to the many people who gave their time to be interviewed in the course of researching this book; without their extraordinary patience and generosity, there would be no story. Of these, I owe particular gratitude to Diana Kuh, who spent hours letting me pick her brains; and Michael Wadsworth, who was so amazingly generous with his time and knowledge and offered insightful, detailed feedback on my draft. I am tremendously grateful to everyone who took time to speak to me during my research, a list that includes but is not limited to: Eva Alberman, Evrim Altintas, David Barker, Mel Bartley, Yoav Ben-Shlomo, Jo Blanden, Andrew Boddy, Nicky Britten, Peter Brocklehurst, Bess Bukodi, Paul Burton, John Bynner, Lisa Calderwood, Iain Chalmers, Philip Cheetham, Steve Christmas, John Colley, John Cooper, Jane Costello, Claire Crawford, Janet Currie, Angela Dale, Colleen Daley, Ronald Davie, Shirley Dex, Carol Dezateux, Ian

Diamond, Brian Dodgeon, John Douglas, Rachel Douglas, Greg Duncan, Peter Elias, Jane Elliott, Hilary Emery, Alan Emond, Leon Feinstein, Elsa Ferri, Emla Fitzsimons, Ken Fogelman, John Fox, Jonathan Gershuny, Gail Gleave, Jean Golding, Harvey Goldstein, John Goldthorpe, Alissa Goodman, Hilary Graham, Paul Gregg, Toni Griffiths, Louis Hancock, Rebecca Hardy, Diane Iles, Hazel Inskip, Michael Jay, Heather Joshi, Elaine Kelly, Frank Kelly, Yvonne Kelly, Kathleen Kiernan, Mike King, Mark Klebanoff, Jack Kneeshaw, Peter Kuh, Catherine Law, Debbie Lawlor, Annette Lawson, Kit Leighton-Kelly, Rona McCandlish, Alison Macfarlane, Stephen Machin, Lindsey Macmillan, Patricia Malvern, Michael Marmot, Barbara Maughan, Robert Michael, John Micklewright, Lynn Molloy, Amy Murdoch-Davis, Jeremy Neathey, Nigel Paneth, Alison Park, Samantha Parsons, Catherine Peckham, Marcus Pembrey, Doria Pilling, Steve Pischke, Philip Pizzo, Lucinda Platt, Barry Pless, Diana Pomeroy, Christine Porter, Neil Porter, Chris Power, Gillian Pugh, Jugnoo Rahi, Caroline Relton, Marcus Richards, Sue Ring, Euan Ross, Michael Rutter, Stephanie von Hinke Kessler Scholder, Ingrid Schoon, Vanessa Shenton, Peter Shepherd, Alwyn Smith, George Davey Smith, Camilla Stoltenberg, Alice Sullivan, Ezra Susser, Deliang Tang, Nicholas Timpson, Anna Vignoles, Morten Wahrendorf, Jane Waldfogel, David Ward, Peter Wedge, Rebecca Wood, John Wright, and Vikki Yip. Several of the people on this list also gave me wise and invaluable comments on my draft. The British birth cohorts would not exist without the loyalty and participation of the cohort members and their families. Their identities are confidential, as is the data that is collected on them. The cohort members that I interviewed for this book agreed to have their stories included, and are remarkable for their openness and honesty. In some cases, names or details were changed to maintain confidentiality. I would also like to thank the participants that I interviewed during my research whose names I have not included here to respect their confidentiality. I hope I have the opportunity to meet more cohort members in the future, and hear about their extraordinary lives.

The feelings I have for my family defy words. My parents, Kate and Don Pearson, and my sister, Elizabeth Pearson, have offered unquestioning encouragement and help. This book would not have been written at all without the many days of childcare that my mum provided. No one believed in it more than my partner, Peter, who gave me his unwavering faith and support. My sons, Ashby, Lynton and Edwin, were a source of delight and inspiration. Please forgive me the many days that I spent on this book, when I wanted to spend them with you.

Index

air pollution 91–2, 94, 167, 318–19
alcohol dehydrogenase gene 198
annual conference, Royal Economic Society 231
antenatal care 28, 149, 259, 282
antibiotics 95, 140, 143, 322, 352
Archer, Jeffrey 85
atherosclerosis 118
Attlee, Clement 30
autism-spectrum disorder 324
Avon Longitudinal Study of Parents and Children *see* Cohort Study-1991 (Avon Longitudinal Study of Parents and Children)

baby boom 27, 29, 64, 302, 316
Barker, David 172–80, 182–4, 200–201, 289
Barker Hypothesis 178
Bedford 117
Bee Gees 125
Ben-Shlomo, Yoav 185–6
Beveridge, William 29, 39, 57, 183, 302
Big Science projects 289, 310, 324
birth
    caesarean 141–2, 290, 322–3, 352
    stillbirths 44–5, 142
    weights 174–5

see also childbirth; maternity; perinatal mortality rate; placentas; pregnancy; stillbirth
birth cohorts laboratory 311–2, 316, 331, 333–6, 350
birth rate 19–20, 27, 325
Blair, Tony 190, 220, 258
Blanden, Jo 229–30, 233–6, 245
blood pressure 101–2, 171–2, 175, 178–9, 197, 200–201
Born to Fail? (cohort report) 75–7, 269–70
Boyd Orr Cohort Study 195–6
Boyd Orr, Sir John 195–6
Boyle, Sir Edward 63
'Bradford Hill's criteria for causation' 101, 106
Brazil 197, 291, 322
breast cancer 180
breastfeeding 196–7, 282–4, 286, 291
British Births 1970 (book) 86
British Empire 19–20
British Eugenics Society 20–21
British Household Panel Survey 257
bronchitis 90–93, 113
Bucking the Trend (Blanden) 245
Burton, Paul 350
Butler, Neville
    and the 1982 video shoot 153–5
    and Carol Dezateux 317

387

in favour of a new cohort study
84
held party for the third cohort
297
and Kellmer Pringle 64–6, 72
and the Perinatal Mortality
Survey 47–56
a presence on both 1958 and 1970
cohorts 258
responsibility for the 1970
Cohort Study 130–34, 135–9,
151–2, 159
set up International Centre for
Child Studies 134–5
and smoking 103–5, 107–8
sought help for the 1970 cohort
216–17
study of births and perinatal
deaths in Cuba 288
survey of the 1970-born children
206, 229, 236
Butterfield, John 114–18, 171
Bynner, John
encouraged scientists to use
Essex data archive 334–5
directed 1958 and 1970 cohorts
229, 236, 258
investigated lack of cohort data
usage 210–214, 217–19
making cohorts relevant to
policy 238–40
plan for a millennium cohort
261–2
sample data sets for new
scientists 285
survey of reading/maths skills
of 1958 and 1970 cohort 237

trajectories of 1970 cohort 240–41
trajectory of disadvantage 244,
271
and the work of Glen Elder 244,
244–5

Cameron, David 232, 276, 315
cancer
breast 180
and adult cohort studies 109
deaths from 96
and genetic sequencing 164
lung 96–101, 104, 106, 112, 210, 321
carbon monoxide 108, 319
Cardiff Birth Survey 141
cardiovascular disease 89, 101–2, 171,
175, 181, 302
carpet survey (1968) 207
case-control studies 97–8
Central Advisory Council for
Education 63
Centre for Longitudinal Studies
258, 345, 352
Chalmers, Iain 140–45, 151–3, 220
Chamberlain, Geoffrey 85–6
Chamberlain, Roma 85–6
Charles, Prince 32
Cheetham, Philip 88–90, 185, 298
Child Health and Development
Study (US) 94, 112
child poverty 268
childbirth 28–9, 31–2, 39, 55, 86–7,
141–2, 144
See also birth
Children and Their Primary Schools
(Plowden Report) 67–8, 74,
105

chloroform 31
cholera 31, 94–5
Christmas, Steve 72–3, 77–8, 245–7
Churchill, Winston 30
Clean Air Act (1956) 91–2
Clegg, Nick 232, 235
Clinton, Bill 190
Cochrane, Archie 144
cohort studies
  birth 5–10, 147–9, 275
  birth cohort study (Pelotas,
    Brazil) 197, 290
  birth cohorts laboratory 311–12,
    316, 331, 333–6, 350
  British Doctors' study 100, 103, 112
  Child Health and Development
    Study (1959) 94, 112
  'Children of the 90s' 161
  See also cohort study (1991)
  children in California studies 94,
    242–3, 319
  China-Anhui Birth Study 290
  Collaborative Perinatal Project
    94, 112
  'Dutch Hunger Winter' natural
    experiment 176
  explanation of 33–9
  Framingham Heart Study 102–3,
    112, 175
  French child cohort study
    (Growing Up in France) 290
  Hertfordshire Cohort Study 175,
    177
  Human Genome Project 162–64,
    190–1, 199–200, 289
  Mandela's Children cohort study
    288

National Children's Study (US)
    292, 295, 328
  Netherlands child study (Genera-
    tion R) 290
  in New Zealand 188, 291
  Norwegian Mother and Child
    cohort study (MoBa) 290, 294
  plans for a 1982 cohort 146–53,
    159, 253–4, 315
  Second Generation Study of the
    1946 birth cohort 115
  Whitehall (1967) 181
  Whitehall II 181
  William Kermack study (1934) 176
Cohort Study (1946)
  and the 11-plus 59–61
  and the 1982 video shoot 153–4
  Barker's ideas lead to new lease
    of life 179
  a biomedical cohort 254–6
  birthday party (2011) 296–8,
    304–5, 307, 317, 343
  current status of 345–7
  and Diana Kuh 184, 295–305,
    341–4
  discovery of wide inequalities
    between children 27–9, 41–7,
    271
  and divorce 81
  and early adult years 118
  funding for DNA sample
    collection 191–2
  longest running birth cohort in
    the world 291, 341, 345
  medical disorders over time
    revealed 301–3
  memorabilia in time capsule 353

and Michael Wadsworth 114–5
needed to adapt 111
and obesity 192–3, 311, 332–3, 348
reinstated as a dedicated research
    unit 297
requirement for giving 'consent'
    264
size 289
and smoking in pregnancy 104,
    106, 108–9, 130, 148, 269
study of high blood pressure
    171–2, 175
unit moved back to London 180,
    182
unit moved to Bristol 120–21, 125
wide breadth of study 109–110
work reviewed by MRC 170–72,
    297–8
Cohort Study (1958)
    Alissa Goodman took charge
        (2012) 28
    bibliography of 219
    birthday party (1979) 125–6
    and *Born to Fail?* book 75–7,
        269–70
    brought to light widespread lack
        of basic skills 237
    and children with psychological
        problems 352
    considered consequences of
        family break-ups 81–4
    contained unparalleled data
        about smoking in pregnancy
        105, 147
    current status of 345–7
    data stored at Essex University
        206–7, 209

increasing government interfer-
    ence in 128–9
Jane Elliott took charge (2004)
    285
Jo Blanden's research 229–30
and John Bynner 210–216
and Kellmer Pringle 71–6, 78
located in Gordon Square 286
NIH provided funding 215
and obesity 333
plans postponed 64
questions about schooling 78–80
and smoking in pregnancy 104,
    106, 108–9, 130, 149, 269
and social science 128, 254–6
taken over by John Fox 214
used to assess social mobility
    228–34, 236
Cohort Study (1970)
    Alice Sullivan took over (2004)
        285, 338, 348
    bibliography of 219
    birth survey 85–6
    celebration party for at Alton
        Towers (1989) 139, 297, 338
    current status of 349–51
    data at Essex University 206–7,
        255, 257, 334–5, 339
    disadvantaged children analysis
        by Blanden 245
    and Facebook 337–9
    and home ownership 338
    Jane Elliott took charge (2004) 285
    and Jo Blanden's research 229–31,
        233–6, 245
    John Bynner took charge (1990)
        218

and Leon Feinstein's research
221–5, 227
located in Gordon Square 286
and Neville Butler 130–6, 216–18,
and obesity 335–6
plan to collect DNA (2016) 192,
348
reading and maths skills testing
236–42
sexuality question asked (2012)
248
and social science 254–6
uncovered widespread lack of
basic skills 238, 241–2
used to assess social mobility
229–34, 236
Cohort Study (1991) (Avon Longitudinal Study of Parents and
Children)
a biomedical cohort 254–6
and cot deaths 188–9
current status of 349–51
establishment of 159–70
recruiting the children of the
cohort members 202–4
viewed as an outsider 254
Cohort Study (2000) *see* Millennium Cohort
Cohort Study (Life Study) 317–31,
352–3
Collaborative Perinatal Project (US)
94, 112
Colley, John 119–20
comprehensive schools 62–3, 78–9
Concern (journal) 79
Cooper, Rachel 344
corporal punishment 64, 68

cot deaths (sudden infant death
syndrome) 188–9
Crick, Francis 161, 353

Davie, Ron 66
Dearden, Lorraine 228
death atlas (Barker) 172–3
Declaration of Helsinki 165
delinquency 115
dementia 304, 344–5
Dex, Shirley 269–71
Dezateux, Carol 278–280, 314–5,
317–19, 325–9, 331, 352
diabetes 96, 102, 162, 171, 181, 279,
302, 322, 333, 348
Type 2 114, 116–18, 162, 178
Diamond, Ian 309–12
digital video recordings 324
divorce 7, 81–2, 111, 115, 221, 264, 285,
DNA 161–7, 190–91, 197–9, 322–3, 329,
340, 348, 350
Doll, Richard 97–100, 106, 210
Domesday Book 33–4
Douglas Babies 40, 68, 90, 298
Douglas, James
and the 1944 Education Act 59–60
and the 1982 video shoot 153–5
and breastfeeding 282–3
clever and curious 317
death of 180
determination to span both
social and medical science 254
and early deaths of children 35
early life of 22–4
and educational reforms 63,
69–72, 74–5, 78
and good parenting 81, 244, 271–2

lessons on use of data by
politicians 25, 236
and maturation of 1946 cohort
study 110–111, 115–16
an outsider by attempting to
bridge disciplines 312–13
and Neville Butler 132
and Patricia Palmer 57, 59
predictions on class differences
over time 301
and respiratory diseases 92–4,
113–14
retirement prospect 119–20
review by MRC 298
second nationwide birth survey
45–52
setting up 1946 birth cohort
16–19, 25–32, 38–44, 325
size of 1946 study 40, 289
smoking in pregnancy dilemma
148
technology held him back
318
and the 'waste of talent' 89
Dutch Hunger Winter 176

Economic and Social Research
Council (ESRC)
and bid to the Large Facilities
Capital Fund 310–3
funding the 1958 and 1970
cohorts 214–15, 254, 345
investigated use of 1958 cohort
data 210, 212
Ian Diamond became head of
309–10
Jane Elliott became head of 287

and plans for a new birth cohort
257, 260, 327–8
see also Social Science Research
Council (SSRC)
education 220–21, 245
nursery school 68, 76, 268, 275
Education Act (1944) 30, 58–9, 63–4
Elder, Glen 242–4
electromagnetic radiation 321
11-plus exam 57–61, 79, 89, 114, 183,
245, 305
Elias, Peter 260, 310–312, 316
Elizabeth, Princess 32
Elliott, Jane 285–7, 331
emphysema 92, 183
epidemiology
and Life Study 323, 327
calculating rates of disease or
death 35–6
cohorts an unshakable place in
the field of 94–7, 103
genetic 161–2, 164, 190
glass-half-full approach to 333–4
impetus for a millennium cohort
289
life course epidemiology 185–7,
243
and Michael Marmot 180
and origins of chronic disease
171–182, 184–8
perinatal 263
plans for a new birth cohort 321–3
search for causation in 95–103,
106, 162, 164, 172, 178, 194,
197–8
a victim of its own success 194
epigenetics 199, 350

Index

Escape from Disadvantage (Pilling) 5, 244

eugenics 20–21, 77

Eugenics Society 69

evidence-based policy-making 220, 238

Facebook 337–9

Farr, William 36–7, 96, 100

Feinstein Graph 222–3, 224–6, 235–6

Feinstein, Leon 221–7, 232–3, 235–6

Ferri, Elsa 82–3

Field Survey of Air-Raid Casualties 24

Finer Committee on One Parent Families 81–3

fish consumption in pregnancy 189, 202

Fitzsimons, Emla 283–4, 286, 340, 351

foetal development 174–5, 178, 182–4, 189, 191, 200

Foetal Origins Hypothesis *see* Barker Hypothesis

foetal programming 175, 183, 200

fog/smogs 91–2

Ford Foundation 69

Fox, John 214–15

Framingham Heart Study 102–3, 112, 175

Framingham, Massachusetts 101–3, 112, 175

Framingham Risk Score 103

Francis Crick Institute 353

Frankel, Stephen 196

Franklin, Rosalind 161

FTO gene 190–92

gas and air 31, 52

'Genetic Studies of Genius' (Terman) 38

General Register Office *see* Office of the Registrar General

genetics 161, 190, 193, 199, 350

Gershuny, Jonathan 257–8, 260

Gibb, Andy 125

Glass, David 22, 25, 32, 38–40

Gleave, Gail 138–9

Golding, Jean
  ambitious plans for a 1982 cohort 146–53, 253–4, 259–60
  and the Avon Longitudinal Study of Parents and Children (1991 cohort) 159–70, 187–95, 201
  early life of 145–6
  perinatal survey in Jamaica 288
  planned for a new birth cohort study 147–53, 341
  research on urine samples 201–2
  retirement 194–5

Goldstein, Harvey 106–8, 153–5

Goldthorpe, John 233–4

Goodman, Alissa 286–7, 345, 352

grammar schools 57–63, 78–9, 110

Great Depression 101, 242–3

Great Ormond Street 47, 69

gynaecology 144

'Haldane Principle' 128

Haldane Report (1918) 128

Hardy, Rebecca 192–3

Head Start Program (US) 76, 225

Health Education Council 108

heart disease,

and the 1970 cohort 348
and cohort studies 109, 112
and the Framingham Heart
    Study 101–2
and high infant mortality 173–5
large increase from the 1920s
    onwards 96
and overweight children 279,
333
and poor nutrition 178
and smoking 100
Hill, Austin Bradford 97–101, 106,
    143–4, 194, 210
Himsworth, Harold 69
home births 31, 52–5, 141
Home and the School, The (Douglas)
    61–3
'human agency' 243
Human Genome Project 162–70,
    190, 289

Iles, Alex (son) 156, 158
Iles, Diane 156–8
in utero experiences 176–7
income,
    and the 1970 cohort 348
    and childbirth 29
    and deprived children 75–6
    and the Pilling interviews 2–3
    and property prices 336
    and social mobility 228–30, 232–6,
        269–70, 330, 334
independent schools 80, 232
inequality 30, 73, 219, 221, 228, 261,
    268, 268–9, 275–6, 279, 320,
    329–30
inherited wealth 336

International Centre for Child
    Studies (ICCS) 134, 217
International Classification of
    Diseases (ICD) 36
iodine 202
IQ 197, 202, 232

Jay, Michael 247–9
Jerrim, John 225–6
Johnson, President Lyndon B. 76
Joseph Rowntree Village Trust 48
Joseph, Sir Keith 76, 127
Joshi, Heather 262–5, 287, 341

Kermack, William 176
King George Hospital, Ilford 326,
    354–5
Kuh, Charlotte 183
Kuh, Diana 8–9, 182–6, 296–305, 307,
    341, 343–4
Kuh, Peter 183

Lamont, Norman 134
Large Facilities Capital Fund
    309–10, 312–13
laughing gas *see* gas and air
Lennon, John 60
Leopold, Prince 31
life course epidemiology 185–6, 243,
    296
literacy 236–41
Local Fuel Overseers 92, 319
lung cancer 96–101, 104, 106, 112, 143,
    147, 210, 321

Machin, Stephen 228
Macmillan, Lindsey 232

Major, John 220, 232
Mandela, Nelson 288
Mandelson, Peter 258–9
Marmot, Michael 180–81, 295
'marshmallow test' 346
Mason, James 134
maternity
  care 28–30
  grants 21, 29
  survey (1946) 19, 25, 27, 32–4, 39,
    43
Maternity in Great Britain (Douglas)
    27
*Maternity Letters from Working
    Women* (Women's Co-opera-
    tive Guild) 317
Maxwell, Robert 135
MC4R gene 193
Medawar, Peter 23
Medical Research Council (MRC)
  birth cohorts laboratory
    proposal 311–2, 316, 331, 333–6,
    350
  funding of cohorts 69–71, 97, 110,
    126–8, 133, 148, 213–4, 225, 238,
    287, 299, 309, 347
  and James Douglas 69, 113
  little interest in a protracted data
    collection exercise 163
  moved 1946 cohort to Bristol
    119–20
  parties held for 1946 cohort 298
  performance assessments 299
  debate about future of 1946
    cohort 119, 152, 253
  pressure to control its costs
    296–7

reviewed the 1946 cohort 170–72,
    299–300
  tobacco and lung cancer link 100
Medical Research Ethics Commit-
    tee 264
'Memorandum on the Procedure'
    18
Mendel, Gregor 197
Mendelian randomization 197
microbiome studies 322, 352
middle-classes 28, 61, 74, 93, 107, 145,
    197, 223–4, 228, 232, 302
midwives 16, 31–2, 53, 104, 168,
    281–2, 325
Milburn, Alan 232
Millennium Cohort
  comparison with earlier cohorts
    265–71
  current status of 308–310, 314, 316,
    318, 340–1, 345, 351
  decision to create 257–63
  Emla Fitzsimons takes charge
    283–4, 286, 340, 351
  and Heather Joshi 262–5, 287, 341
  inequality still a topic of
    discussion 275–6
  and obesity 278–81
  and parenting 273–8
  planned diary study 351
  and summer-born children 282
Ministry of Home Security 24
Mischel, Walter 346
Moser, Sir Claus 239
Much Hadham (village) 174

National Birthday Trust Fund 48,
    85

National Bureau for Co-operation in Childcare 65
National Children's Bureau 65, 67, 74, 79, 82, 125, 211
National Coal Board 48
national fertility 20–22, 27, 36, 303
National Health Service (NHS), and the 1946 cohort 267, 344, 330
a British institution 344
and cohort studies 6, 39
design and launch of 30
and Diana Kuh 183, 303
and inequality 51
and pain relief in childbirth 32
and pregnancy 293
restructuring of 330
spiralling costs of 45–6
and middle- and upper-class women 302
National Heart Act (US) 101
National Institutes of Health (NIH) 215, 292
national insurance 29
National Perinatal Epidemiology Unit 139, 144
Netherlands 176, 290
neural tube defects 146
non-achievers 3–4
Norway 45, 290, 294
Nuffield Foundation 69
nursery education 68, 76, 268, 275

Obama, Barack 330
obesity 102, 176, 190–93, 196–7, 279–80, 302–3, 311, 332–3, 338, 348
obstetrics 51–55, 130, 140–1, 144, 263

Office of the Registrar General 36, 99–100
Osmond, Clive 173

Palmer, Derek (son) 14
Palmer, Edith (daughter) 14
Palmer, Gertrude Mary 13–15, 18, 57, 156, 264
Palmer, Ken (son) 14, 58
Palmer, Patricia (daughter) 13–14, 57–9, 72, 115, 305–7
parenting 81, 244, 271–8
Pembrey, Marcus 164, 190
perinatal mortality rate 45–6, 51–2, 105–7
Perinatal Mortality Survey (1958) 46–9, 55, 141, 145
pethidine 52
Philip, Prince 32
phonics 80
Pilling, Doria 1–7, 244
Pinch, The (Willetts) 316
placentas
cotyledons 201
David Barker's fascination with role of 178
plans to study in Life Study cohort 324
in storage, as part of 1991 cohort 6, 157–8, 168, 195, 200–201
Plowden Committee 63–4, 66–7, 71
Plowden, Lady Bridget 63
pneumonia 90, 92–3, 113, 140
pollution 91–4, 109–110, 113, 167, 318–20, 323
Population Investigation Committee 19, 20–22, 85, 284

Porter, Christine 131–3
poverty
  and the 1946 cohort 13, 29, 36,
    42–3, 81–3
  and the 1970 cohort 241
  in 1999 261, 268
  and Life Study 329, 331
  link to reading 245
  and parenting 275–8
Poverty: A Study of Town Life
  (Rowntree) 42
pre-eclampsia 288
'prediabetes' 117
pregnancy
  alcohol consumption during
    198–9
  fish consumption in 189, 202
  and Life Study 324–6
  and foetal growth 178
  and increased medical interven-
    tion in 141
  and Jean Golding's plans for 1982
    cohort 149–50, 198–9
  and pollution 320
  prematurity 27, 44, 51, 75, 149
  and smoking 103–9
  and starvation 176
  working during 43–4
  see also birth ; childbirth;
    maternity; perinatal mortality
    rate; placentas; stillbirth
primary schools 64, 67, 239
Pringle, Mia Kellmer
  and the 1958 cohort 71–2, 74, 78,
    152
  and the 1982 video shoot 153–5
  celebrated 21st birthday of 1958

cohort 125–6
  death of 155, 214
  life of 64–6
  plan for an institution to mount
    cohort studies 154, 312
  provided typed notes for use of
    1958 cohort 212
  retirement 129–30
  secured government funding for
    1958 cohort 127
  and Sir Keith Joseph 76
punched cards 26–7, 38, 70–71, 120

qualitative/quantitative methods
  211
Queen's Diamond Jubilee 313
questionnaires 17–19, 25–6, 49–50, 73,
    99, 129, 132, 138, 165, 170, 184, 293

randomized controlled trials 143–5,
    151, 194, 220, 253
rationing 45, 196, 265, 298, 320, 330
Reed, Howard 228
'Report upon the Mortality of
    Lunatics' (Farr) 37
Research Councils UK Executive
    Group 309
Research and Experiments
    Department, Ministry of
    Home Security 24
Research Unit Bicycle 70
respiratory diseases 92, 113
'risk factor' for chronic disease 102
Roosevelt, Franklin D. 101
Rothschild Report 127, 213
Rowett Institute for Nutrition and
    Health 195

Rowntree, Griselda 16
Rowntree, Joseph 48
Rowntree, Seebohm 42

Sabates, Ricardo 269–71
schizophrenia 113, 118, 177, 180
secondary modern schools 58, 60,
    77–8
Skills for Life programme 239–40
Smith, George Davey 195–201, 284,
    291, 350, 371
smoking 49, 96–101–9, 112–13, 182–3,
    210, 302, 321, 335, 340
smoking in schoolboys survey 210
Snow, John 31, 95
social mobility
    role of private schools and elite
        universities 348
    absolute and relative 227–8
    Golden Age 227–8
    in the 1958 and 1970 cohorts
        227–36
    and the millennium cohort 269
    parenting as the new law of 276
    strategy 235
Social Sciences Research Council
    (SSRC) 71–2, 127, 209, 213
    see also Economic and Social
    Research Council
South Africa 288
Stiglitz, Joseph 183
stillbirth 44, 142
streptomycin 143–4
Struggle for Population, The (publica-
    tion) 20
sudden infant death syndrome
    (SIDS) *see* cot deaths

Sullivan, Alice 285–7, 338–40, 348,
Sunday Times 74
Sure Start programme 225, 268
Sutton Trust 232–3

Tawney, R. H. 76
Terman, Lewis 37–8
'Termites' 38 *see* 'Genetic Studies of
    Genius' (Terman)
Thatcher, Margaret 74, 79, 127–8,
    133–4, 151–2, 213, 220, 315
tissue store (Bristol) 157–9
Tobacco Research Council 48
Toynbee, Polly 7
Truman, President 101
tuberculosis 92, 95, 101–2, 143–4
Twilight of Parenthood, The
    (Charles) 20

UK Data Archive at Essex Univer-
    sity 206
'Unequal Start, The' (*Sunday Times*)
    74
United Kingdom 27, 168, 197
United States
    and autopsies of American
        soldiers 118
    and the baby boom 27
    and Caesarean-section births
        325
    and cardiovascular disease 101–2
    Child Health and Development
        Study (1959) 94, 112–13
    and cigarette smoking 96, 107
    and Collaborative Perinatal
        Project 94, 112–13
    Head Start Program 76, 225

and National Children's Study 291–5

NIH provides money for 1958 cohort 215

and nursery education 76

and 'prediabetes' 117

small studies to trace cohorts of young children 37

social mobility in 230

University of Essex 205–212, 255

University of London 70

upper-classes 20, 28, 58, 61, 68, 223–4, 227, 232, 268, 301–2

urine test 116, 171, 202

Variety Club of Great Britain 48

Vibrio cholerae (bacterium) 95

Victoria, Queen 31, 95

Vignoles, Anna 225–6

village life in Hampshire survey 209

Wadsworth, Michael

and the 1946 cohort 113–16, 125, 152, 179–80

and the Bedford diabetes survey 117–18

blood pressure study 171–2, 175

and Diana Kuh 182–4

funding for DNA samples for 1946 cohort 191–2

glimpsing early signs of chronic disease 118–21

MRC reviews 1946 cohort 170–71, 298

and Neville Butler 132, 217

retirement of 296

and the Whitehall Study 181

video shoot (1982) 153–5

war brides 18

'waste of talent' 62, 89

Watson, James 161

Wedge, Peter 76–7

Wilkins, Maurice 161

Willetts, David 315–17, 330–1

William I, King 33–4

Wilson, Harold 62

Wood, Rebecca 266–7

Wood, Thomas 266

working mothers 43–4, 280

working-classes,

and antenatal care 28

and Carol Dezateux 317

and the eugenics movement 20

and Harvey Goldstein 107

and James Douglas 61–2, 74–5, 89, 93, 272

and Leon Feinstein 223–4

Patricia Palmer 305

and reading 241

and social mobility 227–8, 232

World Health Organization (WHO) 159–60, 319

World Medical Association 165–6

Young, J. Z. 22–3

Youth Opportunities programme 217

Zuckerman, Solly 23–5, 97